Written/Unwritten

Written/Unwritten

Diversity and the Hidden Truths of Tenure

Edited by

Patricia A. Matthew

The University of North Carolina Press *Chapel Hill*

© 2016 The University of North Carolina Press

All rights reserved

Set in Espinosa Nova and Alegreya Sans by Westchester Publishing Services

The University of North Carolina Press has been a member of the Green Press
Initiative since 2003.

Library of Congress Cataloging-in-Publication Data
Names: Matthew, Patricia A., editor.
Title: Written/unwritten : diversity and the hidden truths of tenure / edited
  by Patricia A. Matthew.
Description: Chapel Hill : University of North Carolina Press, [2016] |
  Includes bibliographical references and index.
Identifiers: LCCN 2016008742 | ISBN 9781469630168 (cloth : alk. paper) |
  ISBN 9781469627717 (pbk : alk. paper) | ISBN 9781469627724 (ebook)
Subjects: LCSH: Discrimination in higher education—United States. | College
  teachers—Tenure—United States. | Diversity in the workplace—United States.
Classification: LCC LC212.42 W75 2016 | DDC 378.1/214—dc23
  LC record available at http://lccn.loc.gov/2016008742

This book is dedicated to Georgine Leonie
and William Owen Matthew
"train up a child . . ."

Contents

Manifestos

Hierarchies

Activism(s)

Preface

It's not just us. This is happening everywhere:
On CVs and the Michigan Women

The catalyst for this project—for my decision to add a focus on diversity in higher education to my work on nineteenth-century British fiction—was hearing about the four women of color at the University of Michigan denied tenure in the same year. I heard about the case while I was in the middle of my own tenure battle, planning for a meeting with my university's provost to ask him to reconsider his decision to recommend against tenure. Until I reached the provost's review, my tenure process had gone well, so I was surprised by his denial. He ignored the recommendations of my department committee, the department chair, the (interim) dean, and external assessments from three senior colleagues in my field that I was advised but not required to submit. He even ignored his four previous, full-throated recommendations for reappointment.[1] His denial was based on the fact that my accepted essays and the special issue of a journal I had coedited were forthcoming but not yet in print. My appeal was based on the fact that neither he nor anyone else assessing my work had told me that "in print" was the standard. To be clear, it wasn't necessarily the standard I objected to but the fact that I didn't know it existed; if "in print" was enough to get me fired, I argued, I should have been told. Instead, I had been told that my institution was looking for a "scholarly disposition" and that I should show steady, sustained progress in my research agenda. When I asked the now-retired provost if my file showed a lack of scholarly disposition or steady progress in my research agenda, his "no" was unequivocal. He approved of my research, my work pace, and where my work was being published.

In the week between his initial denial and his final decision to uphold it, I, along with colleagues from my department and the College of Humanities and Social Sciences, worked on an appeal. We spent the Thanksgiving holiday reading the faculty manual, looking at other tenure cases, and reading the provost's guidelines posted in different areas of the university's website. Senior colleagues from different departments wrote to the provost to explain that they had been tenured, promoted, and won university research awards based on forthcoming work. A former junior colleague wrote from Ireland and sent me an e-mail from one of the three deans we'd worked with in the four years prior to my tenure review. In this e-mail, she specifically explained that "in print" was not the standard. I put together documentation from different editors making clear that my work was actually forthcoming along with proofs of my various essays. Faced with a contract that would end with the conclusion of that fiscal year (my institution does not have the "grace" year), I was also looking through the MLA job list for the first time that season. Since I had received four positive recommendations for reappointment from this provost and had sailed through the department, chair, and dean reviews, I hadn't planned a job search. It was during this period that I received an e-mail with Andrea Smith's CV attached.[2] The e-mail itself was brief and with only a few facts and one claim. The facts: four women of color at Michigan had all been denied tenure in the same cycle; Smith was denied tenure by Women's Studies, which was its own department at Michigan and not a program. It included the following claim: "It's not just us. This is happening everywhere."

It's a story I still find difficult to believe. In 2007, five assistant professors (four women of color and one white man) who all had joint appointments in the same department program at the University of Michigan at Ann Arbor went up for tenure. Only the women of color were denied tenure by their major departments. Generally speaking, joint appointments are tricky to navigate. They usually assign a faculty member to both a full-fledged department and a fledgling program or institute. In theory, a portion of the faculty member's time is spent in each academic unit; she will be split fifty-fifty or sixty-forty. The reality is that each academic unit needs its faculty to give 100 percent, so those with joint appointments tend to have twice as many service duties, student advisees, and colleagues to manage. They are expected to explain and defend the value of the program's contributions to their institution's mission. Other things make these appointments tricky. The emerging field usually has an explicit advocacy component to it, requiring faculty to use additional time to develop special programs and sponsor student groups. Finally, and perhaps most important, it is often difficult for faculty in more traditional fields to fully appreciate and assess the value of scholarship in emerging fields. The faculty workload makes it difficult, if not impossible, to take the time to learn about areas outside one's own specialization. In other words, a department's specialist in a more traditional field simply might not have time to understand the intricacies of an emerging one.

Since the Michigan Women (as I immediately came to think of them) had joint appointments in the program in American Culture and more established departments including History, English, and Women's Studies, I assumed that their heavy loads had hampered their scholarly production. Universities such as Michigan at Ann Arbor have reputations for valuing publication over *everything* in their faculty; it's the kind of institution the phrase "publish or perish" was probably invented to describe. I didn't know the women who had been denied tenure, and—despite my own experience—my initial thought was to give the benefit of the doubt to the institution. I was suspicious, but I also know that there are some universities that simply don't award tenure to new faculty (Harvard and Yale come to mind immediately), and I assumed that Michigan was one such school.

I wanted to know what the standard for tenure was and how it had been explained to the Michigan Women. It's not an easy thing for me to admit, but my very first question at the time was, what might *they* have missed in the years leading up to their final review? Then Andrea's CV showed up in my Gmail inbox, and it was the beginning of my understanding about how capricious the academy can be. I started by looking for evidence that she had somehow fallen short of Michigan's standards or, to be more precise, what I imagined those standards to be (what I should have done was look to see how much her colleagues had published). But as I skimmed the twenty-three pages of her tenure CV, entries such as "Nobel Prize Nominee" and "Address to the United Nations General Assembly" jumped out. She had authored two books and coauthored one, with her most recent book due out from Duke University Press. She had edited or coedited three books and two special issues of journals in her field. She matched this scholarly output with the kind of service and activism that faculty of color regularly take on. I couldn't keep track of all she had done, even though it was right there in print for me to read.

I burst into tears.

You should know that I'm a sentimental, weepy person, and some of those tears were surely projections of my own sadness and anxiety (I read her CV as I fully faced the reality of losing a job I loved along with the salary, the health insurance, and the professional security that came with it), but most of those tears were ones of deep, almost all-consuming sadness at the realization that as faculty of color we can never be good enough to gain tenure if someone (or an institution) simply decides we don't belong. What Andy's CV brought home to me was that it wasn't about being "good" enough or collegial enough or *anything* enough. She—and by extension faculty in general and faculty of color in particular—was subject to the feelings and biases of senior faculty and administrators dressed up in the rhetoric of objective evaluations or the maddeningly opaque "academic judgment." They can deny you tenure and then twist the process and make up reasons along the way. It was a problem that called for a study of some sort, and soon after my university president overturned the provost's decision and I got tenure, I talked about editing an anthology one day.

I might have forgotten about this project if I hadn't been accused of lying by an interim dean who flat out refused to believe that I had drafted three of the five chapters of my book about Romantic-era fiction (never mind that I'd included a draft of the book with all of those chapters in the tenure file she supported)—and this a year after getting tenure. Even still, I might have let the project fall by the wayside if my own experiences in my fairly progressive institution felt purely anecdotal. When I started working on this project, I didn't know the term "microaggression" was available to describe why I was regularly confused with our department secretaries (we look nothing alike) and found myself having to provide more documentation than my white peers whenever I submitted reports about how I was progressing with my research agenda. I wasn't particularly interested in questions around affirmative action, mostly because these days, when it comes to hiring in the academy, it's either window dressing or a bogeyman more than an active policy.[3] And it wasn't just because whenever I was in the company of other academics of color they regularly noted two things—that they faced more scrutiny with less support than their white counterparts, and that any error on their part was viewed as a sign of incompetence or intellectual inferiority. Blogs such as *Conditionally Accepted* and anthologies such as the massive *Presumed Incompetent* put to rest, once and for all, the idea that the problems around diversity are because faculty of color aren't good enough, productive enough, or collegial enough. It wasn't just because I didn't see this issue being addressed.

The reason I kept at the project is because the more I read and talked with faculty of color around the country, the more I came to understand that we still need to figure out the ways in which the academy is structurally hostile to diversity and how to unpack the unwritten codes that underscore various personnel processes (formal and informal) that make it difficult for faculty of color to succeed. I set out to discover whether or not the Michigan Women were anomalies or if this was, indeed, "happening everywhere." I wasn't looking for anything specific, so the invitation I sent out was pretty open. I asked scholars of color from different fields in the humanities (social sciences, literary studies, history, anthropology, etc.) to write or talk about what they experienced, what they learned, and to share any advice or perspective they might have for the academy—not just for academics of color but for white faculty who might want to support a diverse academy without knowing quite how to do it. They were invited to reflect on any part of their careers, to write openly about their subject position in this twenty-first century iteration of the academy and its complicated relationship with diversity. While I had a sense of the kinds of stories that were out there, my primary goal was to gather an array of perspectives from faculty far enough along in their careers to reflect on how they started, stumbled, and survived. I wanted their individual stories to be read in the context of other narratives.

My sense was that while there certainly can be malice at work when faculty of color are assessed and evaluated, formally and informally, it is also the haphazard nature of these different processes that they are more structurally complicated for faculty of color than for their white counterparts. To use my tenure battle as an example, I don't think that provost looked at me and thought "She's black; I'm not going to treat her well" or "She's black so she's incompetent" (I don't even know if he knew who I was before I showed up in his office with my appeal in hand). I wouldn't try to argue that there was explicit bias. But what I've found is that there are codes and habits that faculty of color often don't know about because those unwritten practices are so subtle as to seem unimportant until something goes wrong, and then the assumption is that the person of color is incompetent, lazy, or lying. In my case, the assumption was that I was dishonest or disorganized, though neither of those things is true. The fact that I am a Black woman played some role in that tangled-up process, and I still see the same patterns that were in play in my reappointment and tenure reviews whenever I am assessed. More important, I now know that those patterns are at work all over the country. It's not just me. It's not just us. This is happening everywhere.

The essays collected here show how faculty of color always have to do at least two things at the same time as they go about their work: figure out how to cope with (confront, deflect, or absorb) the daily micro-aggressions of the academy while trying to navigate structural obstacles that everyone faces in environments that are either maddeningly indifferent or hostile. Faculty of color will find strategies here that they can borrow. They'll also find articulations of rage and be inspired by those who have thrived. White academics who might care about supporting faculty of color will learn that it's not enough not to be racist or to have Lucille Clifton on the syllabus or offer a sympathetic nod when they see that faculty of color are being treated unfairly. They'll find examples of what to do (and what not to say) and a fuller understanding of what their colleagues of color face as they try to do the same work that matters to everyone who undertakes the work of being an academic.

Written/Unwritten isn't just about a CV, my struggle to get tenure, or the Michigan Women. The stories here certainly reflect my experiences and observations, but more than that they reflect the questions those experiences and observations have left me with: What kind of structural problems hinder meaningful diversity? What can we learn from groundbreakers and canon builders? How can the project of Women's Studies make any progress when white feminists fail to see the ways they dismiss their "sisters" of color? What can we learn from the painful process of tenure denials? What can white allies do? How does activism line up with institutional goals? How can social media transform the work of diversity in the academy? The essays and interviews here can't answer these questions fully, but they can point us toward a way to consider different paths to meaningful diversity and to a fuller understanding of what faculty of color contribute to the academy and the work it takes for them to survive.

Patricia A. Matthew
Brooklyn, New York
June 2015

Notes

1. At Montclair State University, tenure-track faculty are required to go up for reappointment every year until they apply for tenure at the start of their fifth year.

2. From the start of this project until the end of June 2015, I and others involved in this project took for granted Andrea Smith's claims to Native American identity. Smith, along with nine others, is listed as an author of the *"Talking Tenure"* newsletter (see Appendix A), and she granted me permission to publish the newsletter a few weeks before challenges to her identity appeared on blogs,

Tumblr posts, newsletters, and online magazines. In an "Open Letter From Indigenous Women Scholars Regarding Discussions of Andrea Smith," a dozen indigenous women from around the country wrote: "[O]ur concerns are about the profound need for transparency and responsibility in light of the traumatic histories of colonization, slavery, and genocide that shape the present. . . . Presenting herself as generically indigenous, and allowing others to represent her as Cherokee, Andrea Smith allows herself to stand in as the representative of collectivities to which she has demonstrated no accountability, and undermines the integrity and vibrancy of Cherokee cultural and political survival."

At the time of this volume's submission, Smith's response has been through her private blog.

"I have always been, and will always be Cherokee. I have consistently identified myself based on what I knew to be true. My enrollment status does not impact my Cherokee identity or my continued commitment to organizing for justice for Native communities . . . . what is most concerning is that these social media attacks send a chilling message to all Native peoples who are not enrolled, or who are otherwise marginalized, that they should not publicly work for justice for Native peoples out of fear that they too may one day be attacked. It is my hope that more Indigenous peoples will answer the call to work for social justice without fear of being subjected to violent identity-policing."

All of the comments and references to Smith in this anthology are based on Smith's claims that she is Native American.

3. See Katznelson, *When Affirmative Action Was White* (2005); Walesby, "Facts and Myths of Affirmative Action."

Written/Unwritten

Introduction

Written/Unwritten: The Gap Between Theory and Practice

Patricia A. Matthew

Montclair State University

"With the Negro Marine, officer and private, fighting side by side with his white brother, with Navy ships manned by mixed crews, with Americans of all creeds standing side by side at the factory bench, it was no longer a daring thing . . . for a college to add a Negro to its staff."

—Fred G. Wale, 1940s[1]

"I don't know if I want to work with a black on a permanent basis."

—Faculty member reviewing Dr. Reginald Clark's tenure file, 1984[2]

"While we'd like to diversify the department, we will make an appointment on merit, and will look for the best candidate."

—Faculty member to a Black job candidate, 2006[3]

Mat Johnson's novel *Pym* begins with a tenure denial: "Always thought if I didn't get tenure I would shoot myself or strap a bomb to my chest and walk into the faculty cafeteria, but when it happened I just got bourbon drunk and cried a lot and rolled into a ball on my office floor."[4] Despite a positive recommendation from his colleagues for tenure, low enrollments have hurt protagonist Chris Haynes's tenure review. He has also, according to the college's president, strayed from his original research focus on African American literature into a consideration of Edgar Allen Poe and hasn't won any major fellowships to burnish his professional profile. Hired to be the department's "Professional Negro," he has "gone off the farm" and, perhaps most damningly, he has also assiduously avoided the college's diversity committee, recognizing it for the window dressing such committees often become: "The Diversity Committee has one primary purpose: so that the school can say it has a diversity committee.

They need that for when students get upset about race issues or general ethnic stuff. It allows the faculty and administration to point to it and go, 'Everything's going to be okay, we have formed a committee.' People find that very relaxing. It's sort of like, if you had a fire, and instead of putting it out, you formed a fire committee."[5]

It is clear from Haynes's confrontation with the college president that he has been hired not so much to fill a position (specialist in African American literature) as to fill a role (Black male academic) and, moreover, to fill that role in the language and affects that already fit his white colleagues' image of what it means to be a Black male academic. It's an image that Haynes thinks his former institution will undoubtedly see in Mosaic Johnson, the new hip-hop scholar hired to replace him: "You're hired to be the angry black guy. . . . You're here so you can assuage their guilt without making them actually change a damn thing. They want you to be the Diversity Committee. Because every village needs a fool."[6]

Pym's first chapter almost perfectly encapsulates the multiple issues that bubble up to the surface when the processes of evaluation and the issue of race intersect: the erosion of faculty governance; the narrow subject position academics of color are expected to occupy; the fact that while faculty of color might be hired because of an institution's stated commitment to diversity, that commitment often buckles under the need to only reward with tenure those who conform to their institutions' preconceived notions of what it means to be a successful academic. And as the first chapter ends and Haynes begins (descends into) his journey, Mosaic Johnson is at the beginning of the tenure-track journey that every person of color in the nonfiction world knows is fraught with complicated expectations, sets of opaque policies, conscious and unconscious individual bigotry, microaggressions, and institutional racism.

Written/Unwritten is a collection of tenure-track journeys recounted by faculty of color from humanities departments around the country. The scholars here theorize about identity politics and ideologies of immigration at the same time that they discuss the nuts and bolts of working within academic systems that are often structurally hostile to diversity. They are pointed, angry, sometimes funny, and often poignant. They hold the academy to account, but they do so from the vantage point of those committed to its success. Taken together they illustrate the wide gap between the language of diversity (the written) and practices of individuals and institutions that work against its goals (the unwritten). This is not a new problem, and, as I discuss later in this introduction, there is a pattern to how this gap is maintained, even as we see signs of progress. *Written/Unwritten* joins a series of conversations about the experiences of faculty of color and extends that conversation by showing precisely what faculty of color have contributed to the academy and, in some instances, the price of those contributions.

For marginalized faculty in *English, Power, Race and Gender in Academe: Strangers in the Tower* (2000) was, perhaps, the best book to begin the most current conversation around diversity and inequity in higher education. It invited many of us to understand our personal experiences in the context of patterns that cut across race and gender. Moreover, it provided substance to the inchoate sense that faculty of color had that everything was not as equitable as everyone claimed.[7] Since its publication in 2000, the conversations about inequity in higher education have been a mix of the theoretical, the confessional, and, with a growing sense of urgency, the practical. In my review of *Mentoring Faculty of Color: Essays on Professional Development and Advancement in Colleges and Universities* (2013), I note that the Michigan tenure denials "mark a shift in the structure and tone of books and anthologies about the experiences of faculty of color in higher education."[8] The titles are telling. The books about diversity in higher education published before the Michigan cases have milder titles with an eye toward offering context and naming the problem: Christine Stanley's *Faculty of Color: Teaching in Predominately White Colleges and Universities* (2006), Stephanie Evans's *Black Women in the Ivory Tower: 1850–1954* (2007), and Deborah Gray White et al.'s *Telling Histories: Black Women Historians in the Ivory Tower* (2008). There is a sense of urgency and anger in anthologies and collections published following those cases: *Tedious Journeys: Autoethnography by Women of Color* (2010) edited by Cynthia Cole Robinson and Pauline Clardy; *Racism in the Academy: The New Millennium* (2012), a collection of essays that grew out of the American Anthropological Association's Commission on Race and Racism in Anthropology (2010); Sarah Ahmed's *On Being Included: Racism and Diversity in Institutional Life* (2012); and *Presumed Incompetent: The Intersections of Race and Class for Women in Academia* (2013), an encyclopedic recounting of the trials women of color face. This shift is due in large part to the high-profile nature of the Michigan cases and, as I discuss in this anthology's conclusion, the way social media is shaping the narratives of faculty of color during tenure battles, even if it doesn't change the outcome of those struggles. *Mentoring Faculty of Color* joins guides such as the almost canonical *The Black Academic's Guide to Winning Tenure—Without Losing Your Soul* (2008) and pushes the notion that the academy is a minefield that can be successfully navigated. The most recent anthology, *Beginning a Career in Academia: A Guide for Graduate Students of Color* (2015), makes clear that at the same time that faculty of color are, indeed, successfully climbing the academic ladder, those on its lower rungs need help understanding what it really takes to successfully navigate each rung. It's a sad and frustrating truth that in addition to the superearly professionalization that all graduate students face, graduate students of color face that process while being forced to battle assumptions by professors in their programs and disciplines that they are only in the programs because of white liberal guilt and assumptions by peers who assume that white liberal guilt will result in job opportunities they might not otherwise deserve. They will think this despite any number of studies that suggest that it's the lack of jobs and not an increase in minority applicants that shapes job markets.

Of course, to invoke numbers is to suggest that they can offer us concrete evidence about the state of diversity today. The problem is that tracking diversity with any nuance is not a major goal in higher education. Take, for example, the most recent numbers from the National Center for Education Statistics. In that counting, 4 percent of full professors are Black, but they don't designate how many are women and how many are men. If we could track attrition rates of faculty of color across the country and have a concrete number, then we might gain a greater scope of the problem. Although everyone seems to know that attrition is a problem, what Marcia Chatelain explains about her experience in Oklahoma seems to happen at many schools around the country: "No one had a conversation about why people were leaving. The assumption was that faculty of color don't want to live in Oklahoma, but a lot of us enjoyed our lives in Oklahoma." This is part of the reason why instead of large-scale studies we have snapshots that usually only emerge after cases such as the Michigan Women make troubling patterns public.

Consider what we learned about DePaul University when Namita Goswami, a philosophy professor, and Quinetta Shelby, a chemistry professor, were denied tenure in 2007.[9] We learned that in the 2008–09 academic year, seven professors from marginalized groups were denied tenure; in 2009–10, five of ten marginalized faculty of color were denied tenure. In 2011, six faculty of color were denied tenure. In 2012,

University of Southern California (USC) International Relations Professor Mai'i K. Davis responded to her tenure denial by working with USC political scientist Jane Junn to collect data (see Appendix B). Their findings show that between 1998 and 2012:

> Ninety-two percent of white men in the social sciences and humanities were awarded tenure.
>
> Fifty-five percent of women and faculty of color were awarded tenure.
>
> Eighty-one percent of white junior faculty (this includes men and women) were awarded tenure.
>
> Forty-eight percent of faculty of color were promoted to associate professor.
>
> Sixty-six point seven percent of white women were awarded tenure compared to 40 percent of Asian-American women.

The USC numbers are stark, and they reveal troubling institutional practices that hide behind languages and processes that seem neutral. They suggest that the problem of substantive diversity is an institutional problem and not one that might seem like a series of coincidences or a reflection on the candidates up for tenure. The USC data show where the commitment to diversity ("USC is an AA/EO employer and is seeking to create a diverse community") bumps up against practices of discrimination, and the analysis shows the difference between theory and praxis by pointing out the gap. According to USC's manual of the University Committee on Appointments, Promotions, and Tenure (UCAPT): "UCAPT's recommendations are made individually on a merit basis. Analysis of the data between 2005 and 2009 shows no statistically significant difference between minority and non-minority candidates in success rate for promotion to tenure. (The success rate for minority candidates happens to be five percentage points higher.) During the same period, over a quarter of UCAPT's members were themselves minority."

But as Cross and Junn show: "These figures are inconsistent with results of tenure cases in the Social Sciences and Humanities at USC College observed during this time period. Between 2005 and 2009, there were [forty-two] cases, of which [twenty-six] were white scholars and [sixteen] were minorities. White junior faculty were awarded tenure at a rate of 88.5 [percent], while 56.3 [percent] of minority junior faculty were awarded tenure. The relationship between race and being awarded tenure during this time is statistically significant at .017."

In 2013, *Insider Higher Education* reported that of the fourteen professors who went up for tenure at the University of Texas–Austin, five out of six faculty members from interdisciplinary programs were denied tenure. Although the university did not release information about race or ethnicity (they cited privacy concerns), faculty confirm that all six were from marginalized groups. At a university where twenty-three of thirty-six of the faculty working in the Center for Asian American Studies are not on the tenure track, the loss of even one faculty member is a problem. Critics of the institution's decision note that the problem in these cases was partly structural. The faculty up for tenure were not assessed by the interdisciplinary centers and institutions that relied the most on their work. They could provide letters of support but could not contribute to the review process. This, in addition to budget cuts, undoubtedly contributed to the drop in tenure rates from 81 percent in 2012 to 57 percent in 2013. A letter in response to these decisions sums up what the numbers here reveal, but only to a limited degree: "In these deliberations, important venues of interdisciplinary and ethnic studies, such as Centers and Institutes, did not have the opportunity to contribute their views and enrich the discussion and decision-making of the College Tenure and Promotion Committee. Unfortunately, this process remains limited by the boundaries of disciplines and departments; while at the same time the University publicly highlights the value of innovation and interdisciplinary research."[10]

While the temptation might be to begin a discussion about diversity in higher education with an overview of affirmative action, given that this is a book about patterns rather than policy, it's more useful to consider key moments that shape how we think about diversity in the academy today. The first PhD earned by an African American was awarded in 1876 to Edward Bouchet in physics at Yale. The first African American woman to earn a doctorate was Sadie Tanner Mossell Alexander in 1921 in economics. It would take another twenty-six years for an African American scholar—William Boyd Allison Davis—to be appointed to a permanent position. Hired as a professor of education at the University of Chicago, Davis earned tenure in 1947—just seven years after the American Association of University Professors (AAUP) moved to make tenure a more integral part of hiring and retention practices.[11] According to James D. Anderson, "Until 1941 no African American scholar, no matter how qualified, how many degrees he or she had earned, or how many excellent articles and books he or she had published, was hired in a permanent faculty position at any predominately white university in America."[12] In 1942, Berkeley statistician Jerzy Neyman tried to hire mathematician David Blackwell but, according to Blackwell, the university wouldn't hire him because he was Black. A few years later, in 1954, he was hired and went on to be the first Black professor tenured at the university.[13] In 1945, Fred G. Wale embarked on a project to place African American faculty in predominately white colleges and institutions (PWIs). In the late 1960s, amid protests against Vietnam and for women's liberation, African American students demanded that humanities curricula represent a broader world experience, specifically their own experiences. As a result, the first Black Studies Department was founded at San Francisco State University in 1968. The following year, Harvard University's law school, partly in response to protests by Black students, hired Derrick Bell. He went on to become the first tenured law professor of color in the law school in 1971 and, through protests of his own, ensured Lani Guiner's tenure in the law school in 1998.[14] It took until 2010 for an African American woman to complete the tenure track in the College of Arts and Sciences at Washington University (founded in 1853).[15] Not until 2015 did Princeton University approve a bachelor's degree in African American or Africana Studies.

Of all of these milestones, it is Wale's project that offers perhaps the most useful way to think about how some of the same ideas and attitudes against hiring faculty of color in the 1940s remain in place today, especially when tenure is at stake. Wale's campaign was launched at a historical moment of promise, at a time of progressive change on the national level and in institutions of higher education. A constellation of events informed his optimistic view that an integrated military could lead to and be a model for an integrated professoriate. It was, after all, the same historical moment that saw the founding of the Tuskegee Airmen (1941) and Executive Order 9981 (1948), the law making segregation illegal in the military. In 1940, the AAUP moved to codify tenure processes that resemble what most colleges and universities practice today. Four years later, the Serviceman's Redistribution Act of 1944 (the GI Bill) was passed. It's tempting to see the evolution of tenure and the first move to integrate the faculty of PWIs as an accident of history, but tenure and the push for diversity in higher education increased because of an influx of white World War II veterans using the GI Bill to fund their college educations.[16] According to Anderson, in the first forty years of the twentieth century, enrollments in higher education increased 529 percent. This was at a time when the nation's total population increased by only 73 percent, and the population of college-aged citizens increased by 63 percent. This influx of new students resulted in a need for more faculty, particularly in English departments (Anderson shows that there was a demand for 142,982 new faculty), and the AAUP argued that a shorter tenure clock would be a compelling inducement to recruit faculty.[17] Wale saw in the shortage of faculty an opportunity to convince presidents, provosts, and deans at PWIs to hire Black faculty, hoping that the integration evidenced in the military could be replicated in colleges and universities.

With funds from the Julius Rosenwald Fund,[18] Wale compiled a list of African American scholars with the credentials he believed would make them competitive for faculty positions at PWIs.[19] He sent letters to 600 presidents of PWIs with a list of 150. A third of the presidents replied. As chronicled through his correspondence with the presidents, his efforts showed that—even at a time when an increase in student enrollment meant more professors needed to be hired—college presidents found a variety of reasons why hiring faculty of color wasn't feasible: institutional needs, geography, population, and local community attitudes. Almost to an administrator, the claim was that the lack of faculty of color was not by choice or design but by accident: "We have no negroes on the Bryn Mawr faculty at present but we should be glad to consider candidates on the same terms as any other," the president explained to him. The president of Pennsylvania State University promised, "In appointing members of the faculty we shall continue to try to select the best person irrespective of color, race, or religion." The acting president of UC Berkeley responded, "I assure you that the university has steadily sought to choose its faculty, and its students as well, solely on the basis of their qualifications and without regard to race, ancestry." The responses continue along those lines, almost without fail. As Anderson explains, Wale's project allows us to see the "interrelationship of race, meritocracy, and institutionalized discrimination"[20]—a trio still at work today in colleges and universities across the country. While a few college presidents were candid enough to tell the truth—the president of Heidelberg College in Tiffin, Ohio, said plainly, "Our college is not ready for it yet"—most fell back on the opaque language of false meritocracy. It must have been difficult, if not impossible, for them to face the fact that foundationally and structurally their institutions might be hostile to diversity. It's not that different today, but instead of institutions resisting hiring faculty of color, they are hostile to awarding them tenure, even as they benefit from the unique contributions faculty of color make to those institutions. The list of reasons the presidents came up with in 1945 are still used today, especially the rhetoric of meritocracy. It's not difficult at all to imagine why it took more than a hundred years for an African American woman to make it through its tenure process at the college of arts and sciences at Washington University.[21] It suggests that underneath all of the diversity initiatives and the "we are an affirmative action institution" and "women and minorities encouraged to apply" statements, that despite all of those diversity committees, the academy still hasn't figured out how to maintain meaningful diversity.

In part this is because, even though personnel processes are inherently subjective at every level, those who are part of those processes deploy the language of meritocracy in the belief they are being objective. Words such as "merit" evoke notions of fairness. The "best" or "most qualified" person is offered the tenure-track position, and evaluation processes rely on words such as "excellence," "rigorous," and "innovative." These ideas and words are not in and of themselves discriminatory, but they are more subject to cultural forces than many in the academy will allow. In much the same way that race is a social construct, so are notions of excellence, and those notions are constructed by people who often unknowingly seek only to acknowledge and reward those qualities they see in themselves or wish they possessed.[22] This is not to suggest that the idea of having standards is racist, but when those standards are invented by the majority culture, it is a mistake to assume that diversity gaps are a result of a lack of qualified faculty of color. On one level, we know this, which is why personnel decisions are made by committees. This structure acknowledges that multiple viewpoints are necessary when it comes to assessing faculty, but it still ignores that terms meant to indicate merit are often used uncritically and, whether they want to or not, committees reflect the same biases that shape the larger culture's view of people of color.[23]

As Anderson points out in his discussion of Wale's project, "Usually meritocracy is viewed as the antithesis of racism, ethnic, and religious prejudice, and related forms of exclusion and discrimination. . . . The practice of proclaiming one's devotion to meritocratic principles, while actually perpetuating traditional patterns of ethnic discrimination and exclusion, transformed theoretical enemies (i.e., racism vs. meritocracy) into pragmatic friends." However, he continues, "Over time there developed in the American academy an ethic which held that African American scholars were justifiably excluded from faculty positions because somehow there was always a mismatch between their circumstances and the particular needs of the white-dominated academy."[24] Washington University's Shanti Parikh is right to say, "I've worked very hard, and I do feel honored. However, I think it's a bit embarrassing for Arts and Sciences that this is only happening in the year 2010."[25] An anthropologist with degrees from the University of Virginia and Yale, she has sterling credentials, but that isn't always enough, and, worse "enough" can be a vague, moving target. One wonders how many academics of color were hired before she was but failed to make it to tenure not because they were lacking in any substantive way but because the institution has been caught up in fixed ideas of what merit looks like and has convinced itself that those ideas don't need to be examined.[26] Perhaps its personnel committees comforted themselves with the same argument that W. C. Giersbach, president of Pacific University in Forest Grove, Oregon, used in 1945 when he claimed that his institution "had no written or unwritten rules concerning the employment of colored folk."[27]

Of course this wasn't true then, and it's not true now. The academy thrives on unwritten rules. Personnel processes in the academy are particularly opaque at almost every stage—from the processes departments use to decide what areas they want tenure-track positions in, to the composition of search committees, to mentoring of junior faculty through the tenure process. In many instances opacity is a result of trying to accommodate for the different reasons why faculty are hired in the first place; departmental needs tend to be specific, while institutional evaluative measures are more broad, and this gap widens when the time comes to evaluate tenure candidates. In addition, curricular discussions (which courses count toward a degree and which are electives) and institutional cultures build up and tear down faculty (sometimes actively and sometimes simply by neglecting them) based on a complicated code that can be impossible to crack. In the essay "Women and Minority Faculty in the Academic Workplace: Recruitment, Retention, and Academic Culture," Adalberto Aguirre makes a claim that, on the surface, seems self-evident: "The academic workplace is characterized in popular thinking as a place of enlightened thought and discourse that is immune to influences from the outside world. Its perceived immunity to the outside world has resulted in a perception that the academic workplace is free of conflict and stress. The reality, however, is that the academic workplace is characterized by struggles over the definition of knowledge and about what it means to be a knowledgeable person. To survive in the academic workplace, faculty members must align themselves with and participate in institutional networks that define one's position in a knowledge hierarchy."[28]

The challenge for untenured faculty is to figure out which networks matter and—more important—how to read the individuals who make up those networks. Navigating those networks can be difficult for anyone, but add race to the mix and it is all too easy to end up in a minefield with colleagues and administrators who use tenure not to reward accomplishment and potential but as a way to weed out those who simply don't fit in intellectually, socially, or, culturally. The first landmines can appear as soon as the interview process begins. Graduate school can teach all manner of important skills (in and out of the classroom), and job workshops[29] can help with cover letters and teaching portfolios, but there is no class on how to respond when someone says to a candidate of color, during a campus interview, "While we'd like to diversify the department, we will make an appointment on merit, and will look for the best candidate," a statement made to a Black South African assistant professor of psychology during a campus visit. It can't teach faculty members how to respond to jokes like the one told to an African American associate professor of education who reports: "While walking with another colleague of color to a faculty meeting, a colleague said in jest, 'This side of the hallway sure is looking darker lately.' My colleague and I exchange[d] glances with each other. This same colleague observe[d] the noticeable exchange and trie[d] to make light of the comment. 'You ladies know I was just kidding, don't you?' "[30]

This exchange highlights several tensions that can bubble up when faculty of color come up for tenure. The problematic "is looking darker" while telling is perhaps less interesting than the final question, "You ladies know I was just kidding, don't you?" It's not a question at all, of course, but a kind of dare, one that marginalized people face all the time. It demands that statements that are problematic at best and racist, sexist, or homophobic at worst be given a pass by the very people who rightly feel they are its target. The "ladies" are put in charge of managing the moment, and it's not only possible but highly likely that if they don't laugh it off or "let it go," their colleague will be offended and uncomfortable around them, and if this colleague has any part of their personnel review,

this discomfort will shade his evaluation of their work. Their very subject position as "racialized other" can trigger anxiety and a kind of racist
Tourette's syndrome in white colleagues who haven't done the work of
thinking carefully about race. Moments like this are not just annoying
or demoralizing to academics of color and their allies but, the case can
be made, they lead to statements like the second epigraph to this introduction: "I don't know if I want to work with a black on a permanent
basis." This statement is not startling just for its blatant racism but for
how much it reveals about how a candidate's tenure file is reviewed. At
the end of the day, merit had little or nothing to do for this vocal member of a review committee and more about whether or not this member
is willing to "work with a black" for the long term. Perhaps even more
stunning is the fact that he felt wholly comfortable making this prefer-
ence clear to his colleagues.

In response to an anonymous column written by a Black woman for
Insider Higher Education about the "gray balloon" feeling of being reduced to a statistic, a commentator writes: "Thank you for writing this
with such feeling. Unfortunately, I was recently part of a hiring panel
where I was the lone vote for hiring the *most experienced, educated, qualified* candidate for our university. Instead, I listened to my fellow pan-
elists tout the least qualified candidate and eventually hire her, I am
certain, because she is African-American. In addition, her attitude has
proven out to be 'you owe me.' This is how the gray balloon is inflated
time and again, but the bigger impact is that I've lost all respect for my
colleagues." (*emphasis added*).[31]

It's not difficult to imagine how this anonymous commentator treats
the African American colleague and what this attitude could mean for
her tenure review. Is that anger carefully masked? Does it leak out
in ways she doesn't quite understand? If the commentator is not simply
being hyperbolic and actually no longer respects the personnel process,
what does that mean if her tenure case comes to a departmental vote?
More important, can she ever do enough to overcome that initial resentment? When people like this commentator genuinely believe the bar
has been lowered to hire faculty of color, then those faculty are viewed
suspiciously and even external reviews and evaluations from the commentator's colleagues won't be enough. Hired under a cloud she had no
part in creating, this new faculty member faces obstacles that cannot be
overcome by any amount of publishing or collegiality or any number of
external reviews or professional accolades. For at least one colleague, her

tenure case has already been decided. And the cruel irony is that while her colleague will claim with conviction that she was only hired because she is African American, he will also claim he only finds her unworthy because she is not "qualified."

Given how much of the tenure process is kept from candidates up for review, it is all too easy for the resentment that soaks this comment to hide behind language that seems neutral on the surface. Since "higher education institutions are greatly influenced by, and cannot be analyzed apart from, the larger social, historical, and cultural context,"[32] and we have documented evidence that faculty and administrations hold problematic attitudes like the one on full display in the comment under discussion, how can they fairly evaluate their colleagues of color? Further, how can they value the unique contributions faculty of color make, especially when those contributions are not easily quantified? When faculty of color are hired, they are expected to accomplish different things than their white counterparts: to "diversify" institutions with their very presence, to serve as role models for students of color in particular and for the student population in general, to represent an alternative perspective on matters ranging from curriculum development to faculty governance by serving on an array of committees, and to represent the concerns, habits, and histories of whatever ethnic group to which they happen to belong.[33] Unfortunately, in the bean-counting model of evaluating faculty, these contributions don't really count. Denied tenure by USC's religion department, Jane Iwamura explains, "There are certainly additional demands on faculty of color. We are asked to serve on more committees, help out students groups, and mentor and serve as role models to graduate and undergraduate students, because of our unique experience and positionality. . . . It can be a real balancing act, since it is work we obviously feel is important and necessary," she continues, "but oftentimes, such work is not 'counted' by the university as far as tenure is concerned."[34] At the same time, they are expected to fit in to the department's and institution's dominant culture and not raise any difficult questions or they run the risk of being labeled "uncollegial"—academic jargon for calling an uncooperative person hostile or angry.[35]

Some of the work that faculty of color are called on to do is the bridge-building work of simply being present. Sometimes the institution needs them to do the kind of work that is easier to ignore or easier to place solely on the shoulders of faculty of color. Take, for example, a list of duties included in a 2006 report recommending the approval of a bachelor's degree in African American Studies at Princeton. Forty-three years after the first Black Studies program was founded, Princeton was on the verge of making it possible for students to major in the subject. The authors of a five-year plan advocating for the major explain some of the duties of faculty currently affiliated with the certificate program: "Our faculty will have to conduct multiple searches, enrich the University's certificate program, oversee renovations to the Program's physical home, and assist in fundraising." They know it's a lot: "That is a tall order."[36] At the 2010 symposium "Race, Tenure, and the University: A Public Forum," Cynthia Young, also denied tenure by USC, talked about being hired by Boston College to resurrect a floundering Black Studies program. In his report on the symposium, Liam Drislane notes Young's claim that "scholars in Ethnic studies do an inordinate amount of program building." Program building in emerging fields of study is part of the workload for many academics, but the preponderance of emerging fields of study are organized around questions of race and developed by faculty of color. The time and energy to do this work means time away from building and maintaining a research agenda. More important, while this work requires a great deal of effort, it often does not count in any meaningful way toward tenure, and it is rare to find a department of colleagues who will argue for valuing that work—not because whole departments are racist but because the work of building diversity, especially at the curricular level, is hard, thankless, and largely invisible (see Appendix C).

At the same time, if, as is often the case, faculty of color work in new or emerging fields of scholarship such as Ethnic Studies, Latino/a history, Afro-American literary studies, or new areas in existing fields, their colleagues in more traditional fields may lack the basic understanding necessary to accurately and fairly evaluate the quality of their scholarship.[37] When these elements are part of evaluative processes that are largely invisible, vagueness rather than clarity reigns. In other words, while faculty of color often rightly feel they are being held to different standards than their white counterparts, the language of evaluation is so opaque as to leave these professors and their allies confused, frustrated, and, worst of all, paralyzed. Although the subjective nature of evaluation makes fair reappointment and tenure reviews difficult, charges of unfairness are difficult to prove. There has yet to be a denial of tenure that begins, "We are denying Candidate X tenure because she is Hispanic" or "Because Professor X is Black, we'd rather not grant him a lifetime appointment." Terry L. Leap explains in the essay "Tenure, Discrimination, and African-American Faculty" that "most accusations of race discrimination are difficult to prove because of their subtle nature."[38] This is, in part, because tenure cases are rarely black-and-white. Even when race is a clear factor in tenure denials, it is rarely the only reason. When the four women of color at the University of Michigan–Ann Arbor were denied tenure in 2007, it's unlikely that the departments blocking their path to tenure saw this as anything more than a coincidence. The data we have for USC is not widely available at other institutions. It is lucky then that Reginald Clark happened to overhear the consideration of his tenure file in 1984 when a colleague said, "I don't know if I want to work with a black on a permanent basis." It's lucky that this comment was one of a string of incidents that proved to a court's satisfaction that he was being discriminated against. According to court records and Leap's reporting, Clark, who has a doctorate in education from Wisconsin–Madison, was told by his department chair at Claremont University Center that he should focus his research on issues of multiculturalism. Hired in 1979, he was the only Black faculty member at Claremont and published and developed courses in the area. When he came up for tenure, five scholars in his field praised his publishing record and recommended tenure. His teaching reviews were mixed, but no other potentially mitigating factors were mentioned in the tenure file. The court decided in his favor, awarding him $1.4 million. They list six reasons, including the fact that two other non-minority faculty with "inferior" publishing records received tenure and "Claremont used unwritten, changing publication standards to justify its denial of tenure to Clark."

Evaluation processes are, however, often hidden, especially at private colleges and universities,[39] but Lisa Sánchez ("In Search of Our Fathers' Workshops") found the paper trail that detailed her tenure process. She utilized the Freedom of Information Act, and one of her colleagues had an attack of conscience and sent her the e-mails a nemesis had been circulating about her to derail her tenure review and her attempts to find another position. Sometimes carelessness on behalf of the committee opens a window for the candidate. When a member of the tenure committee reviewing Vassar professor Kiese Laymon's tenure file inadvertently sent an e-mail about his file to the wrong person, Laymon learned that his colleague was investigating his credentials to see if he had earned the degrees listed on his vita,[40] even though his pre-tenure reviews were overwhelming positive. Absent damning evidence, sometimes a proven pattern of tenure denials can spark questions.

It is not exaggerating to say that every academic of color has a story about how their subject position clashed with an institution's vision of itself. And while the temptation might be to place the blame solely on an academy dominated by white men, white women in the academy can be as oppressive as their male counterparts, even though we might assume that Women's Studies departments are more inclusive than traditional departments. Given the activist history of Women's Studies and the oppression that white women face in the academy, it can feel counterintuitive to see women as enacting the same discriminatory practices they have worked against, but as Audre Lorde explained in her address to the National Women's Studies Association conference, it can be precisely because white women face sexism that they are blind to their own oppressive conduct. In 1981 she posed a challenging question: "What woman here is so enamored of her own oppression that she does not see her heel print upon another woman's face?" It's a question that women of color still ask today as they report a lack of support or aggressive hostility from white feminists who purport to share a common struggle. This results in blind spots that force women of color to wrestle with explicit racism and microaggressions under the additional burdens that come with the call for solidarity that characterizes mainstream feminism. An assistant professor at a small, Midwestern liberal college shares how her department chair and dean responded to poor teaching evaluations: "Neither woman, both putatively concerned with inequality, used their sociological imaginations to interrogate why a young, African American female professor who, through their own admissions, had never displayed what was being described in course evaluations from white middle-class students who, as one expressed to me in class, thought it 'weird' that he had an African American woman for a professor. Indeed, it was not until three years later, and in a comment directed towards someone else, that my chair said that she thought that my evaluations were shaped by the constellation of my race, age, and gender."

Despite numerous studies that prove that women of color are viewed more harshly than white men and white women,[41] this assistant professor's white female colleagues saw no need to use their intellectual and academic training to understand the gap between what they knew about her and how students perceived her. They are perfect examples of what Mariana Ortega describes in her essay "Being Lovingly, Knowingly Ignorant"; white women who "are actually involved in the production of knowledge about women of color—whether by citing their work, reading and writing about them, or classifying them—while at the same time using women of color to the perceiver's own ends."[42] What this suggests is that in all corners of the academy, even those spaces that explicitly work to reveal systemic oppression, faculty of color face obstacles that disrupt their research agendas, teaching, and service to their institutions.

The narratives here offer snapshots that are proof of larger patterns at work. As the blog that extends the project beyond traditional ink and paper publication shows, there are more stories to tell, more questions to ask. While the stories here fall under the broad categories of race, gender, and sexuality and also take on the issues we've come to associate with conversations about diversity, I have paired them based on how their narratives reflect the different modes and models of academics of color so that we can better understand not only what they bring to the academy but also what the academy demands of them.

Foundations

In an interview with Ayanna Jackson-Fowler ("Responding to the Call-(ing): The Spirituality of Mentorship and Community in Academia"), Houston Baker recalls his first year at Yale in the 1960s when, in response to a trio of graduate students who told him they "need[ed] him for a revolution," he decided to apply his training as a Victorianist to the study of African American literature. In addition to recalling the different communities that have helped him from his time at UCLA to his current position as Distinguished University Professor in English at Vanderbilt, Baker reflects on the progress and challenges of diversity in humanities in and out of the academy.

Rashida Harrison ("Building a Canon, Creating Dialogue: An Interview with Cheryl A. Wall") recounts her conversation with Cheryl Wall, the Board of Governor's Zora Neal Hurston Professor of English at Rutgers University, whose career has both shaped and followed the contours of the rise of African American literary studies. In the early 1970s, when Wall joined the faculty at Rutgers, discourses and methodology about African American literature were in their formative stages. Wall simultaneously broke new ground in the classroom and in the field. As she remembers it, "I would tell students in the African American course that there were not shelves of books or a consensus about what we were teaching. All our opinions were valid as long as they were based in the text. . . . Part of my role as a teacher was really to help create a critical language that would allow the text to be discussed."

Navigations

Leslie Bow ("Difference without Grievance: Asian Americans as the Almost Minority") argues that Asian Americans hold a precarious place in the American imagination and within academic institutions as well. The simultaneous erasure and celebration of cultural difference, its uncertain capital, and the ambiguity about where Asian Americans stand in the history of social injury and its redress are, Bow explains, all inseparable from the ways in which they are located on American campuses. In her essay, she explores the ways in which this climate might impact the ambiguous place that Asian Americans inhabit within academia as "overrepresented" minorities.

Lisa Sánchez González ("In Search of Our Fathers' Workshops") explores the highlights and lowlights in her journey from kindergarten to tenure as a Boricua feminist scholar deemed "radical" in U.S. academia. Her essay charts the challenges that she (and many other Latina girls identified early in their education as "gifted") overcame in public schools and the pattern of racial, class, and gender stereotyping that perpetually repeated itself in her academic career, as well as how it uniquely deformed the shape of her first tenure review.

Identities

In her essay ("Tenure in the Contact Zone: Spanish is Our Language Too"), Angie Chabram charts her negotiations of higher education, her own brand of cultural politics, and her interdisciplinary path toward bilingual Chicana/o Studies and interdisciplinary cultural studies to winning tenure. Rather than overpersonalizing her story or providing celebratory closure, she invites readers to consider how the language and tenure struggle that intersect in higher education reflect the struggles of everyday people in different geopolitical and educational venues.

Andreana Clay ("'Colored' is the New Queer: Queer Faculty of Color in the Academy") and a small group of queer faculty of color reflect on E. Patrick Johnson's experiences at Amherst College, which are recounted in his essay "In the Merry Old Land of Oz: Rac(e)ing, Quee(r)-ing the Academy," as they discuss how things have and have not changed for LGBTQ faculty around the country. In addition to the challenges that all faculty of color face, this essay shows the struggles unique to queer faculty—from coming out in the classroom to being viewed as super minorities, to working in departments all too willing to ignore the invisible labor they do as they work to build communities in and out of academia.

Manifestos

The overall inquiry of the essay by Jane Chin Davidson and Deepa S. Reddy ("Performative Testimony and the Practice of Dismissal") can be understood as an investigation of the tyranny of dismissing women of color in Women's Studies communities by silencing them. This essay looks empirically at specific experiences in Women's Studies for what they are—attempts to delimit voice, speech, naming, and ultimately, contestations made by minority women in the community. Chin Davidson and Reddy conceive of "dismissal" as a practice that is inextricable from the speech act and through a consideration of Crenshaw and Derrida seek to renegotiate actions that subordinates expression, participation, and membership in a community that is called "women's studies," the name itself signifying a particular, narrow membership that fails to recognize the shifting constituencies that make up its community.

Written in the wake of her tenure case at the University of Michigan ("Talking Tenure: 'Don't be safe. Because there is no safety there anyway'"), Sarita Echavez See's essay reflects the various subject positions she has held in the academy from untenured and therefore vulnerable assistant professor to a powerful advocate and organizer calling for institutions to closely interrogate what is at stake when faculty of color face tenure battles. Reflecting the challenges of writing about the unwritten record of racism and sexism in the United States academy, this essay documents and juxtaposes two radio segments with the radio collective "Asian Pacific American (APA): A Compass"—a rant and an interview—that See did as part of two national tenure justice campaigns on behalf of women of color academics that she helped organize at the University of Michigan in 2007–08 and at the University of Southern California in 2010–11.

Hierarchies

With an essay that challenges the notion that processes can ever be neutral ("Still Eating in the Kitchen: The Marginalization of African American Faculty in Majority White Academic Governance"), Carmen Harris addresses the issue of bureaucratic racism and the resultant marginalization of African American faculty in historically white colleges and universities through processes of faculty governance. The essay illuminates the consequences of tribalism and bias masquerading under the guise of professional objectivity in an environment in which overt racism is frowned upon but also one in which systems intended to thwart inequality are applied by members of the majority to the disadvantage of people of color.

In his essay ("Contingent Diversity, Contingent Faculty: Or, Musings of a Lowly Adjunct"), Wilson Santos, a relative newcomer to the academy, discusses how he came to understand the exploitative nature of contingent faculty. Santos's narrative is more about class than race, though his writing and teaching reflect his experiences as a man of color. Folded into Santos's stories are the experiences of two other adjunct faculty. Doctoral Candidate X, a queer Black woman, talks about how the intersection of class and sexuality shape her choices as she considers whether or not to continue her academic career, while Dionne Bensonsmith discusses how she has fashioned a scholarly community for herself so that she can forward her research agenda even though she doesn't have the resources enjoyed by tenure-track and tenured faculty.

Activism(s)

In her essay ("Balancing the Passion for Activism with the Demands of Tenure: One Professional's Story from Three Perspectives"), April Few-Demo demonstrates what is possible when senior faculty work with junior faculty throughout the tenure process. She discusses the challenge of balancing her commitment to diversity and social justice with the demands of tenure and reflects on how racism and sexism within the classroom have defined her professional identity as an activist scholar. Her colleagues Fred P. Piercy and Andrew J. Stremmel discuss how they advised her throughout this process, and they ask us to think more carefully about how we assess junior faculty, providing a model for how to make the case for faculty of color who might feel a different pull toward activism than their white counterparts.

"When you get to my age," E. Frances White told me in the months before she retired, "you can tell your history in many different ways." In this essay ("Cast Your Net Wide"), White's history and reflections are juxtaposed against the questions and aspirations of two junior scholars—Ariana Alexander and Jennifer Williams—who are developing academic careers on and off the tenure track at a time when student protests demanding more diverse faculty are moving from campus to campus at the same time that wealthy universities are announcing multimillion dollar programs to develop diversity. The essay poses more questions than it answers but addresses the question Alexander poses as she completes her doctorate: "How can I see my intellectual work manifest itself in real ways?"

The anthology concludes by looking forward and considering how social media, especially Twitter, is shaping how faculty of color manage their careers by discussing the possibilities and risks of engaging with complicated ideas and taking on the work of activism outside of academia while in full view of those who evaluate our work.

As historian Deborah Gray White notes, "Things have changed, but some things have only been altered and there is a big difference between change and alteration."[43] With an increased presence of faculty of color on campuses, it is easy to confuse alteration for change. It is easy to ignore how many faculty of color are clustered in contingent ranks, often as diversity fellows, visiting assistant professors with short-term contracts, or untenured assistant professors.[44] In these precarious positions, they often struggle more than those who fit the traditional profile of an academic to gain tenure-track positions, tenure, and promotion. Hired for their difference, they are often penalized for not being like their white peers, not only on the level of identity politics but also for the roles they are often expected to take on in their departments and for the methodologies and focus of their scholarship. The result has been a tenuous diversity, and as the specter of the economic crisis continues to erode the budgets of colleges and universities, it is more important than ever to attend to the persistent problem of bias in the evaluative process and its effects on sustaining a diverse professoriate. This collection shows that the academy is somewhere between two poles. At one end, it seems as if Derrick Bell's claims about Black people still apply to those who have done the hard, often isolating work of earning the chance to write, teach, and work in American colleges and universities: "Black people are the magical faces at the bottom of society's well. Even the poorest whites, those who must live their lives only a few levels above, gain their self-esteem by gazing down at us. Surely, they must know that their deliverance depends on letting down their ropes. Only by working together is escape possible. Over time, many reach out, but most simply watch, mesmerized into maintaining their unspoken commitment to keeping us where we are, at whatever cost to them or to us."[45]

At the other end, there are successes—just as there were in 1945. Fred Wale's campaign resulted in twenty-three faculty of color joining predominately white institutions. Some of the presidents said yes, and there are moments of positive diversity today—invariably these moments happen where faculty of color are spread out among the ranks, when there are senior faculty to mentor junior faculty, and where they have helped institutions move beyond the limits of their racial imaginations. There are programs designed to prepare future graduate students from marginalized communities for the culture of academia: the Moore Undergraduate Research Apprentice Program (MURAP) at the University of North Carolina at Chapel Hill, African American Literatures and Cultures Institute at the University of Texas at San Antonio, and the Rutgers English Diversity Institute (REDI), cofounded by contributor Cheryl Wall.[46] More than just offering the kind of intellectual engagements that all scholars are expected to perform, these programs aim to demystify processes and practices that might seem like second nature to many academics. As faculty face increased pressure to publish more and faster in a tight tenure market, programs for faculty of color are becoming more common. The National Center for Faculty Diversity and Development offers a broad array of services for new faculty who can afford the annual membership fee of $480 or $3,400 for four months of coaching via the web. Duke's Summer Institute on Tenure and Professional Advancement (SITPA) is the most promising and is a program that should be replicated around the country. Hosted by Duke's Center for the Study of Race, Ethnicity, and Gender in the Social Sciences and funded by the Mellon Foundation, the program pairs new faculty in their first or second year on the tenure track with senior faculty in their fields for twenty-four months. It is unrealistic to expect that the gap between the written and the unwritten will ever be completely closed; institutions rely on methods of exclusion to distinguish themselves, but it is possible for institutions to understand their own fallibility so that they can develop fairer processes—perhaps to let diversity committees do meaningful work.

Notes

1. Anderson, "Race, Meritocracy, and the American Academy during the Immediate Post-World War II Era," 6.

2. Leap, "Tenure Discrimination, and African-American Faculty," 104.

3. Stanley, "Coloring the Academic Landscape," 722.

4. Johnson, *Pym*, 8.

5. Ibid., 18.

6. Ibid., 20.

7. See Bramen, "Minority Hiring in the Age of Downsizing."

8. Matthew, Review of *Mentoring Faculty of Color*, 283–84.

9. Several of the DePaul professors won their discrimination suit. See Flaherty, "Women and Tenure at DePaul."

10. Straumsheim, "Interdisciplinary and Out of a Job."

11. According to Ryan C. Amacher and Roger E. Meiners, the current model for tenure went into effect in 1915, but 1940 marks the date when the AAUP worked to change the probationary period from ten to seven years, which is the period at most colleges and universities today. See Amacher and Meiners, *Faulty Towers*.

12. Anderson, "Race, Meritocracy, and the American Academy during the Immediate Post-World War II Era," 4.

13. David Harold Blackwall, "National Visionary"; Grimes, "David Blackwell."

14. In 1988, the Black Law Students Association occupied the outer office of the dean of the law school: see Gold, "Black Students End Occupation."

15. Levitt, "Wash. U. Finally Gives an African-American Woman Tenure."

16. While the 1944 GI Bill has been touted for the access it provided World War II Veterans to an array of resources (money for a college education and money for housing), the intentions of the law could not move around a host of legal and socially constructed practices designed to limit African Americans' access to education and stability. For a full accounting, see Mencke, *Education, Racism, and the Military*, and Katznelson, *When Affirmative Action Was White*. I am grateful to Ta-Nehisi Coates for pointing me toward a more nuanced understanding of the law in his post "A Religion of Colorblind Policy."

17. Anderson, "Race, Meritocracy, and the American Academy during the Immediate Post-World War II Era," 6.

18. Belles, "The College Faculty, the Negro Scholar, and the Julius Rosenwald Fund," *Journal of Negro History* 54(4) (1969): 383–92.

19. The candidates he put forward had doctorates from elite institutions, including Columbia, the University of Chicago, Northwestern University, the University of Pennsylvania, Harvard University, the University of Wisconsin, Oxford University, and Yale University.

20. Anderson, "Race, Meritocracy, and the American Academy during the Immediate Post-World War II Era," 5.

21. Marcal, "Tenured Professor Overcomes Obstacles of Race and Gender."

22. Jaschik, "Hiring Themselves."

23. A contributor to Christine Stanley's study on the connection between racism as a system of institutional oppression explains: "As do all institutions of higher education, the university I joined reflects the majority culture. Historically excluded from the academy, minority faculty have been admitted as guests within the majority culture's house . . . expected to 'honor their hosts' customs without question, keep out of certain rooms . . . and . . . always be on their best behavior'" (Turner, "New Faces, New Knowledge," 85). Minority faculty are subject to the expectation that they will think and act as do their white colleagues.

24. Anderson, "Race, Meritocracy, and the American Academy during the Immediate Post-World War II Era," 16. See also *Journal of Blacks in Higher Education*, "No blacks in the pipeline: The standard explanation for low percentage of Black faculty continues to be much of a red herring."

25. Jaschik, "Hiring Themselves."

26. To be clear, Parikh is the first African American woman to succeed all the way through Washington University's tenure process as an initial hire. According to university officials, faculty of color who have received tenure in the past have been hired from other institutions.

27. Anderson, "Race, Meritocracy, and the American Academy during the Immediate Post-World War II Era," 173.

28. Aguirre, "Women and Minority Faculty in the Academic Workplace," 3.

29. Cornelius et al., "The ABCs of Tenure"; Baez, *Affirmative Action, Hate Speech, and Tenure*; Evans, *Black Women in the Ivory Tower*; Laszloffy and Rockquemore, *The Black Academic's Guide to Winning Tenure*; Mabokela and Green, *Sisters of the Academy*; White, *Telling Histories*.

30. Stanley, "Coloring the Academic Landscape," 722.

31. Anonymous, "Not Just a Diversity Number."

32. Allen, "The Black Academic," 112–13.

33. See Baez, "Race-Related Service and Faculty of Color."

34. Banh, "Professor Denied Tenure Despite Decade of Service."

35. See Haag, "Is Collegiality Code for Hating Ethnic, Racial, and Female Faculty at Tenure Time?"

36. Princeton University Reports, "Program in African American Studies."

37. Drislane reports that David Lloyd (professor of English at USC) explains, "Decisions are being made not just by peers in [the candidate's] fields, but by committees and provosts who potentially know nothing about your field."

38. Leap, "Tenure Discrimination, and African-American Faculty," 103.

39. In a column for *Religious Studies News* published by the American Academy of Religion, Andrea Smith argues that the secrecy surrounding tenure processes can be especially damaging to faculty of color.

40. Laymon, "Recipe #150: How to Lay Claim to Dignity," kieselaymon.com/p =1697.

41. See Dukes and Gay, "The Effects of Gender, Status, and Effective Teaching"; Fries and McNinch, "Signed Versus Unsigned Student Evaluations of Teach-

ing"; Hendrix, "Student Perceptions of the Influence of Race"; Rubin, "Help! My Professor (or Doctor or Boss) Doesn't Talk English."

42. Ortega, "Being Lovingly, Knowingly Ignorant."

43. Conference marking the sixtieth anniversary of the Radcliffe Institute for Advanced Study's Arthur and Elizabeth Schlesinger Library on the History of Women in America.

44. The National Center for Education Statistics reports that of 728,997 professors in 2013, 21 percent were Black, Hispanic, Asian/Pacific Islander, and American Indian/Alaska Native.

45. Bell, *Faces at the Bottom of the Well*, epigraph.

46. I have sent several students to the REDI program; all of them have gone on to graduate school.

Foundations

Responding to the Call(ing)

The Spirituality of Mentorship and Community in Academia:
An Interview with Houston A. Baker Jr.

Ayanna Jackson-Fowler
Tarrant County College

Houston Baker Jr. has taught in the academy for more than forty years in institutions such as Yale, the University of Pennsylvania, and Duke. Born in Louisville, Kentucky, in 1943, he initially wanted to be a lawyer because, as he said during our conversation, "In the segregated world of Louisville, there did not seem to exist a world of professions or professional opportunities for Blacks. It sort of boiled down to doctor, lawyer, teacher, preacher, or undertaker. Though I knew very little about what a legal career might entail, it seemed the most glamorous of available choices." In his second year of college at Howard University, Baker decided to major in English because of the influence of his mother, who was a teacher. He notes that she would "walk around the house quoting Chaucer and Tennyson and Langston Hughes." "From my mother," he continued, "came my love of literature and of reading." During his first year as an assistant professor at Yale in 1969, Baker would experience a major shift in his career by leaving behind his training as a Victorianist to research African American literature, a field of study that was virtually nonexistent at the time. This shift in his research was the result of a "calling" from a group of Black students at Yale who insisted on a community-wide Black revolution. Baker responded to this call and would go on to be not only a preeminent figure in Black literary studies but also the first African American president of the Modern Language Association. He is currently Distinguished University Professor of English at Vanderbilt. Over the course of this conversation, he not only talked about his career but also about the way different communities are part of his academic career. He also reflected on the role of mentorship, the risks and rewards of an academic career, and the role of Black intellectuals at a time when they are called on to contribute to public conversations.

Beginnings, Connections, and the Calling

Although the "inferable connection between family and vocation" largely contributed to Baker attaining his first position as an assistant professor at Yale, his connection to African American student activists at the university allowed him to help them position a Black revolution in New Haven. For Baker, both of these connections enhanced his first job more than the "affirmative action" and "tokenism" that he says seemed to be the reason he was hired at Yale. Content with his decision to pursue a career in academia, Baker says, "I would have lost, in a figurative sense, my life's joy if I had not gotten the [first] job that I did and stayed on."

How did you get your first job?

My first job was a matter of changes in society and things that were going on vis-à-vis the appearance of African American men and women in places where they had not traditionally been present at all. My older brother graduated from Howard University Law School in 1965, the same year that I got my BA degree from the same university. He went off to work in New York and ended up in one of the top Wall Street law firms. He was the only Black person in this firm. I went off to Edinburgh, Scotland, my third year of graduate school to continue studying and to write my dissertation. While there, I got a letter from my brother in which he said that he had been talking to his white colleagues at the firm, and they told him that, with affirmative action and the things that were then going on in the United States, if I was going to get my PhD, I should start by applying to Princeton, Harvard, and Yale because these universities were looking for Black PhDs. I looked at that letter in disbelief and thought, "He's lost it up there in New York. The Ivy League is not looking for black PhDs." I wrote to my dissertation adviser at UCLA, and, in his response letter, he told me that it would not be good for me to apply to those schools because they only hired their own. He advised me that I should just stay focused on the dissertation. On the evening of the same day that I received this letter, I showed the adviser's response to my wife, who had been teaching in Edinburgh. She looked at the letter, put it on the table, and said, "Apply to Princeton, Harvard, and Yale. Listen to your brother." So, I did, and I got a telegram from the chair of the Yale English Department saying, "Meet me in London at the British Museum for lunch, an interview, and a job offer." And, there it is. The rest is history.

One of the things that characterized the achievement of my receiving my first job was my decision to go abroad and write my dissertation in Edinburgh. My wife and I decided to go to Edinburgh because I was studying English Literature, but I had never been to the United Kingdom. In fact, I had never been abroad. I first applied to Sussex University to spend a year in the [United Kingdom], but that did not work out, and Edinburgh wrote back with open arms. The National Library of Scotland is in Edinburgh, so I knew I would have access to very useful archives for research. Edinburgh was a personal and an intellectual adventure that turned out very well, indeed. I wrote almost the entirety of my dissertation while abroad, and my wife and I made good friends. Going abroad accelerated my job search and put it outside the normal process of going to MLA, interviewing, and so forth. I went to several places and wrote to a few places in April or May of the year that I was taking off to go to Edinburgh, which was 1967. I visited places and actually talked to people on board at different universities, and I think that there were a couple of offers that came out of that process. In some ways, the times were flush. There was a lot of money around in the academy at that time. When I asked my adviser how I was to go about conducting my job search, he handed me the Modern Language Association directory and said, "Just look in there and find out the places you might like to go, write to the chairs, and tell them you want a job." Of course this method has been unheard of for many years in the academy. But, getting started early had amazing advantages, and I guess, in one sense, there is an inferable connection between family and vocation. What I mean by this is: Because my older brother (hence "family") had found his way to Wall Street and had come in contact with a network of well-endowed and well-placed white professionals—he learned what the then "professional marketplace" was looking for with respect to Blacks. His access to information from within the system, as it was, and his passing it on to me resulted in my amazing first academic post. I was lucky just to get the early start and then to get information from a person who knew what the employment scene was within the U.S. academic economy.

What, if any, kind of work do you feel you've been called to do because of your race or gender?

The calling was from a group of amazing graduate students who were based in architecture, drama, and elsewhere on Yale's campus. They were intent on a Black revolution to be situated in New Haven and at the university. A group of three of them came to me one day, and I thought they were coming to hear about Oscar Wilde or my achievements in the white academy. When I finished my dissertation and left UCLA, I was a trained and committed English literary Victorianist, and my dream was to write a definitive biography of Oscar Wilde. The woman in the group, Pam Jones, looked at me and said, "Brother Baker, did anybody tell you how much you look like Malcolm X? We need you for the revolution." I thought that revolution was a pretty good idea given the fact that I came from segregated Jim Crow Louisville, Kentucky, which was very scarring to body, soul, and psyche. So, this group of committed folks was, as it turned out, affiliated with Black faculty and with the Black activists in the communities surrounding Yale. The Black Panthers were extremely active in New Haven at that time. So, the call came from activities that were very much in process, and, in many ways, far outside my acquaintance or knowledge. It was just one of those serendipitous blessings. I had colleagues, and I had a location in my standard English literature credentials. When I say that about "credentials," I mean actually to emphasize "standard" because the study of English Victorian literature was, in itself, a recently flourishing field. But still, Victorian studies were flourishing within what Thomas Kuhn[1] would call the "normal practice" of a venerated discipline, namely, English literary study as approved by the likes of Harvard and Oxford, Princeton and Cambridge. Most of my peers and superiors in my first academic post made it clear that my Victorian literature credentials were preeminent in whatever positive proof they had of my intelligence. I was young, though, and perhaps too naïve, and felt I could convert to an energetic Black aesthetic activism without professional consequences. The Black national mood was heady. I was blessed to be a part of that. I felt I was called in ways that are obvious from the story of affirmative action I just related. I was called to be involved in a certain politics of representation that can be interpreted, in not uncharitable ways, as a certain tokenism that was being engaged to show off the commitment, post–Dr. King's assassination, of a particular institution. By "tokenism" I mean that I can only speculate on the causes for my hiring at Yale, but one eager male spouse of one of the white cohort that was hired with me was happy to tell me one day: "You know you were only hired here—and my wife knows because she was a Yale graduate student when it happened and is now your colleague—because you are black." This cannot be a great surprise to many, right? A great number of us have gained entry—no matter what our IQ or EQ—as spooks expected to sit by the door forever. But, there was so much more than tokenism that graced my first academic post. It was quite an extraordinary moment.

Misconceptions and Tensions Surrounding Race, Gender, and Diversity

In response to my questions about tensions related to diversity in academic departments, Baker not only offered examples of his experience with such situations but also discussed specific ways that faculty of color can effectively respond to them. He explained that the biggest mistake departments make while hiring faculty is to believe that "there can somehow be a quantifiable number that is called 'enough difference'" and thus cap "the organizational imagination and the intellectual imagination" of a particular program. Baker discussed how he responded to a variety of racial misconceptions by being a part of activist organizations at both Yale and the University of Pennsylvania as they sought to work with minority organizations in the surrounding community to create a "university without walls." He also emphasized how mental and physical health is especially important for Black faculty as they encounter these tensions in their careers.

What are the biggest misconceptions about race, diversity, and affirmative action you feel still inform the academy's relationship toward people of color?

The very first misconception would be that there's a difference between affirmative action, the seeking out of difference to infuse and energize a program, and merit. There is the assumption that if an African American scholar is found, sought out, or placed in essentialist ways, then the department can say, "We have placed a black woman in a particular department. Therefore, we don't need a black man, and we don't need another black woman here. We've taken care of everything." Also, I have heard these types of misconceptions in the statements from my colleagues. I've been doing this for more than four decades. So, I have had a lot of contact with a lot of different people. One familiar remark, and we can keep it generic, is: "You know . . . when we hired Susan (the hypothetical black woman) for the department, I was really glad that we had done that outreach gesture because we were such a white department and this has just really made a difference. I was reading something of hers the other day and you know . . . she's really smart. I am really surprised." To which I have been known on more than one occasion to respond: "You know that is so interesting because Susan just told me she had been reading your work, and she was almost certain you had the canniness to understand her work. Susan is prolific. I think she is probably the most terrific hire we have made in recent years, don't you agree?" I think the big, enduring misconception is that programs that strive to institute difference in their student body, the faculty, and their curriculum are just the opposite of doing meritorious work to enhance the program, department, faculty, etc.

What mistakes do you see departments making with regard to the issue of diversity?

The biggest mistake departments make is that they believe there can somehow be a quantifiable number that is called "enough difference." The hiring process in our very beleaguered humanities in the United States today is difficult, and one doesn't have the same kind of fluidity and flexibility that were available when there were abundant resources. But it seems to me that there should never be a cap on one's imagination or aspiration with respect to difference. And by imagination, I mean the model of the cluster that will enrich the offerings of a department; the notion of collaboration with neighboring schools in the same vicinity; and the idea of connecting with Black, Asian American, South Asian, and other minority community organizations to enhance the offerings of a given program or department. For departments not to do such incorporative thinking and outreach is for them to put a cap on both their organizational and intellectual imagination. The other mistake that departments make, which is allied with the above, is to think that an increase in difference is purchased at the expense of merit.

How did you cope with tensions that came up around race and gender?

In the first instance, at Yale, I was able to be part of a community that was addressing racial tension in activist, creative, and resistive ways that in some sense changed radically and dramatically traditional academic protocols. Traditional modes of classroom authority and address gave way to collectives that were sometimes called "liberation schooling." The actual walls and structures that kept out the surrounding community were literally and metaphorically breached in the notion of a "university without walls." The audience for teaching and learning included rich and poor, Black and white, young and old. Black drama school students set up community theater events. "Defense funds" and legal counsel for radical activists were prominent features of the spirit of the times. I didn't find that type of community again until I went to the University of Pennsylvania, where there was a large critical mass of people. Penn was in an urban setting, and there were some really shrewd logistical men and women on faculty and in the student body who brought the noise in very effective ways. There were clear material gains in terms of structure and space, and there were clear intellectual gains in terms of programming and resources as a result of Black activism. Given the monumentally, exponentially higher number of whites in the academy (I think Black faculty constitute maybe 5 or 6 percent in the U.S. academy now), there's always going to be a cause of friction, perhaps anger, annoyance, and contestation on any given day. You can end up destroying yourself, wrecking your brain and your health by focusing too much on this tension. There is a storied legion, sort of lost to "official academic history," and charitably protected by kind anonymity, who have been undone, at least in part, by the burdens of race in the academy. One of the brightest and most beautiful graduate students I ever knew succumbed to mental illness and became a sort of token of "Black failure" to the white majority rather than a figure deserving compassion. It's probably good to go to the gym or for a run at the end of the academic workday. Health is really important, and physical healthcare is so necessary, particularly for Black academics.

Curriculum, Collaboration, and Other Changes in Academia

Along with discussing the inclusion of African Americans' work in the curriculum of departments and various other changes, I asked Baker about how certain factors of academia have changed since he began his career. He emphasized how the current formation of collaboratives across race and generation have made a positive impression on him. The national and international collaboration among current minority graduate students causes him to recall his experience as one of four African American graduate students at a predominately white UCLA without any "Black support system." He also discussed how the current "fusion" of older and younger generations has allowed him to revise courses and classroom strategies. In reflecting on the benefits of this union, Baker says that had he not engaged in "the endeavors of a new generation [he] would not be as happy as [he] currently [is] in the classroom." These innovative collaborations that Baker details seem to be a formidable foe to the individuals who he calls the "unchangeables" in academic society: neoconservative academics who denigrate any variation from "Western knowledge."

> *What has changed most visibly since you first started your career?*
> *What remains the same?*

The curriculum and the canon have certainly changed. There's been an increase in the work of African Americans in the curriculum and canon. When I was in graduate school, few Black works were taught. I remember reading one or two books by Black authors. One, of course, was *Invisible Man*. The other, I think, may have been by Frederick Douglass. Now myriad books by Black authors are the coin of the realm, and African American Literature classes are now standard offerings in the curriculum. This is very different from forty years ago and even twenty years ago.

Also, it's an interesting phenomenon to look at where we are now in terms of collaboratives like reading groups and national and international collaboration among minority graduate student groups like Asian Americans, Latinas and Latinos, and South Asian students. There were no collaboratives of this kind when I went to graduate school. I went to UCLA from Howard, and it was like going through a black hole and coming out in another universe. I always wanted to go to California. So being at UCLA was a dream come true. But, it was an all-white dream once I got there. It was as if there were no Black people in Westwood. In the graduate program, there may have been an unseen three or four Black people who were not literally in residence but were working on dissertations or projects. There were only four Black people in my program who were visible. Being so definitively and numerically separate from the white majority—and certainly implicitly held to a more rigorous standard of performance and achievement—sets one's nerves on edge. And when there is a miniscule pool ("we four") rather than lightening the pressure, the pressure can be even greater because you are set by the dominant group in competition. The old "Battle Royal" protocol of "Who is the Best Negro?" and "Who will be the last Negro standing?" Ralph Ellison's novel *Invisible Man* offers a brilliant fictional representation of the strife staged by dominant power among the minority. And indeed, rather than becoming friends or aiding one another in tight spaces of scrutiny and segregation, Blacks sometimes battle furiously to be "adopted" by the white majority, to doff the burdens, as well as the populace, of "race." Even though my fellow Black graduate students in that first year at UCLA were companionable, we never really socialized as a "group of four." I found one of the numbers incredibly smart and amiable, and he commenced my introduction to Black expressive culture. That person was Addison Gayle, who went on to become the veritable dean of Black aesthetic theorists and critics. Still, having perhaps no Black support system or Black interlocutors or Black social or study groups can leave one treading furiously in a Sargasso Sea of whiteness. But in that sea one can sometimes find great white friends. I found such in the UCLA professoriate and among the white graduate student body, and I am still in touch with one or two of them.

In terms of what remains the same, I think there is a large constituency of what we can call "unchangeables." These are white and sometimes Black, Asian American, and other neoconservative academics who continue to feel that there is a signal and exclusive body [that] is called "Western knowledge" that proceeds from almost godly epistemologies, ontologies, and sanctions. These people believe that this knowledge is God-given and that any variation from this body of work and its miraculous source is a misstep, if not actually in league with "devils of inferiority." I don't think that this constituency is going anywhere. For anyone who wants to explore these matters further, I am going to suggest the book I published a few years ago titled *Betrayal: How Black Intellectuals Have Abandoned the Ideals of the Civil Rights Era* (2008), which issues a pretty thoroughgoing critique of neoconservatism, centrism, and the intellectual cadre that enlists under such banners.

Also, I suspect that there has been no exponential increase in the numbers of specifically African American undergraduate students on major university campuses in the past ten years. I don't have that as an exact statistic, but the numbers at UCLA, for example, in the wake of King's assassination, did increase due to the campus community and Los Angeles community activism. However, the last time I was at UCLA, it wasn't at all the same level of visibility of Black students that marked the campus in 1969.

What subtle changes have you noticed in academia?

One of the changes that can be so easily missed is the kind of fusion of my generation—what Sterling Brown called the "old heads"—and younger generations. These younger constituencies are working particularly in what largely can be defined as Black and African diaspora cultural studies, particularly with Skip Gates and his work on the Atlantic and the kind of work others are doing across the eighteenth century. So the fusion of people of my generation and people of younger generations, including current graduate students, is energizing.

This fusion reminds me of the calling that I had at Yale, and my continuing role as a mentor is a great privilege and honor. As a result of the exchanges of mentorship, I've revamped my own pedagogy. For the past six years I have been building and revising, expanding and refining a course called "Transatlantic Crossings." I have read in depth in the expressive cultural, historical, sociological, political, and polemical texts of the trans-Atlantic slave trade. I use films, videos, music, visiting lecturers in the course and work transnationally and across time to probe the relationships between commerce and culture, colonialism and slavery, race and modernity, fungibility and modernism. Had I not been fortunate enough to engage—through mentoring and by invitation—the endeavors of a new generation, I would not be as happy as I currently am in the classroom. I don't think everyone sees this fusion of older and younger generations because formal mentor evaluations are not a regular part of the mechanics of a department. So this change is subtle in that sense. Mentorship is absolutely important, and although it comes with benefits, it also has its incumbencies and obligations for the person who seeks out the mentor. The ability for those mentored to seek out mentors and seriously to listen to them and to make the connection is hugely productive and gratifying. I don't believe there is a "one size fits all" protocol of mentoring. Some mentoring situations are quite formally prescribed. The age, venerability, personality, and high achievements of the mentor can preserve a formal distance between mentor and mentee. Other relationships can be casual and almost informal. I recently read a beautiful eulogy for a mentor delivered by a now senior and established professor. This senior colleague greeted the eulogist when he first joined the faculty as an assistant professor. The senior colleague offered to read one of the assistant professor's essays. By turn, the assistant professor got to know the senior's brilliant intellectual insights and to admire his scintillating prose. They commenced to have lunch—never formally set down as "an appointment"—nearly every day. They became mutually supportive and mutually respecting friends for life.

During my academic career, I have found that setting rigorous standards of intellectual production always entails an obligation to read, edit, conference endlessly with those who seek me out and are willing to do the work. What has been most surprising and gratifying in recent years is what might be called "the return" upon mentoring. Within the past year and a half, four of my students have published first-rate books and have received tenure and promotion at fine academic institutions. And, of course, there are prior groups of my students who have done the same. But it is particularly gratifying at this advanced stage of my career to still be, as it were, "in the game" and blessed by the labor, achievements, and friendships of a younger generation. I think a principal consideration in any mentor–mentee interaction is empathy—a reading out of the best intentions and cultivation of the most outstanding performance that one can imagine. This constitutes, I think, a fine brand of intellectual and personal honesty.

Have you seen shifts in attitudes about race among students?

Yes, good and bad. White people in large measure have a lot of "legacy wealth," while African Americans, by and large, would not even get into the bottom bracket of this wealth classification. So, when African American students enroll at places like Yale, Penn, Vanderbilt, University of Texas–Austin, and University of Virginia, they come in and they're flummoxed by the fact that they don't have the material advantages that white students have. So, what I have seen African American students do is assume the "attitude of entitlement" of whites and then look at me, the Black teacher, and say things like, "You don't even make as much money as my daddy. He's a doctor," or "How can you give me a B? I went to private school." Briefly put, what might be called the new Black university and college student elite are likely to be just as blasé about their advantages and as naïve about what constitutes a truly well-educated person as those students from any other blasé "racial elite."

There was a time when educational advantages were scarcer for Blacks and when there was a Black social mission for the "educated" to "uplift" the Black majority. Black college and university students during those times worked more earnestly and honestly and, I think, were not blasé—and it must be said—not nearly so willingly undereducated and un-self-educating as a privileged group of Black college and university students today. W. E. B. Du Bois's wonderful chapter in *The Souls of Black Folk* titled "Of the Coming of John" offers a compelling portrait of what might be called earnest Black educational ideals and practices. There is a current trend for some Black college and university students to self-fashion themselves as "postracial," beyond definitions, boundaries, and burdens of racial identification with the concerns and conditions of the Black majority. And, I suppose, if you feel no obligation to educate yourself for service to a vastly underserved community that bears the same color as you, then there is only one outcome to be expected. That outcome, as Carter G. Woodson so excoriatingly demonstrated, is a "miseducation" that produces a frivolously uncaring Black elite.

The positive side of the shift in students' attitudes about race is that I have seen undergraduate and graduate students come to campus and immediately begin to build "community" without the leadership of "senior personnel," as it were. It's like these self-starters believe that every man and every woman is "their own Moses" or Harriet Tubman. They are not in waiting for a great campus race leader to come along. These students, whom I have the pleasure and honor of knowing and teaching, have done this community building in really energetic and smart institutional ways. They've built alliances across race and ethnicity and brought in people of color across class. They have introduced questions of sexual orientation, religious affiliation, and environmental sustainability into formal and informal curricula. These are the kind of mini rainbow coalitions on campuses that are arising, and they are a pleasure to behold.

How did your scholarship shift as you became more established?

I guess I'll give two things. The first is that if you work hard, get your credentials in place, and your work is receiving favorable critical attention, then you feel freer to investigate things that are not in a straight line. I think you get a lot more freedom in your pedagogy and in your scholarship, and you get to take on things that are risky. The second thing is that, as you accumulate experience, you begin to have the license or have the daring to bring together the personal, the political, and the professional. In one sense, this translates as the memoiristic impulse in one's writing and scholarship, and, in another, it is the kind of actual fusion of those things in the real world, where the personal is always political. Certainly an earned rank of achievement has freed me to write at least *how* I want to write. The same is true for my teaching. I believe that writing for publication in refereed venues is quintessential to the process of intellectual growth, to academic and personal self-confidence. As in the enduring annals of Black expressive culture, the literacy and eloquence of published production is the road to freedom, both of person and expression.

Mentorship, Community, and Advice for Minority Scholars

Baker continued his discussion of the benefits of the fusion of the older and younger generations by noting how mentorship played and continues to play a vital role in his academic career. He notes how his mentors— Addison Gayle, whom Baker calls his "salvation and keeper of [his] sanity" and Leon Howard, without whom Baker says he would not have been able to complete his program of study—created a sense of community for him while he was at UCLA. Gayle, the literary critic, educator, and purveyor of the Black aesthetic, introduced him to African American literature and culture, and Howard, professor of American literature at UCLA, nurtured his development in American literature and culture. Through mentorship, Baker explains, individuals can seize the notion of "Black community" despite the argument that, as a result of the plight and blight that have faced so many Black neighborhoods, "community" is no longer a reality. For Baker, community is "an archive of feelings" made available through "intellectual endeavor, mentorship, and spiritual kinship." Along with detailing the connection between mentorship and community, Baker discussed how his "passion, commitment, and love of the work" has allowed him to stay in the academy when times have gotten hard, thus giving sound advice to faculty members of younger generations. He ended the interview on a hopeful note, discussing how the opportunities available to all individuals entering the academy allow for the present to be "a good time, in many ways, to be doing what we do."

What are your thoughts about mentorship?

I guess I would have to start with the fact that Addison Gayle was my mentor, and in many ways my salvation and keeper of my sanity. Suppose there had just been three Black people and Addison had not been one of them in my UCLA years? I would, on a personal level, have suffered enormously from the absence of community. At the level of coming through my graduate school days at large, I had the blessing of a very famous Americanist named Leon Howard. I was the only Black person in his seminar, and he helped me as much as anybody has helped me in my life. He took me under his wing with commendations, recommendations, and suggestions for the way I should work. His role, in a great and important spiritual sense, was a matter of love. He gave me love, and I wouldn't have made it successfully through the program if it had not been for Leon Howard and his deep interest, despite my concentration in Victorian literature. My true grounding in American literature and culture was born under and nurtured by Leon. I had other mentors as well. My dissertation adviser, despite his fear that I would embarrass the institution by applying to Harvard, Princeton, and Yale, was staunch and steadfast. He was a fortress, and he wouldn't let anybody mess with me. The flip side of this is that he would not let me slack off even a little bit. Of course, I had wonderful people at Howard as well. Along the way, people have reached out and said, "I want you to contribute to my volume," or I've had amazing editors who've said, "I want you to start a series" or "I want you to contribute a book to the series." So I've been very fortunate in the world of mentors. In mentoring other people, I'm glad for any accolades that come my way, but I certainly do reciprocate these accolades to my mentees. I have learned so much from people I've been in collaboration with.

Where did you find community?

I had several really good friends at UCLA who were white and who were graduate students as well. They were steadfast, and they were particularly a blessing to my wife and me. A couple of them were further along in their lives and finances than we were, and so we had some good dinners and good camaraderie at their invitation. It was when I got to Yale that I gained a notion of activist Black community, motion forward, responsibility, and commitment. That really was a life-altering event for me, and it introduced me to African American literature and culture. The Yale moment also opened that vein, which goes back to the days of my observing my mom teach, of reading and writing with a sense of passion, love, and absolute pedagogical commitment. The Yale community also showed me scholastic commitment in the sense that we must rewrite the canon and the books and alter the epistemologies of a form of knowledge production and dissemination that has been inimical and harmful in its racial terror to the Black majority.

What do you think of the whole notion of "community" as an idea or a reality?

Black community is something that is sometimes glibly put forward. People sometimes look at the really rotten, under-resourced, horrifically violent neighborhoods in a city in which Black people live and will say,

"Black community is not even a reality. It doesn't exist. It used to exist." Usually they then recall the pre-*Brown vs. Board of Education* days and talk about how the middle class lived in the community. But Black community is, as Langston Hughes said, "a flame of the spirit burning through the ages." So, if you think of that as the notion of community and see it as an archive of feelings and a set of structures of feelings that are always available through sometimes prayer and often through intellectual endeavor, mentorship, and spiritual kinship, then the notion of Black community cannot be denied simply because the physical venues of Black life in any given city are depressed.

What mistakes do you see faculty of color make?

One thing that may be a problem is to equate financial matters with matters of well-being, possible advancement, tenure, and everyday life. I see graduate students think that they are being entirely canny by saying to a university committee, "Well, I've read your benefits book, and I know what the salary scale is, but you're going to have to adjust my salary." While the tangible things like salary, teaching load, and leave policies are very important, the whole question of what is the "habit of mind" of the department in which you're going to spend twenty-four, seven physically, intellectually, and spiritually is vastly more important, especially for one's health and longevity.

What privileges do you see faculty of color enjoying that you may not have benefited from at the start of your career?

The privileges and possibilities that are there for people, not just African Americans, but people coming into the field of study in the academy today are exponentially expanded beyond what we were working with in what some people call "the pioneering days." In the early days, we were hard pressed. Now people throw out the agenda, or the "itinerary" as it is called, for splendid visits that I have been honored and privileged to take. It's a good time, in many ways, to be doing what we do. There are abundant resources, and new technologies have made access to information much less arduous than it was a few decades ago.

The Future: Public Intellectuals, Black Studies

Asked to talk more about these new technologies—not just technologies that give more people more access to archives but also the way technology shapes how scholarship is shared—Baker turned his thoughts to the complex role of Black intellectuals at a time when so much of what passes for discourse is filtered through social media, especially in the wake of current conversations about old patterns of violence. Whether he's talking about the tensions between Black academics and Black activists; current debates about what it means to be a Black public intellectual; or how social media is shaping the careers of emerging scholars of color; and whether he's thinking about Steven Salaita, Dyson versus West, popular culture, or the history of the Modern Language Association, Baker sees it all through the lens of someone who has seen the academy wrestle with ideology and scholarship since the 1960s.

What this means is that instead of seeing specific moments between individuals or groups or platforms, Baker understands all of these moving parts as part of a long history of systems that undermine attempts at unity: "There have always been systems that have worked to separate people from one another," he explained: "When you have some people who woke up to another day of trying to keep the family together while others wake up saying 'I'm running a bit late' you have completely different sensibilities." Baker sees these two different sensibilities at play as Black intellectuals and Black activists face increasing pressure to contribute to and shape conversations around attempts to stem the police violence that has gained more national attention. For Baker, the "huge state of emergency" we are in right now requires more than what this current model of the public academic has to offer. He talks about how the current construction of the Black intellectual community, especially the fixation on a single voice as representative of all Black intellectuals, "differs from the grassroots community with conversations across class, status, and locale" that marked a time when thinkers and activists like Erika Huggins and Stokely Carmichael added important layers and nuance to a vibrant dialogue.

So, on one level, he sees this moment—the violence and the call to Black intellectuals to respond—as the "same old story" amplified not only by the role of social media and a new level of urgency but also by a larger commentary culture where writing op-eds for various publication is as much a goal as publishing in peer-reviewed journals. Baker points out that what used to be considered a rare moment, a "Michelin Star for the academic to get out of the hermetic circle," is now almost de rigueur, and he worries about how this shapes both political efficacy and the intellectual integrity of what Black intellectuals are trying to do. He argues that "the entire project of the academy is still in some large measure, cliques, cabals, and intimacies" that can't be breached with op-eds and television appearances.

His concern is not simply theoretical, and he does not seem simply cranky about progress. When Baker talks about answering to a calling, he is not being rhetorical and he sees the same urgency in this moment as he did at Yale in the sixties. For him, strong Black Studies programs across the country are vital movements, and he worries about the cost of pursuing the spotlight. One the one hand, he thinks about how the pull toward "the public" is incompatible with the life of sustained academic work: "The bleed of energy between the academy and social media is nearly fatal for those giving sixty hours a week." He is also concerned about how this focus on a few public Black academics undermines the values of those whose work is essential but often overlooked. Beyond this he sees how this focus on the few makes it easy for institutions to opt out of supporting faculty of color and Black Studies. "There are very few Black Studies programs that are secure . . . they sit on foundations that are built around a cult of personality and in other ways within themselves are scattered and dispersed," he explains. "If you can just hold up just one person and say 'This person is ideal,' then other institutions can feel safe and free to say no."

Baker's most recent book is *The Trouble with Post-Blackness* (edited with K. Merinda Simmons). It takes up the kinds of questions that have occupied Black Studies since its inception and reads those questions at a time when Obama's election has pushed the question of whether or not America is postracial to the forefront of too many conversations. It is a collection of essays that demonstrates the kind of intellectual community and engagement Baker has sought and built his entire career, and it wrestles with the current tragedies and questions with the depth that Baker sees as missing from the op-ed and commentary culture. But most important, like Baker himself, it offers a model of the way that emerging scholars can engage with urgent questions.

Notes

1. American historian and philosopher whose book, *The Structure of Scientific Revolutions* (1962), influenced both academic and popular culture.

Building a Canon, Creating Dialogue

An Interview with Cheryl A. Wall

Rashida L. Harrison
Michigan State University

While preparing for my conversation with Dr. Cheryl Wall, I came across recordings from the "Black Women in the Ivory Tower: Research and Praxis" conference held at Rutgers University in March 2009.[1] I was particularly interested in the title of a panel Wall introduced: "What Does It Mean to Be a Black Woman Who Reads Books for a Living in the 21st Century?" The question is one I am familiar with as a Black woman immersed in academia for more than ten years as a student, instructor, and administrator. Wall reminisced with me and explained the similarity of the question to Alice Walker's 1974 inquiry about Black women as artists in "our grandmother's time." The 2009 version of the question focused on Black women's contributions to the humanities, specifically the value placed on their scholarly interpretations and interventions and their larger bodies of knowledge.

In her introduction to the panel, Wall highlighted a discussion from the *New York Times* about the relevance of the humanities in the twenty-first century that suggested "the humanities would become the province of the leisure class that it was a century ago."[2] Wall—now Board of Governors Zora Neal Hurston Professor of English, affiliate faculty to the Department of Women's and Gender Studies, and Cochair of the President's Council for Institutional Diversity and Equity at Rutgers University—remarked dryly, "If that were true then it would be anomalous, indeed, for Black women to read books." The remark shows Wall's shrewd analysis of the precarious relationship she continues to observe between Black women in the humanities and the academy in general. It is a relationship she has observed from different vantage points: as one of the only women of color in Harvard's graduate program, as a doctoral candidate teaching for the first time, as a trailblazer in African American Studies, and as a passionate advocate for meaningful diversity initiatives.

Throughout our conversation, Wall emphasized the value of good mentorship and the importance of maintaining balance in an academic career. We talked about her personal experience with feeling marginalized in graduate school at a predominately white institution, the contrast of being a junior scholar in a relatively diverse department, and the impact that working in supportive departments had on her teaching and research. Her experiences, coupled with her love of teaching and scholarship, form the foundation for her diversity work, which challenges the traditional institutional approach of support and retention of faculty of color. In the model Wall works with, support for underrepresented members of the academy begins not at the professorial level but with targeted efforts that encourage historically disadvantaged students to pursue academic careers by providing them with opportunities.

My conversations with Wall happened while I was in a transitional moment, an academic liminal space. I was in the midst of completing my dissertation, making the transition from graduate student to junior faculty member and later launching my research agenda with the help of a postdoctoral fellowship. Like the work of many scholars of African American literature, Wall's scholarship informs my own research, and I saw this as an opportunity to not only talk about her work (as specialist in African American literature) but also her role (as African American scholar). I was curious to know how she maintained such an active career. In my attempt to start with a general question, I immediately went right to the heart of the matter: "What does it mean to be a Black woman teaching in the humanities at Rutgers University at this moment in history?" She replied, "I think it is a fascinating time because of the presence of Black women. We have achieved a toehold as Black women in the humanities. It is just a toehold, but I do not think that anybody is surprised to see us here. Which, in my experience, was certainly not the case when I started. When students would come into the classroom they would be surprised to see me, a Black woman, as their professor. I think that is less likely, at least in the humanities."

Wall's sentiments resonated strongly with me. While finishing my dissertation and two years thereafter, I taught in an interdisciplinary humanities and social science residential college in a large research university. Out of fifty faculty members, only two of us were African American, and I was not on the tenure track; as a result, I was often an anomaly. My presence was one that provoked a variety of responses from surprise to fascination, skepticism, and sometimes disbelief. The truth of Wall's assertion sheds light on academia's slow evolution when it comes to maintaining meaningful diversity. Over the course of our conversation, Professor Wall offered an example of how that toehold was achieved and described her experience in the academy from the naïve way she went about her first job search to the "sheer dumb luck" that resulted in a teaching position at Douglass College.[3] She was fortunate to join a department that already had some established courses on the Black American experience and to meet another woman of color who served as a mentor. Though she did not realize it immediately, she was in a rare place.

Mentorship as a Cornerstone

Early in her career, Wall learned the value of having a good mentor, the challenges and rewards involved with being a Black woman in the academy, and the hard work involved with building a Black women's literary canon. Throughout the conversation, she unpacked a variety of components that continue to matter for successful mentoring relationships. After spending two years taking courses at Harvard where, she explained, being a Black woman in a graduate program really was an anomaly, she decided to leave Cambridge, Massachusetts, and find a job while preparing for her oral examinations and writing her dissertation. She said she left because she "felt alienated." As I made my way through graduate school and faced a similar sense of alienation, I often found that the exercise of debriefing with more senior scholars about my experiences, particularly those from African American and Latino communities, was very helpful. I made sure to seek out a variety of perspectives, including those from my peers. The act in itself offers a sense of visibility and voice that risks disappearing in states of alienation that make graduate school particularly challenging for Black women.

Wall finished her coursework and was not obligated to stay in Boston. She wanted to explore the teaching profession and was in the process of trying to figure out her career when she joined the faculty of Douglass College, a school that had a structure in place that allowed for more mentorship and guidance. Douglass College's small academic units (as opposed to large departments) and already established core courses made it easier for new faculty to find their footing. It's clear when Wall talks about finding her first job that that she lacked a sense of guidance in graduate school: "I found my job through the *New York Times*. I was so naïve, Rashida. And I did not go to my adviser at Harvard. They did not know I was looking for a job. I had a four-year Ford Foundation fellowship, so I had no financial imperatives to find a job. I just felt so alienated where I was." Not only was Wall the only Black woman in her department but she also could not see herself in any of the scholarly conversations. This lack of representation and a craving for a different space are some of the reasons why she left Boston: "I had finished course work so it was possible for me to be someplace away from the campus. I felt that I needed to figure it out. I needed to know whether I wanted to be a teacher at the university level, and that is really how I thought about it—as a teacher, not as a scholar. I had never heard of an 'MLA.' I did not know there was a system where people went to a convention in December to interview for jobs that had been advertised earlier in the fall. When I think about it, that kind of thing that would be almost impossible to do today. But it was really a less rigidly structured system at that time and, of course, a far less competitive one. I was able to come here, be hired, and figure out everything about how institutions work once I was part of the institution."

One thing Wall's story illustrates is the importance of having representation in the midst of the hierarchical muddle that characterizes the ivory tower: "I think I came to Rutgers—or Douglass College specifically—in order to determine if this was what I wanted to pursue. I was very fortunate because Douglass College at that time was one of the foundational places for the development of Women's Studies. When I first arrived, there were people who were working, not in my field specifically, but in what was then called 'Black literature.' I knew I wanted to work with women writers. When I arrived, I found that there were conversations that I could see myself in, which was very different from my experience in graduate school." Wall's pivotal moment of "seeing herself" was evident to me much earlier in my career. Black women professors were still anomalous in my undergraduate university, but early experiences offered insight into the possibilities of placing my experiences at the center of scholarly endeavors. Wall continued: "One other thing I should say is that I have never been the only Black woman in my department. Even when I came to Douglass College in 1972, there was already another Black woman there, Adrianne Baytop. She was a senior colleague who really was prepared, at least institutionally, to be my mentor. We worked on very different things. She was a specialist in the English Renaissance. But institutionally she was a mentor. I have just been incredibly fortunate to have always had some assistance in negotiating the academy. And in turn, I have certainly tried to be a mentor to women and men who have come after me."[5]

Wall's experience as a new professor with senior colleagues of color to offer informal and formal mentorship is unique, and she knows it. She pointed out that that many young professors of color entered departments in predominantly white institutions without advisers, so they faced a lack of cultural familiarity and understanding from colleagues. Her observations are not merely true about the early 1970s but also applicable to the experiences of junior faculty today. It is important to note, however, that mentorship must be balanced between making clear the difficulties of the academy without pushing people of color away from it. I have often heard from faculty of color in particular that they had experiences that they wanted to help students of color avoid. They are referring to the difficulty of traversing an institution where people of color have no previous framework to provide context for their experiences. While I was in graduate school, for example, I met women of color who strove to provide what many would call "safe spaces" for their graduate students of color. Their mentees could ask questions about scholarly endeavors while also challenging sociocultural issues particular to them. I understood early on that Black women saw their role as preparing me for faculty life at a research-intensive university. Much of their guidance was about making clear that to be a woman of color in the academy is to be in an almost constant state of negotiation, grappling with issues of race, gender, and scholarship. My position teaching as a post-doctoral fellow often left me vulnerable to colleagues who dismissed culture and race as insignificant to everyday interactions. I often walked the halls of a residential college and had colleagues look past me without a greeting because I did not look as if I had the status they might be inclined to respect. The propensity for marginalized students of various backgrounds to seek me out even when they were not enrolled in my course was a constant source of curiosity for other faculty. In addition, there was little advice offered by white colleagues about how to navigate the disproportionate demands on me as a Black woman to provide mentorship and service for students. Even as the demands were ones I answered willingly, the lack of an institutional wherewithal to nurture faculty of color creates a cycle of marginalization in which faculty of color, in an attempt to protect future academics of color from oppressive practices, unintentionally exude energy that might also push future academics of color away. It is so important to tell difficult truths with care. Despite the struggle of balancing these perspectives with my own experiences, having Black women who offered guidance about maneuvering professional politics and my perceived social responsibilities was pivotal. My support network is one that I continue to intentionally construct, one that encompasses multiple perspectives.

Embracing the Teacher-Scholar

I wondered what additional factors kept Wall at Rutgers. It's clear that what has sustained her is passion and commitment to teaching. In our discussion, I identified with some of her early circumstances as a novice professor (Wall explained that at twenty-three she looked the same age as many of her students) and the particular impact a young Black woman often can have on predominantly white classrooms. She discussed a love for teaching from "the very first day." She left graduate school "abruptly" and did not have any experience, but she understood early that she was good at it. "It was enormously interesting and gratifying. I had a passion for the material and I was eager to share what I knew and to learn more about what I was teaching." Wall was fortunate in that the school already had Black literature courses on the roster. The first course she taught was "Black Music and Black Literature," established by A. B. Spellman, a leading jazz scholar. She also taught developmental English, which she saw as a challenge because she had never taught writing. Wall confessed, "I did not know what I was doing." She talked of developing a pedagogy that grew out of the tenets of feminism. "For example," she explained, "the idea that there is no one authority in the classroom and having people keep journals. I would tell the students in the African American course that there were not shelves of books or a consensus about what we were reading. All our opinions were valid as long as they were based in the text. I loved it because I found it really energizing. I was trying to figure out what I thought about the books myself as they were figuring things out. That is the kind of approach that is dependent on being young. In those days I was unsure, yet it was a very free, exciting, and open space for thinking in the classroom. It felt like a very experimental time in higher education." Wall's assertions still ring true. She is talking about the challenge of building a critical tradition I currently identify as pivotal to holistic understandings of African American literature.

As we talked, I reflected on my own experience as a graduate student and now as a junior scholar in Africana Studies. Even a field that professes a distinct cultural competency faces challenges by the structures of academia that do not always value fields like mine, even though the library shelves are filled with research that show its importance. Some subfields of Cultural Studies still strive for legitimacy, and their frameworks of operation are often experimental and their institutional support unstable. Wall discussed this further: "Most of the students I taught had never read African American texts before. Some of the writing like *The Bluest Eye* or *I Know Why the Caged Bird Sings* were presenting situations and histories that people did not know, ones with which they were very uncomfortable. Part of my role as a teacher was really to help create a critical language that would allow the discussion of texts. These fictions spoke directly to people's everyday lives and indeed to my own life. I was concerned that they also be read as literary text because I understood that there was something powerful about the way that a Toni Morrison or an Alice Walker wrote. It was not just *what* they wrote, but it was *how* they wrote. Trying to come up with some language that would allow that to be discussed in the classroom was a challenge."

While the academy tends to split the world into teachers and scholars, Wall has come to see the two roles as deeply connected: "I do think I have come to really appreciate the dual roles; they are really mutually reinforcing roles, being a teacher and a scholar. However, initially, it is being a teacher. You are in the classroom. People are looking at you with certain expectations." She also described the challenges of working in an emerging field, which often means doing specific kinds of publishing that are not initially valued and about the need to create a balance, writing for journals and later her first book, with more reference and encyclopedic publishing pieces. It was all the foundational work that may have been undervalued in her early career but is now an essential part of Black women's literary studies: "I fell in love with my project. I certainly enjoyed the research. I love—and I still love—being in an archive and doing that kind of work. The writing of the dissertation was a bigger challenge. But it took me much longer to write the first book. I do not think that made me unusual among my cohort of scholars. It was very difficult to really gain the confidence that I had something worthy of being said in a whole book. It took me a long time to work through that. When I finally was able to complete my first book, I realized that I very much enjoy writing."

Wall's experiences illustrate historical privileges within established disciplines and fields of study. She did not have a scholarly vantage point, and scholars of her cohort worked to establish conversations and arguments about African American literature at a time when it was still new. She described publishing steadily, though she explained that she published more chapters in books than single-authored articles. The field was still forming, so she was frequently invited to contribute to anthologies and references book and didn't realize at first that they are not as highly prized as journal articles and books. It's this kind of institutional marginalization that faculty in emerging fields face. The foundational publishing they do to provide a critical framework for their fields goes largely unrecognized by too many institutions. In my graduate experience, I was encouraged to contribute to encyclopedic reference sources as a way to practice preparing for a publication, but, as Wall explains, "It is much more important to write an original journal article than a reference article on, say, Zora Neale Hurston. But of course there were very few reference books on Black writers or women writers. Eventually I understood that to be essential in the establishment of the field, you have to have dictionaries of women writers or notable American women. I contributed to *African American Writers*; I edited the Library of America volumes on Zora Neale Hurston. If you are going to create a canon, then you need to do that."

She acknowledges that her path to publication would not lead to tenure at Rutgers or most other research institutions today: "I was tenure track from the time I finished the degree in 1976. And then I came up for tenure in 1981. I was in the process of writing the book, but I had not written one and I was still tenured. The chances of that happening today at my institution are nil; it just could not happen. And because of the shrinking of the faculties at colleges and universities and the increased number of scholars who are seeking these slots, the expectations for tenure have increased dramatically. The possibility of enforcing the rules with any flexibility has decreased dramatically, so it is a much a tighter tenure decision for young people today. The expectations are higher. The clock is shorter and there is no give." All of this is tied to the job market. Wall joined the Rutgers University system in 1972 at a time when you could find and get a job by simply reading the *New York Times* and be more exploratory with teaching. I am working in era that requires a consistent awareness of the job market if I want job stability. Tenure-track jobs are rare, especially at research institutions, which are the kinds of jobs young scholars are often being prepared to seek. I went on the job market for three years. The first year I got a better grasp of what different types of institutions sought in their faculty candidates. For some, a successful teaching record and diverse experiences with students was desired. First-tier universities saw research and publication experience as a primary factor in determining their interest. Fortunately, I had mentors who understood and articulated these distinctions for me and also offered support while I developed experiential knowledge. The limits of those efforts, however, became apparent when I entered a job market even more tenuous than the one previous generations faced, and I did not have the kind of resources necessary for a sustained job search or the kind of primary income from a partner that often makes adjunct work possible.

Diversity and the Institution

In addition to being a scholar of note in the field of Black women's literary studies, Wall has built a reputation as a leading advocate for diversity. Rutgers' Council for Institutional Diversity puts its resources to good use, and Wall is the co-chair. I asked Wall about her work at Rutgers, but she commented more broadly on institutions of higher education and the tenure and promotion process. Concerning historically marginalized faculty, I was interested in the following questions: What are the causes of major discrepancies when a faculty person of color comes up for tenure? How much of the responsibility is on the institution and how much should faculty shoulder? Wall's response illustrates what is needed to successfully navigate the road to tenure and the need to be proactive about creating a supportive environment. She also discussed the historical disjuncture between people of color and women generally in the academy and the need for the institution to diversify its faculty body in response to the undergraduate student body's growing diversity. She argues, "If the university is going to continue to produce new knowledge, it needs to diversify the people who are seeking new knowledge." She elaborated:

> I think that diversity is an absolute critical part of the academic mission of universities as well as whatever is left of a commitment to social justice. When I began, I was trained in American literature and culture, and when I started teaching courses in nineteenth-

century American Literature—nobody typically taught *The Narrative Life of Frederick Douglass*. All the writers were white. And most of the writers were men. The transformation of American literary study has had a lot to do with the incorporation of text by Black authors. Now, when we hire a nineteenth-century Americanist, the expectation is that they will teach Harriet Jacobs as well as Frederick Douglass and maybe David Walker. And [the presence of Black faculty] has changed the field's understanding of itself. Now do I think that would have happened had Black professors not been in English departments? No. I think, if you look at the way that American or U.S. history is now taught or understood, it looks differently than it did forty years ago. I think that is because you had, by now, two generations of women historians, two generations of African American historians, increasing numbers of Latino and Asian American historians who just ask different questions, who go to different archives. They also discover and recuperate different texts. It changes our understanding of what the past has meant, what the present means. If the university is going to continue to produce new knowledge, it needs to diversify the people who are seeking new knowledge; that includes scholars of color.

Wall further discussed dramatic changes in the student population at Rutgers and other public universities and predicted that it will continue to change over the next thirty years. "It will become less and less tenable for those people to be taught by a faculty that is 90 percent white." Such concerns are what led Wall and other faculty from across the country to work toward developing pipeline programs that encourage historically underrepresented people in the academy to pursue academic careers early in their education. One initiative she currently works with is the Rutgers English Diversity Institute (REDI). This one-week program introduces undergraduate students to graduate study by pairing them with a diverse group of scholars in their general field of interests. Participants in the program have been accepted for graduate study in competitive English programs at Yale, Columbia, UCLA, Princeton, and Northwestern. Tricia, who has recommended several students for this program, explains that the program not only demystifies the work of the academy but helps students decide whether graduate school is right for them before they find themselves floundering and taking on even more debt. Although Wall describes this as a modest effort, it is indicative of the types of programs essential to the restructuring of the current state of the humanities. The makeup of a faculty body that is only 4 percent African American and 3 percent Latino nationally "is not going to be acceptable."

Wall firmly believes that mentoring relationships must be pivotal in navigating these institutional inequities: "I really am interested in helping people figure out how to prepare for this change and how to make it happen. And some of that has to do with establishing mentoring programs. We have had several hiring initiatives that have been sponsored by the President's Council on Institutional Diversity here [at Rutgers University]. Some of it focuses on strategies for hiring and identifying best practices for more inclusive faculty appointments. Next, we have to come up with strategies for retention. Some of the things needed are less tangible things like helping those scholars create community once they are here."

Wall is referring to communities of support. Throughout our discussion, she made clear the various factors that contribute to "support," including formal and professionalization spaces along with larger social support:

> There are many ways to go about that. Sometimes it involves creating places for people to interact with each other outside of departments, where people can come together and have discussions that are academic and that can also generate a social network. I think that academic leaders are going to have to spend some more of their time figuring out how to make these things happen. I had a discussion with a young scholar just last night that is not in my school, Arts and Sciences, but here at Rutgers University. I was thrilled to know that a group of young women, scholars of color, had organized themselves to offer mentoring in terms of preparing for tenure. They are figuring out what is required and what the expectations are of them. A critical mass of them allows that to be possible. When I was a young scholar, there was less than a handful in the college at any one time.

What Wall is describing is the evolution of Black and scholars of color who constitute a growing cohort within university spaces. If they are offered excellent support, they can continue to expand; their presence leads to the creation of inclusive learning environments and more diversified kinds of scholarly inquiries: "There are such groups that exist, and they are at various types of campuses. My work with the project, 'Reaffirming Actions, Faculty Initiatives for Diversity' that was sponsored by the Ford Foundation, allowed me to travel to twelve colleges and universities that had initiatives of various kinds that were given support by the project. We went to large colleges, women's colleges, historically Black colleges, state universities, and elite private universities. In most of those places, [white] women had established a network on the one hand and faculty of color [had established a separate network]. Sometimes they worked in alliance or coalition with each other."

Given Wall's current interest in assessment of diversity, retention, and mentoring, I asked her about concrete advice for junior faculty members who work in isolation. Many faculty of color still feel detached from their departments. They may not have formal meeting spaces or even support at their university. In addition, there are often extra demands on historically marginalized faculty to attend to more service-oriented projects than their peers. This is work—acting as faculty advisers to groups that are often identity based, giving informal talks, and attending campus and larger community events—that is essential but not even considered in the tenure promotion process:

> I can think of no Black woman at the academy who does not carry that extra burden. There may be a couple. Most of us feel ourselves obligated to take on certain kinds of tasks. Sometimes you are called upon to be an adviser to a Black student group. You may be asked to serve on a curriculum committee, and you know your presence on the committee will affect the incorporation of certain types of courses into the program, or to be on an admissions committee or review committee where you know that your voice makes a difference. Whether these are undergraduate or graduate students, your voice would make a difference in the discussion. It is very hard to turn some of those things down. Most of us come into the academy with certain types of emotional and political commitment. Some of that I do not think you can or should decline.

Wall highlights one of the first things I noticed when entering graduate school, teaching for the first time, and moving into junior instructor mode, specifically the need for mentoring of all kind and building an intellectual community:

One of the things I finally did learn is that there were people at other universities who were working on the same topics, and using the same texts, that I was in the 70s. I just did not know who they were. I would urge young scholars to reach out to people who are in their field at other institutions. That is so easy today. Obviously, there was no e-mail when I started. There was no Internet. There were no computers. That seems like I am talking about ancient times, but none of those things existed. When you finally did meet somebody, you spoke to him or her on the telephone. Once I started doing that, it was great. I was able to eventually share my work, find readers for myself, and that was very, very important in the development of my scholarship.

Young faculty can find people through professional organizations. When going to conferences it is important to look for such people who are in the same rank as you are as well senior scholars. *You can identify mentors.* Certainly, a number of young women have identified me in that way. I have tried to be as responsive as I could because there are some people who are on campuses where there still are two Black women faculty in a college. That still exists in smaller colleges in the country, and it is difficult to develop a support network at their institution. I would also urge young people at institutions where there is not another person or a mentor in their department to identify someone in another department that they can call on to ask for advice.

I received such advice at the beginning of my graduate career. The structural makeup of my interdisciplinary program meant that I had to seek out people for support in several departments. That experience offered a more nuanced understanding of the college's political makeup as well as department-specific debates. Wall also reminded me that mentors can be found outside of the small group of faculty of color often available to students.

I would also say the mentor does not have to be the same race or gender as you are. Be open to that possibility. Identify somebody who really knows how the institution works, who knows whom you need to meet, who can answer questions that come up about when you should take a sabbatical or around receiving a competitive fellowship. They can discuss the publishers that the appointments and promotion committee will respect. It is invaluable to have access to that kind of information. As I said, there is no flexibility anymore on the tenure clock. You have to balance your sense of social obligation with "Well, at some point, if I'm going to continue to serve my students and my profession and my area of scholarship, I really need to still be in the profession." Sometimes people have served so much then they are gone and there is a huge void left in the lives of their students. It is a very difficult balancing act.

Wall ended with an emphasis on the value of a good mentor who is able to help faculty think through the tenure process. She also highlighted her philosophy about what it means to be a mentor: "Not somebody giving you orders, but somebody advising can be helpful." This is true for scholars at different levels. As a graduate student, I encountered challenges with mentoring relationships because of an unclear vision between a faculty member's perceptions and my own sense about his or her role in advising me—oftentimes amounting to well-meaning faculty trying to dictate my actions. From my conversation with Dr. Wall, it became clear that mentoring is a dialectical process. Junior scholars as they seek mentors need to think about the type of guidance they require. There must be a mutual understanding about what it means to engage in such a relationship.[6]

On Balance and Community

Much of our conversation centered on career development, and institutional policy, but I also wanted to have a sense of *how* Dr. Wall was able to create a balance between the work she loved and her life in general. She talked of the necessity of a critical community—one that goes beyond the professional. I was interested in the balance of friends, family life, and other communities that nurture the emotional lives of faculty of color. I asked Wall about *her* community, and how it changed or remained the same over time. In addition, I was interested in whether or not her career left anything to be desired. Did she feel like she left anything behind? I was looking for *the* secret of balance:

I think it is important to have a community at least in the profession. Sometimes you have to create a community that is outside of your department but still in the profession. I also think it is very important to have a community that has nothing to do with your professional life. It is important to pay attention to family and friends. I do not think it is healthy to live your life entirely in the profession. You need to try to strike a balance there, too. The academy can be a very isolating place, especially if you are in the humanities, and I think it is probably true for social sciences as well.

Much of what we do as scholars is voluntary. I think that you need a social network to balance all of the time that you necessarily spend alone. I think it is also important to have a community that values you for who you are rather than for what you do. Again, family and friends are important. If you go to a church, that can be a good place to find community. Some people belong to certain social organizations. But just to have a life outside of work I think is important.

I have been very fortunate. I have been married, and I have a daughter, so I do not feel I missed out on something that is a critical component of life. I do not look back and say, "Oh, if I had only done X or not done Y." I do not have those long-term regrets, for which I am very grateful, and I know I am truly blessed. I know other people who would not be able to say that.

There is just so much to do in life. You have so many competing obligations that everybody is trying to balance. It is not just academics. Everybody is trying to balance things. My only point was that because so much of the work we do we do by ourselves, . . . it is even more important to maintain some sense of balance. Other goals I had were as important as professional success was to me. My work is very fulfilling. I love teaching. I love the scholarly writing. I get excited, and I *am* excited to do it. I am proud of having done it. I like seeing my name in print. But I also knew that I cared about other things. I have very big family ties. I need to spend time in the summer with my great-nieces. I have always known when my daughter was growing up that she was my priority. Always. That has allowed me to have some balance in my life.

I also do other things that I enjoy. I love to travel. I travel as much and as often as I can. As I get older, I have learned to reserve time to renew friendships. That is easier to do now because I am not trying to establish myself professionally. When you are in that process, everything is "geared up," and if you have children, it is happening at the same time, there are just a lot of pressures. But certainly, on the other side of that, it is just important to connect with people. That has increasingly become a priority of mine.

Towards the end of our conversation, I found myself thinking about a mix of things. I shared some of my insecurities about transitioning from student to scholar and about politics in the university. My concern at the time was about what it meant to have interdisciplinary training in an academic era where traditional disciplinary training still has seems to have the highest currency on the job market. I was able to identify myself in her history and reflections, and that recognition brought a mix of feelings. As a first-generation graduate student and PhD in one of the younger fields of study in academia, my scholarly and personal responsibilities to a variety of communities come with pressures others might not see at first. Wall was part of the building of a canon, and I want to continue that work. In the interview, I had a keen sense of the path that Dr. Wall and others, particularly Black women, both navigated and paved for my generation.

Because of Wall's candor and encouragement during our conversation I was not only privy to what her continued work is but also to *the way* in which she does the work. A combination of patience and passion is threaded through her commitment to teaching and new research projects and are critical to the building of a field of study. Because even as the journey is somewhat easier for my generation, we still face an uphill struggle. She acknowledged this when she spoke of a recent visit to an event with the Organization of Black Women Philosophers. She remarked, "Wow. My struggles are nothing. I could not believe it. In the meeting was the first Black woman to earn a PhD in philosophy at a majority white institution." Such moments exist even after being a part of the academy for forty years:

> However, I do think it is an exciting time to be a young Black woman in the academy. You began talking about the conference last year. There were 500 women registered for that conference, and the women were overwhelmingly young. There was so much energy in the room. It was wonderful. For somebody like me, it was gratifying to know that there will be a larger cohort in the next ten years than there has been in the previous. There was a moment, in the 1980s, where I would see people and we would lament that there was nobody coming behind us. It was a moment when most of the

bright, young students would go to law school and they would not pursue a PhD. That has changed. Even though the numbers are still not anywhere near what they should be, they are bigger than they have been. And so are the possibilities of creating networks. The more people that are out there, the more it is possible to define new fields.

Wall maintains a vigilant outlook with an eye towards steady progress. She understands the institutional inequities, commits to challenging the academy, and serves as a bridge for historically underrepresented faculty—and even more so for women of color. After we ended our phone conversation, I reflected on the possibilities offered by Wall. I was reminded that my presence as a Black woman in the humanities and academia is not a mere anomaly. I also began to reconsider my sense of Black women's role within the humanities, particularly how their contributions to Black feminist literatures and scholarship are expanding to include larger roles within the university. Throughout my graduate training, I imagined myself as continuing foundation building through traditional academic tracks. The changing social, political, and economic landscape of universities, however, demanded that I revisit my definition of building. Wall talked about constructing canons and introducing African American experiences to traditional fields of study. I would add to this that women's presence continues to grow in diverse spaces within the academy. My work as a Title IX investigator assumes a commitment to putting into place policies at institutions of higher learning that promote intersectional understandings of gender equity. And so the Black feminist criticism that shaped my dissertation research has taken a new form outside of the publishing and teaching track to change the material conditions of Black women's lives. I've also had the kind of mentorship Wall had in her career. In fact, it was a Black woman administrator I developed a mentoring relationship with who offered guidance about the politics of academic administration. To have a seat at a table that was not created with a specific schema intended to include a Black person who was also a woman of color became a new way to engage with the knowledge production of Black women's stories and experiences. Black women like Dr. Wall continue to exemplify the need for our presence within the halls of the ivory tower—to create space and foster dialogue widely throughout—and I see my work in partnership with hers.

Notes

1. Wall, "What Does It Mean to Be a Black Woman Who Reads for a Living?"

2. Cohen, "In Tough Times, The Humanities Must Justify their Worth."

3. Douglass College, originally the New Jersey College for Women, was founded in 1918. In 1973, it was the college for women, a part of Rutger University's federated system. Professor Wall emphasized that it had a complicated system, but Douglass College was for women, and Rutgers College was for men. Today it is a part of Rutgers–Brunswick.

4. Modern Language Association.

5. Wall, "Foreword: Faculty as Change Agents—Reflections on My Academic Life."

6. See Patton, "How a White Historian Nurtures Diverse PhDs."

Navigations

Difference without Grievance

Asian Americans as the Almost Minority

Leslie Bow
University of Wisconsin–Madison

On a good day, I forget I'm Asian.

So proclaimed my fellow panelist. We were at Harvard doing a presentation for Asian American History Month or something like it. Harvard, I say, not out of a sense of self-aggrandizement: it is no doubt the first and last time I will ever be asked to speak there. It's merely to say— *even there*, where there seems to be an abundance of smart people—one runs the risk of being misunderstood. A plethora of smart people, you might say, if you were smart.

On a good day, I forget I'm Asian.

That statement could be taken as a naïve disavowal of the body or as something more hopeful: that, like a white person, my fellow speaker believes that her humanity is firmly intact. That race is inessential to her being.

In 2004, a relatively unknown candidate for the U.S. Senate, Barack Obama, electrified the nation by proclaiming, "There's not a liberal America and a conservative America; there is the United States of America. There's not a Black America and a white America and Latino America and Asian America; there is the United States of America." Never mind that this turned out to be woefully inaccurate. But for Asians in the United States, it was great to be recognized, to receive a shout out on the floor of the Democratic National Convention, to be present and accounted for in this vision of unity. But the current cultural climate is particularly ironic for Asian Americans. Just at the moment that we have been recognized as having racial grievances at all, pundits have declared that we are now "postracial." This declaration does not in any way prevent the strategic invocation of Asian difference within our racially saturated public sphere. In the midst of the 2010 recession, David Brooks trumpeted in the *New York Times*, "Even in struggling parts of the country, Asian Americans do well. . . . The average Asian American in New Jersey lives an amazing twenty-six years longer and is eleven times more likely to have a graduate degree than the average American Indian in South Dakota."[1] What is the upshot of this factoid? Predictably, that public policy doesn't matter: "What matters are historical experiences, cultural attitudes, child-rearing practices, family formation patterns, expectations about the future, work ethics, and the quality of social bonds." In other words, go Asians. They don't need no stinking government programs. When it comes to us, race is no handicap, so there goes your proof.

The so-called postracial proclamation takes place within the context of general skepticism about whether or not Asian Americans are "really" oppressed. For example, Gene Luen Yang was nominated for a National Book Award for his 2006 graphic novel, *American Born Chinese*, which depicted a Chinese American adolescent who undergoes psychic splitting, imagining himself to be white in a fantasy portrayal of race passing. Questioning whether this degree of racial self-hatred would apply to Asian Americans, one book reviewer asked, "Is it so bad to grow up Asian in America? One might be forgiven for asking upon encountering *American Born Chinese*. . . . After all, Asians are widely perceived to have it easier than other minorities in the United States."[2]

Have it easier than other minorities? Yes, I suppose it's a small consolation that there is no Asian version of the tomahawk chop whereby sports fans don conical hats and pull their eyes up in unison at stadiums across the country. That when I enter my white suburb my neighbors most definitely do not think, "Oh shit, the middle-aged Chinese woman is going to jack my car."

I begin with this cultural climate because it continues to inform the ways in which Asian Americans are perceived within academic institutions as well. Asian Americans hold a precarious place in the American imagination. We are immigrants—but not in the tradition of Ellis Island. We are routinely trotted out as proof of national diversity, yet few people can name an Asian person in the United States who does not bear some association to *kung fu*. We are seen as minorities—almost. We have become a source of deep cultural anxiety, resentment, and longing, a template of convenience for liberals and conservatives alike. The simultaneous erasure and celebration of cultural difference, its uncertain capital, and the ambiguity about where Asian Americans stand in the history of social injury and its redress are all inseparable from the ways in which we are located on American campuses. How might this climate affect the place that Asian Americans inhabit within academia?

My focus here will be broader in scope than a consideration of race and tenure, but it nonetheless brings to bear on the larger cultural associations we make about race, our sometimes hidden reservations about compromising academic "excellence," and the ways in which embodied differences challenge assumptions about the value we place on scholarly objectivity. What nuances attend Asian American representation within institutions of higher education? In what ways are Asian Americans the imperfect specimens of diversity, the "almost" minority? In exploring the ways in which the so-called privileges of embodied difference are often indistinguishable from the risks, I highlight a specific paradox: the racial minority who reflects difference without grievance.

"The body has been lost in the language of the academy," laments writer Cherríe Moraga.[3] Yes and no. The body is erased within the language of "objective" knowledge production, but it operates within academia as a visual marker that confers a specific kind of capital. Academic institutions deal with the question of faculty diversity in the same way that liberal businesses do: diversity is a human resources (HR) issue—that is, the question of inclusion represents a problem for HR. The resolution to the problem is indistinguishable from liberalism's horizon: to be successful in diversity recruitment is to mirror the nation's percentage of minority populations in 2000—excluding multiracial individuals, 12.3 percent Black, 0.9 percent American Indian, 3.6 percent Asian, and 11.2 percent nonwhite Latino. Accomplish diversity within this one area (race) and, according to these (modest) numbers, you've done your duty. And if you fail to reach this horizon, you can always create the illusion of diversity. At my home institution, the University of Wisconsin–Madison, officials got into hot water for photoshopping the face of an African American student into a group shot of football fans for an undergraduate publicity brochure. At least they cared enough about integration to fake it.

Proportional representation is problematic for Asian Americans in the academy precisely because we are widely perceived to be overrepresented among the professoriate. (In 2005, in Madison, for example, Asians made up 59 percent of all ladder-rank faculty of color but just 8.9 percent of the total faculty).[4] Within academia, the belief in smart Asian hordes produces a curious duality, the oxymoronic "majority minority." Thus the paradox of Asian overexposure:

To *my detriment*—like other Asian Americans, you are not the best, most valuable specimen of racial diversity. You are "over-represented"; moreover, you are not expected to be militant or aggrieved. You are, like President Obama, "clean and articulate," if something of a grind.

To *my advantage*—like other Asian Americans, you are not the best, most valuable specimen of racial diversity. You are "overrepresented"; moreover, you are not expected to be militant or aggrieved. You are, like President Obama, "clean and articulate," if something of a grind.

Given the simultaneous and contradictory necessity of representing both honorary whites and "right on" people of color, for Asian Americans the risk of racial embodiment is identical to its supposed privileges. Praise and pathology turn out to be different sides of the same coin. This duality is certainly the case within recent, highly publicized media portrayals of Asian Americans in higher education: on the one hand, Annie Le, the Vietnamese American soon-to-be-wed graduate student at Yale whose body was found stuffed into the walls of a basement laboratory ("most likely to be the next Einstein," "a young woman of unlimited potential") and on the other, Seung-Hui Cho, the Korean American mass killer at Virginia Tech (a social loner, a perpetual disappointment to his hardworking immigrant parents). In 1972, writers Frank Chin and Jeffrey Paul Chan coined the term "racist love" as the analog to "racist hate" to describe the duality of racial representation in the United States. Each racial stereotype comes in two models, they wrote, a duality that does not represent a contradiction but is essential to the work of white supremacy: "The unacceptable, hostile Black stud has his acceptable counterpart in the form of Stepin Fetchit. For the savage, kill-crazy Geronimo, there is Tonto.... For Fu Manchu and the Yellow Peril, there is Charlie Chan and his Number One Son.... The acceptable model is acceptable because he is tractable. There is racist hate and racist love."[5]

That racial difference occasions negative affect is now rarely disputed; one has only to gloss Americans' shared history of bondage, incarceration, and genocide. But love—love is another matter. In the violent panorama of race relations, we come to reference it only within catchphrases such as "Be Like Mike" or the inadequate defense "Some of my best friends are—." Racial desire is undertheorized and often unacknowledged. But as literary critic Leslie Fiedler once revealed, homoerotic love for the Other is central to American letters—an ethnic sidekick to grant undemanding, unconditional support to the orphan making his way in the wilderness. From Ishmael to Huck Finn, Fiedler notes, "Our dark-skinned beloved will take us in, we assure ourselves when we have been cut off, or have cut ourselves off, from all others, without rancor or the insult of forgiveness. He will fold us in his arms saying, 'honey' or 'Aikane'; he will comfort us, as if our offense against him were long ago remitted, were never truly *real*."[6] "Racist love" underscores the nation's dependence on and ambivalence about racial minorities who provide, in Diana Fuss's words, the "detour through the Other that provides access to a fictive sense of self."[7] For scholars of color, this is unacknowledged, symbolic labor performed without compensation. Our presence provides proof of democratic inclusion, of equal opportunity, and the aroma of alternative epistemologies, alternative knowledges. Of course—and especially when it comes to awarding tenure—there is a fine line between rage and idealization, a line that Freud's theory of secondary narcissism underscores.

As Freud writes, idealized love is essentially narcissistic insofar as the subject projects the self onto a love object that becomes the temporary repository of his own self-love. "He then seeks a way back to narcissism from his prodigal expenditure of libido upon objects by choosing a sexual ideal after the narcissistic type which shall possess the excellences to which he cannot attain."[8] In popular culture, the love of racial difference—its externalization—takes any number of forms: a desire to possess indigenous people's "oneness" with nature, Asian zen, Black street cred, or Latin passion. The catch is that the ego wants its shit back: how otherwise to explain the phenomenon that was O. J. Simpson? The "prodigal expenditure of libido" on the part of white culture is narcissistically ambivalent as well: I hate the one who withholds my self-love from me. Freud writes, "the re-enrichment of the ego can be effected only by a withdrawal of the libido from its objects."[9] For junior faculty of color, this could be particularly meaningful around year six. The love of difference extends only so far.

What I find particularly prescient about Chin and Chan's 1972 recognition of "racist love" as it applies in particular to Asian Americans is the ways in which it became reflected in what would become our dominant representation, the trope of the "model minority." At one level, the hailing represents the equivalent of "I love your people"—your work ethic, your belief in education, your self-discipline, your yummy food—and this is largely understood not to be "about" Asian Americans as much as a slap in the face to African Americans and Latinos. On another level, the "model minority" construct is a reflection of American narcissism, a screen for those idealized virtues, those "excellences," that are both unattainable and intrinsic to national self-fashioning. This externalization reproduces an imperfect self-reflection, the unresolved interplay between likeness and difference within the self and nation. My thoughts here certainly arise from my recent research into the place of Asian Americans in the segregated South.[10] In 1930, sociologist Max Handman noted that American society had "no social technique for handling *partly colored* races. We have a place for the Negro and a place for the white man: the Mexican is not a Negro, and the white man refuses him an equal status."[11] What does it mean to be "partly colored," partly oppressed? In some sense, this question likewise applies to the raced body in academia: what I uncovered in my research is a narrative about Asian Americans and other anomalies to Jim Crow's racial codes that endures within our now "postracial" moment. The ambiguity of place—neither Black nor white—means that we can be conveniently flexible subjects harnessed to various ideologies and purposes. Asian Americans can thus be coopted as symbols of achievement—as a group *overcoming* an oppressive racial history—when simultaneously met with the disbelief that we ever suffered one. In keeping with a national ethos, it is a narrative that exudes minority exceptionalism. And for faculty of color, exceptionalism (or its failure) is the prevailing narrative.

The schizophrenic role that faculty of color are asked to serve as objects of both desire and suspicion provides the foundation of the not-so-private joke currently circulating on Facebook, an application called "Crappy Gifts for Faculty of Color." Academics can bestow on one another the ambiguous "gifts" that attend embodied difference within institutions that pride themselves on not noticing it. The presents include "Students crying in your office 24/7," "Colleagues congratulating you on being 'articulate,'" and "Department review mentions with surprise that you teach white writers" (she knows what we know—inconceivable!). This racism "that does not exhibit itself in blatant insults"[12] is intrinsic to the academy's subtle upkeep of the borders set around academic "excellence." African American English professor Trudier Harris tells this anecdote about a white colleague's reaction to her being appointed to a named chair: "Now that you're a chaired professor," he asks her, "what are you gonna do? Buy another big ol' car?" She ponders, "It's a wonder we're not all crazy or dead. My major preoccupation in life is managing madness. So, you ask, how do I do that? How do I keep on going on in the face of racism that does not exhibit itself in blatant insults or physical abuse, but in the symbolic 'death of a thousand cuts'?"[13] By no means do I want to discount that overtly racist acts, the bigger cuts, exist within the ivory tower; in this sense, "death of a thousand cuts" represents a weird kind of privilege. But should one draw nuances between the outrage students express when they are unable to understand their chemistry TA's accent and the approving comment that appeared in my Asian American colleague's teaching evaluations—and I paraphrase—"It was a pleasure to hear him speak good English"? One of Harris's colleagues of color wants to write a book titled *The Things They Have Said to Me*. Of course, this imaginary book—like this essay—is a post-tenure luxury.

When I think of racism as it manifests itself on campuses, I often wonder about the resistance of some Asian Americans to seeing it, subtle or no, and their readiness to discount forms of differential treatment. My own "madness" (slight, I assure you) lies in seeing what others do not. (Okay, I'll say it here: is it only because I'm Chinese that I'd never use the phrase "Death of a thousand cuts"?) For example, I have just been reading Yi-fu Tuan's memoir about the pathways that led him to his calling as the father of humanist geography and to his current position as professor emeritus on my home campus. His book *Who Am I? An Autobiography of Emotion, Mind, and Spirit* is also a coming out story, one that makes a significant though at times inadvertent case for the impact of closeted sexuality on the psyche and on every aspect of social interaction, social community.[14] In contrast, Professor Tuan disclaims racial and ethnic identity as essential to his individual development and subsequent life as an academic in the United States. Being Chinese, he asserts, has been a source of pride and self-esteem, the origins of his cosmopolitanism. Self-described "ethnics" (myself included, I suppose) reveal their parochialism by insisting on the designations "Chinese American" or "Asian American," both apparently limiting the ability to see oneself as a world citizen. At what level, however, does glossing over racial identity become a feat of blinkered will? In a review of Tuan's autobiography, Philip W. Porter, his colleague, friend, and former department chair at the University of Minnesota, writes that Tuan's "homosexuality never crossed [his] mind": "Yi-Fu is just Yi-Fu. (I seem always to be the last to learn that a colleague is Jewish, gay, a registered Republican, or recently divorced;

further, I have almost no interest in such information.). . . . Being some thing—Asian-American, homosexual . . . can take on the character of being forced on one. . . . This is identity being stamped down on one by the *other*. Well, I won't have it."[15]

Is it any wonder that the Chinese American did not make an "issue" of his race as a geographer or peer? Or reveal his sexuality to his then department chair? (*"Well, I won't have it."*) I can't help but think about what difference race made in what Tuan reveals as the lack of intimacy in his life and absence of strong social ties, much less a lover or life partner during his years of residence in Australia, Britain, and the United States. He attributes that lack to voluntary behaviors, the better to avoid "temptation." In his attempt to elude homophobic social shunning, he cut himself off but was unable to evade the stigma of queerness within himself. The book self-consciously attempts not to read as tragedy, but it does. It did not occur to his colleagues, however, to wonder about Tuan's wife, partner, or family—because he was Chinese? In other words, as any historian can tell you, failed integration is not always self-imposed. Yet the memoir curiously refuses to locate sexuality and race as parallel systems: the former gives him insight into "human misery and . . . what it means to belong to a disdained minority group,"[16] while the latter's effects are easily countered if, given pride in one's culture, ethnic slurs "have no power to sting."[17] For my Asian American colleague, race only manifests itself as racist acts perpetrated by benighted individuals. Perhaps being an "almost minority" means that you have the luxury of viewing your own experience within the clouded perspective accorded to whites, the inverse of Peggy McIntosh's important recognition, "I did not see myself as a racist because I was taught to recognize racism only in individual acts of meanness by members of my group."[18] In the absence of these acts, one can fantasize that one inhabits that unmarked place of universal abstraction, the place of normative whiteness.

Is maintaining the fiction of disembodiment an unspoken prerequisite to surviving academia? It's not simply a matter of being careful about what you say and how you appear to senior colleagues (universal counsel to any junior faculty person); survival for faculty of color also implies the successful repudiation of the very (marked) body you inhabit. Acknowledging the body announces that you're biased, compromised, partial, irrational—a "wise Latina woman." That is to say, your racial experience counts against you because it is widely perceived to cloud your judgment, your ability to be objective, and, most damning within institutions of knowledge, your access to Truth. Thank goodness that Asians don't have oppressive racial experiences after all!

The upshot of liberal color blindness is the obstinate (if not aggressive) disregard of specificity in the rush to project universal commonality. "I understand the civic ritual that requires us to say in the face of all our differences, We are all one, we are the world," writes law professor Patricia J. Williams. "Yet such a binding force comes from a citizenry willing to suspend disbelief for the sake of honoring the spiritual power of our appointed ideas."[19] Sociologist Eduardo Bonilla-Silva coins the term "racism without racists" to explain the ways in which color-blind rhetoric allows "whites [to] subscribe to an ideology that ultimately helps preserve racial inequality."[20] This careful disavowal—I am not a racist— becomes a hedge against recognizing how the underlying structures of liberal belief perpetuate the racial status quo. Thus the irony of the "postracial" moment and the prevailing HR attitude toward diversity: acknowledging the significance of something that has been willed to have no content. And who better to maintain the fiction of difference without grievance than Asian Americans?

I'd make a distinction here between my identity as an Asian American women in the academy and my fields—Asian American Studies and English. Thus, while I rarely experience a denigration of my person in this politically correct oasis of the Midwest, I normally operate within the context of a slight denigration of Asian American Studies, the projection of a presumably narrow and inconsequential range of competencies that come along with it, many of which are simply attributed to my identity. At one level, identity politics is on my side; identity confers automatic if obviously problematic authority. On another level, that reduction is just plain annoying. As a scholar of color in Ethnic Studies, you are rarely seen as someone who can speak beyond your subfield. In composing a joint evaluation letter for a junior faculty person in Ethnic Studies, the chair of the committee listed the fields of the scholar's intervention as "comparative ethnic studies, American studies, and African American studies," reading them off to us as he composed— well-rounded competencies, to be sure. After a slight pause, the chair's female colleague gently added, "And history." In my case, the inclusion of Asian American literature represents a kind of affirmative action for the field of literary studies; it is situated as a perpetual supplement to the core of English, never as its center. And within the "last shall be first" logic of multicultural curricular inclusion, it can only place a distance third to African American and American Indian literatures.[21] At the same time, neither Asian American literature nor its criticism is yet—it has been stated out loud—very good: both are "emergent."

The latter belief is well meaning, as are a host of other entrenched beliefs about race studies and its practitioners. Affirmative action reproduces soft racist assumptions; for one, the perception that scholars of color will not able to compete with candidates in open faculty searches. And what to do with the all-too-ready acknowledgement that teaching evaluations are going to be lower when one engages racial topics with students coerced into seats by general education "diversity" requirements? Again a paradox: accepting the pragmatic and justifiable acknowledgement of a different context for reading the teaching evaluations of junior scholars whose courses fulfill the Ethnic Studies requirement means accepting that "different" means lower; conversely, to claim that one does not need a differing standard encourages color-blind exceptionalism. Not once have I ever heard that the opposite might be true—that students find discussions of race and literature to be relevant, timely, or powerful—and will reward its careful stewardship, "careful" being the operative word here.

The risk of doing what one might call embodied scholarship might be summed up thusly and with particular ironies given this essay: what white academics do is scholarship, what minority faculty in Ethnic Studies do is polemic.

On a good day, I can forget I'm biased.

But, of course, I keep pushing the rock up the hill, shrilly insisting that race matters to folks who deny that racial discrimination has ever applied to them and to those who claim—I kid you not—that Asians are not discriminated against because their neighbors are Asian and they are both doctors. We in the field soldier on, talking about the history of exclusion laws, denied naturalization rights, the abrogation of civil rights, and, in my case, books my colleagues have never heard of or never plan to read. Like every other racialized minority, we are and have been the targets of rioting, segregation, hate crimes, deportation, and prosecution as traitors to the nation—in spite of widespread belief that none of these things have ever happened to Mr. Lee who runs the takeout place on the corner. In April 1999, on the anniversary of the Third World Strike at the University of California–Berkeley, students occupied a building to protest the university's lack of investment in its Ethnic Studies department. Cherríe Moraga wrote, "The rescue of Ethnic Studies is not, in and of itself, revolutionary. It does not alter the racist *system* of higher education in this country. It is, however, an impressive act of revolt, requiring a radical consciousness. It challenges the unilateral authority of the university to determine *what* and how we learn and by *whom*."[22] The work of minority scholars in the field does not merely address historical erasures in knowledge production, it challenges the foundations of knowledge. At the same time, the value of such scholars seems limited to satisfying the narrow vision of multiculturalism reflected back by the HR department—for Asian Americans, if only ambivalently. It is not so big a leap to shift between understanding the roles that narratives produced by and about Asian Americans play in American culture to understanding those that surround my own visibly and invisibly fraught place in academia. Both involve exposing the hidden and not-so-hidden work of culture, the multiple uses of race, and the ways in which bodies become both targets of venom and screens for the desires of others.

Comedian Sarah Silverman tells this joke about trying to get out of jury duty. A friend advises her to write something inappropriate on the jury selection form such as, "I hate chinks." "But I didn't want to be racist," Sarah cheerfully reports. "So I wrote, 'I *love* chinks.' And who doesn't, really?"

Who doesn't, indeed?

Coda

Since this essay was written, the institution of tenure has undergone an attack in the Wisconsin State legislature. In the context of this volume, I would be remiss not to comment on the structural economic, political, and philosophical implications of this attempt to erode tenure, whether these partisan efforts ultimately prove to be the tip of an iceberg or a blip in the history of higher education.

Governor Scott Walker's proposed changes to tenure and shared governance are folded into a bill that cuts 250 million dollars from the university system budget. These changes do not simply shift tenure policy from state law to the Board of Regents in keeping with most state university systems. Rather, they would effectively dismantle the institution of tenure by including the proviso that "the Board may . . . terminate any faculty or academic staff appointment when such an action is deemed necessary due to a budget or program decision regarding program discontinuance, curtailment, modification, or redirection, instead of when a financial emergency exists as under current law."[23] To the governor, the professoriate represents yet another labor union to be crushed. The Board of Regents, with sixteen of its eighteen members appointed by the governor, adopted this weakening of tenure policy inconsistent with AAUP guidelines without considering modifications requested by UW System faculty. In May, 2016, the UW-Madison Faculty Senate passed a vote of no confidence in President Ray Cross and the UW Board of Regents.

This essay has focused on the ways in which racialized bodies come to be valued or devalued in academic institutions; this book attests to the increased precarity that scholars of color face within them. I take no pleasure in the irony that this precarity has widened, not only within the context of events in Wisconsin, but in the context of the increasing use of contract workers in higher education that erodes the professoriate as a whole. Apparently, as faculty we are now *all* polemical, marginal, devalued. In Wisconsin, particularly in the Humanities, we feel called upon to justify our labor, our perspectives, and our objects of study because the flow of our ideas cannot be easily monetized—precisely what I love about the Humanities. Now the very voice I established in this essay strikes me as a post-tenure luxury. As the contributors to this volume attest, there is always risk in speaking truth to power. Given systemic changes in higher education, this has never been more true.

Notes

1. Brooks, "The Limits of Policy."
2. Vizzini, "High Anxiety."
3. Moraga, *Loving in the War Years*, 175.
4. At the rank of full professor, the percentages are lower. In 2013, the National Center for Education Statistics reported that faculty of color made up only 16 percent of all full professors; Asians represented 9 percent of full professors. (These statistics do not distinguish between Asian ethnicities or citizenship status—American or foreign born.) These statistics do not account for the disparity between the sciences and humanities and social sciences. *The Chronicle of Higher Education* reported that Asians who were American citizens earned 26.2 percent of all biological and biomedical sciences doctorates awarded in 2004, but only 2.8 percent of those in "letters." In 2004, Asian Americans were awarded 5.6 percent of all doctorate degrees in the United States (http://chronicle.com/weekly/v53/io6/06bo1601.htm). Rarely is it mentioned that overrepresentation has anything to do with public policy—for example, post-1965 immigration preferences privileged specific fields—medicine and engineering in particular. (See *The New Asian Immigration in Los Angeles and Global Restructuring*, ed. Paul Ong,

Edna Bonacich, and Lucie Cheng.) Asian American presence in the sciences in the United States has been misinterpreted as genetic proof of mathematical ability rather than as proof of the state's manipulation of its labor pool. Nor does anyone ever seem to mull over the fact that Asians in the United States may choose the sciences precisely because they are perceived to be disciplines in which objective, impartial evaluation is perceived to hold sway. As historian Karen Brodkin has suggested in *How Jews Became White Folks and What That Says About Race in America*, second-generation Jewish American men in the postwar era chose medicine and law precisely because they perceived anti-Semitism to be less of a barrier in these individualized fields.

5. Chin and Chan, "Racist Love," 65.

6. Fiedler, *An End to Innocence*, 150.

7. Fuss, *Identification Papers*, 143.

8. Freud, *A General Selection from the Works of Sigmund Freud*, 122.

9. Ibid., 121.

10. Bow, *"Partly Colored."*

11. Handman, "Economic Reasons for the Coming of the Mexican Immigrant."

12. Harris, *Summer Snow*, 159.

13. Ibid.

14. Tuan, *Who Am I?*

15. Porter, Book review of *Who Am I?*

16. Tuan, *Who Am I?* 89.

17. Ibid., 28.

18. McIntosh, "White Privilege."

19. Williams, *Seeing a Color-Blind Future*, 12.

20. Bonilla-Silva, *Racism without Racists*, 14.

21. The phrase comes from Ann du Cille's discussion of the popularity of African American women's literature among white feminist critics and teachers in the context of canon expansion in the 1980s in "The Occult of True Black Womanhood: Critical Demeanor and Black Feminist Studies."

22. Moraga, *Loving in the War Years*, 187.

23. Nancy Kendall, "What else will we lose when Wisconsin faculty loses tenure?" *The Conversation.* (June 9, 2015), http://theconversation.com/what-else -will-we-lose-when-wisconsin-faculty-loses-tenure-42929.

In Search of Our Fathers' Workshops

Lisa Sánchez González
University of Connecticut

Dedicated, con todo corazón, a mi pai, Louis Sanchez

I'm standing. It's the end of the semester. We've been studying Boricua "coming of age" novels, among other texts. I'm lecturing and leading a discussion about the latest novel in the long line of novels about growing up Boricua. Most of these novels irritate me.

There's a formula in these texts that always revolves around dysfunctional families. The father is abusive, drunk, disinterested, dead, or otherwise absent. The mother is a martyr, a stone-cold religious fanatic, or otherwise helpless, hapless, and hopeless. Foiled by this dysfunction, the child prevails. I'm thinking to myself: *Are these the only types of stories written or are these the only types of stories published?*

A student raises his hand. "Professor, are there any novels in Boricua literary history that have a sympathetic father figure in them, one that isn't a flat character?"

That question knocks the wind out of me. I'd never thought to ask such a question. It's so basic, so simple, so important.

After class I go for a long walk. When I get home I look through my personal library to make sure I have not missed anything. The question is devastating in its own way. It takes me a few days to formulate an answer (I make it a rule never to talk about myself in class).

"The long answer to that question is very long," I tell the class during my last lecture of the semester. "The short answer is 'no.' But let me tell you a little bit about my own father. He was my finest, most exacting teacher. He is my best friend. He taught me how to think for myself, how to solve problems, how to be an ethical person. My father and his workshop," I say, "are the taproot of my radicalism. It was his love that made me a feminist, too."

Silence.

"My father taught me to be suspicious of the paternalism I encountered away from home. He taught me to stand up for myself against racists, machistas, and snobs. He taught me to stand up for others, for those who are weaker, for those who are victimized, for those who are habitually unloved in the world."

But what I'm really thinking is this: *No. The life I save is not just my own.*

Portrait of a Boricua "Radical" as a Young Woman

As far back as I can remember, I had two realms of learning: home and school. At home I learned a lot more in a loving and safe environment with excellent teachers. At school, I had few really good teachers, and what I remember most vividly from elementary school on was watching the big white clocks with the black hands tick-tick-ticking toward recess, lunch, PE, and the last bell of the day.

I grew up in a housing tract built on what was once a citrus grove on the western end of the San Fernando Valley. The town was called Canoga Park back then. My family of six—and whichever relatives were visiting or needed a place to stay—lived in a sturdy three-bedroom house on Schoolcraft Street. There was only one heater in the whole house, one of those wall-mounted electric units that always smell like burnt dust when you turn them on. We had but one shower, too. It seems impossible now in hindsight, but getting everyone up, bathed, fed, ready, and out the door in the morning for school and work ran like clockwork.

When I was a little girl, I didn't know what I didn't know, I didn't have what I didn't have, and I didn't know what I didn't have. We were not poor exactly. I knew that. My mother and father had been poor as children growing up in the South Bronx. Glimpses of that poverty were always a part of the stories my father told me. They were usually funny stories, though. About the linoleum in the kitchen looking like a Fred Murray Dance Studio floor because of all the pieces cut out to replace worn soles in old shoes. About quixotic attempts to race boats made out of newspaper in the gutters when it rained. Stories like that. Lots of them.

Sometimes the stories would start off funny and become serious. My father begging his father for a baseball glove (a real luxury), and the policeman who "confiscated" it from him the very first day he took it outside for a stickball game. My father all giddy to go swimming and, in the end, running to avoid a beating in the attempt to get to the public pool. His friends and their misadventures. Corporal punishment for speaking Spanish in school. Stories about finding the humor in everything while growing up on a single block that might as well have been a reservation.

About the 1940s and 50s and being broke and Boricua in the tenements of the South Bronx.

In California, none of us kids had more than two pairs of shoes at a time, but we didn't resole them by cutting up the kitchen floor. We didn't have much in the way of clothing either, but we were kids and really didn't care. We had regular meals, even if the bulk of most suppers was rice or pasta. We had a small collection of picture books, a lone magazine subscription to *National Geographic*, and library cards, which we used so often they'd become frayed. We were not beaten up when we took swimming classes at the Y or went to the public pool in Lanark Park.

Because California has such a huge Mexican demographic, we got called names like "beaners" on the playground, rather than "spics," and we had schoolteachers who seemed relieved to discover English was our first language. Our greatest luxuries were our bicycles, going to a Dodgers game, or a day at the beach. Our family vacations were camping trips. We went to church every Sunday, and all of us received the Catholic sacraments. We were working-class Puerto Rican kids growing up in the suburbs of Los Angeles in the 1960s and 70s. My father's military service, the GI Bill's home mortgage provisions, the end of real estate redlining in the valley, a lot of hard work, and a bit of luck had made the suburban dream possible for my parents.

My father is a big guy: tall, strong, dark, and, yes, handsome, in an Andalusian sort of way. One of his bowling teams dubbed him "Geronimo," and he does look the stereotypical part of a Native American. Once, in fact, when he was helping me move and our car broke down on a reservation outside Phoenix, the folks there pretty much treated us as family. I also know, to a certain extent, the kind of fear that he often inspires in some smaller, paler people, since I've encountered that kind of automatic intimidation factor myself all too often. I look a lot like my father.

But to know my father is to know a man who is as gentle as a lamb. I never heard him raise his voice. He never beat his children. He never raised a hand to my mother or ever treated her unkindly. He devoted his entire adult life to providing his children with a home that had a lot more than he had growing up, in a neighborhood that had much better public schools than those he attended. He was also a wonderful son to his parents and generous to his extended family, a few branches of which had also moved to Southern California in the late 1950s and early 60s on the heels of an uncle who had found a secure job at a noodle factory in Culver City.

My father is also extremely intelligent. And it's not just his emotional intelligence or his skill with languages—he is fluent in both Spanish and English and can tell a story better than anyone I've ever met—but it's his mechanical skills, too. He can fix anything. He was a straight-A student in high school and dreamed of becoming a physician, but the school provided absolutely no college guidance counseling and he simply didn't know what the college application process entailed or anyone he could ask for advice. He's told me that story many times. The story ends with him doing what many of his friends and cousins did after high school: joining the U.S. military, getting married, and starting a family.

My mother taught me self-discipline, the power of forgiveness, and how to fight back without compromise—lessons that have been invaluable to me in my professional and personal life. My mother is a fierce woman warrior. My two sisters take after her. Unfortunately, I can't rouse that kind of fierceness when I probably should. Instead, I step back and study a crisis, try to find the source of the problem, and carefully fix it. I am my father's daughter.

In fifth grade I was identified as a "special education" student. As an abnormally quick learner, I was, in fact, bored to distraction—even to the point of physical illness (stomach aches)—for most of the school day. I was diagnosed with a "learning disability," the dreadful fate for many gifted girls of color. My mind was in the habit of racing when almost everyone else's mind in the classroom (including the teacher's) was trotting. It was torture.

But outside school I had other classrooms. The public library and my father's workshop—our garage—were the ones I loved most. Reading stories was a joy to me, and I read voraciously. I also loved to "help" my father fix things. And he, with what precious little time he had for leisure on the weekends, would let me watch and assist. When my bicycle got a flat tire or needed adjustments, he'd tell me to take it apart, figure out the problem, and fix it. Of course, he managed to help me through most of my work without really calling attention to that help, making me feel like I had, on my own, solved problems he had actually taught me to solve. This entailed, the first time I "fixed" my bike, putting the whole thing back together (I took his instructions to "take it apart" literally).

The most difficult lesson I learned from him was patience studying a machine—a bicycle, a lawnmower, a lamp—and that identifying the symptoms and sources of a machine's problem was only the first step in solving it. Another important lesson was knowledge of and respect for one's tools, which he kept well organized and maintained. Being a mechanic, in my father's workshop, was an art as much as a science. My father's workshop, in my little girls' eyes, was for me as wondrous as Merlin's.

In school, the major pattern I learned to expect (a pattern that in fact repeated itself over and over again into my college years and beyond) was the one pretty much set for me in fifth grade: teachers or administrators would project very low capabilities onto me (regardless of the evidence before them), I would outperform most if not all of my peers, and some champion would break ranks and step up to defend me. The most important lesson I learned in my twenty-five years as a student was that public educational institutions in the United States are by design racist and elitist, that being female or working class (or both) only compounds a student's experience of racism and elitism, that institutional racism works often in subtle but no less insidious ways than de jure discrimination, that surviving (never mind thriving) in these institutions means fighting your way out of trouble you never authored and treatment you don't deserve, and that, if you're lucky, you might find an ethical and talented teacher (of whatever background) whose mind races too and who not only has something worthwhile to teach but also teaches it well, someone who is willing to protect and mentor you, too. Teachers like my father. Classrooms like my father's workshop.

When the teachers and administrators are the bullies, there's not much you can do except escape to a safe place. Find allies. Study the problem carefully. If you can solve the problem, go back into the fray and fix it. If you can't, save your own life. Run.

Why Angels Fear to Tread in Rat-Infested Places

When I started my first tenure-track job, I immediately sensed an uncanny estrangement from the scene. My powers of intuition are very strong. The faces people make, their casual conversations, their tone of voice, the way they use their bodies in groups—all of this speaks volumes to me. I knew something was "off" from the get-go. It was a large department at a large public university. The department had a reputation for being a place where really big stars would work for awhile and then depart for greener pastures. It was an utterly dysfunctional department, full of cliques, rivalries, hostility, vendettas, and super-strange identity politics, and I intuited the general shape of all that dysfunction almost immediately.

The few stellar scholars and writers I met who were still on the faculty or emerita and emeritus were very kind people, and I was very happy to meet them. I also noticed that they steered clear of department meetings and all forms of department social life. And me being who I am by nature—a studious nerd who prefers a night alone with her cats writing or reading in her home library to, say, schmoozing at a cocktail party—I pretty much kept to myself, though I did make some friends among junior faculty in my own and other departments, primarily through my affiliation with an interdisciplinary Africana Studies program. My friends and I socialized mostly over coffee (to talk about our projects) and at barbeques (to relax for a bit). Rarely did we have the kind of soirees that the more bourgeois-oriented professors seemed to think make an essential part of being a professor. My friends and I were all keeping busy doing our best to produce the scholarship and teach the classes that we were told would be the basis of our tenure evaluations. We also had very heavy service loads, especially with graduate students. For almost every hour of every day—and probably in my dreams while I slept, too—I was working while I was on that tenure clock.

I tried to be friendly with the more "progressive" faculty in the department, but I soon realized that they were heavily invested in an odd dynamic, the kind that makes a group of coworkers add up to a lot less than the sum of its parts. Probably the worst of it (at least what I saw of it) was the ideological turf warfare among tenured faculty who had laid claim to Ethnic and Women's Studies, many of whom were not actually published scholars in those fields. Whenever I voiced my opinion about what I saw as a corruption of due process or decision making, I was warned in private to keep my mouth shut until tenure. By the time I received my glowing third-year review, I was trying my best to find another tenure-track job.

Little did I know at the time that one of my senior colleagues was tracking my job talks and putting in calls that were intended to ruin my chances of being hired elsewhere. So as I watched several senior women colleagues leave and a parade of fellow junior professors—all very talented, all of whom I respected, and all of whom achieved great success after leaving that university—roll in and out of the department's revolving tenure-track door, I also laid plans for an escape. My escape, however, was thwarted by a genuinely evil person who had several accomplices.

Every time I saw this person, he looked like he was afraid I was going to punch him, and he sped off like a rat caught by a light switched suddenly on. In my mind, I nicknamed him "la rata"—the rat. I did not know that his ratlike behavior around me was personal. I just thought he was ratlike by nature. Sadly, there were many such characters in the building and all around campus. There was another one—the department head, no less—who at the end of the day would loudly argue with himself as he walked to his car, his arms flailing in violent gestures. The vain ignorance of many others, expressed as arrogance, was so extreme that they seemed like caricatures rather than real people to me.

My tenure ordeal erupted the week after September 11, 2001. I was convinced then and am still convinced now that the timing of that executive committee meeting had a lot to do with the hysteria that ensued. What should have been a calm, rational discussion of tenure dossiers became, as one informant who was there described it to me, a rendition of *Twelve Angry Men*. I was portrayed as the barbarian in the gates, "the intellectual equivalent of a terrorist." I was the foreign nanny who, when her boss left the room, attacked the children. I was mentally ill and a drug addict. I was a witch who needed to be hung in the public square, the adulteress who needed to be stoned to death by the village.

This was not the first time I had been a hated target there. A few years earlier, in response to a series of incidents that involved the effort to end affirmative action on that campus, I had spoken publicly in defense of it. I spoke on behalf of a group of faculty of color who had banded together with concerned students to protest the dehumanizing rhetoric that had spread like wildfire as a result of the affirmative action issue hitting center stage. Black and Latino students, faculty, and communities at large were being depicted as racially inferior, and a lot of that rhetoric involved the "culture of poverty" theory crudely delivered. The campus climate had become so tense that some students decided to organize a protest teach-in, and their main speaker was the Reverend Jesse Jackson. I stood at the same podium as he did that day and read our faculty position statement, which had been carefully written by all of us. It had taken us a long time to produce it. Our purpose was to exercise our academic freedom to send a powerful message of love and dignity to the students and our respective communities, to express our view that students of color *did* belong on that campus and that they had our full and unwavering support.

That event was the largest protest in the history of that university. The students did a superb job. The media coverage was international. A beautiful and powerful photo of one of my undergraduate students taken at the protest was published in *Time* magazine the next month. But there were serious repercussions. In the months that followed, I received death threats and hate mail. My car was vandalized. My office door was vandalized. My home was vandalized. I assumed the threats and the vandalism had been perpetrated by off-campus groups. I reported all of this to my department head via e-mail, and he never responded. In the hallways, a few colleagues expressed the view that they disagreed with me about the inherent value of affirmative action, but I never thought they could have hated me as abjectly as they revealed they did during my tenure ordeal. The violence later done to me by some of my colleagues may have been epistemic, but it was a violence as equal in its emotional force as the vandalism and hate mail. They may not have threatened to kill me, but as any person who has a scholarly vocation knows, a conspiracy to destroy one's career and professional reputation is tantamount to the threat of a social death.

In the year that followed my department's split tenure decision (I did have some brave colleagues on my side, colleagues who stood up for me not out of friendship but on principle), I reviewed thousands of documents, thanks to the Freedom of Information Act (FOIA), that pertained not just to me but to all the tenure candidates in that department during the previous decade, and nowhere else were there such histrionics focused on a candidate's character as there was in the documentation surrounding my tenure evaluation.

The facts that I was able to glean from the review of the tenure files were straightforward. Based on the criteria that the university had established for tenure, I had one of the most exemplary records of scholarship, teaching, and service among the candidates reviewed for tenure in the preceding decade. The facts were clear. But the facts had been warped by a surreal and vicious depiction of me as an abomination.

I am not and never have been a big fan of "victimologies"—the kind of narratives that revolve around a person's victimization for being female, working class, or nonwhite, and so on—but I had to come to terms with the truth. I had become a victim. Victimhood did not sit well with me; more than probably anything else, I hated being a victim, especially as it became clear that I had very little chance of recourse. As I reviewed the documents I received through the FOIA requests, I had to dissociate myself from the person being portrayed in such vile and libelous ways. When I walked up those stone steps to the tower where the FOIA materials were gathered for me, I told myself it was an archive and the person I was researching was dead. That was how I allayed my rage, tucking it away until I arrived each night at the gym, where I furiously pounded out the anger on the treadmill or the punching bag.

The papers in my files added up to a character assassination complemented by letters of support that had arrived from all four corners of the campus and the country. I discovered who the lead assassin was and, to my dismay (though not to my surprise), found out it was "la rata" and that his accomplices included not just the usual suspects but also another woman of color, a colleague whom I had kept at a distance but naively thought I could trust to write part of my tenure evaluation. That sister sold me down the river. To this day, I still cannot fathom what pleasure or advantage she may have derived or thought she would derive from doing that.

What motivated this character assassin and his accomplices? I thought about this a lot during the preparation of my appeal. There were elements of professional jealousy (the up-and-coming young scholar versus the middle-aged one clearly on the downward slope of a mediocre career trajectory), misogyny (his reputation preceded him), bigotry (try explaining Chicano—or African American—bigotry toward Boricuas to a federal human rights officer), and just plain old meanness of character (I could not recall a single time I saw "la rata" off campus without a beer in his hand). There are also crucial pieces of this story that I cannot tell because they involve the traumas of others and a confidentiality that I, in good conscience, cannot break.

The year 2002 was difficult for me. During that time, I spoke with my parents every week for support. One night, as I was describing the latest wound of the many I had suffered that year, my mom said out of the blue, "Babe, it's not your fault. None of this is your fault." I had not blamed myself consciously for any of it, but my mother's wisdom cut to the bone. I thanked her, hung up the phone, and cried for hours, mourning my innocence, casting into the trash with the tissues all of the messages I had received and internalized that told me that I could have and should have averted this whole ordeal or figured out how to fix it. I hadn't realized how important it was to me that my family might be disappointed, regardless of the obvious injustice I had suffered. I had feared that, in their eyes, I might have to come home a "failure" after nearly a decade of study and my best work.

Trauma has its aftereffects. I have suffered those. Though I now have all the documents I collected and the slide shows that I created for the appeals process safely stored in boxes (down in the cellar), I honestly cannot remember most of the hearing (which lasted for days), yet I refuse to open the boxes or throw them away. I tell myself I am keeping them safe in case someday some researcher needs them. But in a symbolic way, those plastic containers are a tomb where I think I, like Antigone in reverse, buried things I do not love.

In the end, the grievance I presented as an appeal to my tenure case was not successful. It was a kangaroo court, and the issues that were supposed to be deliberated—my scholarship, teaching, and service records—were not deliberated. I also organized a symposium on teaching the next year. I gave a very long talk at that event, but I can't remember a word of it. That lecture and others I gave at that university have never been published. Yet parts of those essays, I recently discovered, live on in the scholarship of those who were in the audience of those events, scholars who were in fact the undergraduate or graduate students who had been the inspiration behind the speech I co-wrote and delivered at the protest. I contacted one of these junior colleagues recently, and she told me I had given her a copy of the lecture. I could not remember that, though I remembered her immediately. Suddenly, my mind was flooded with precise memories of the classroom in which she had studied with me as an undergraduate so many moons ago. I saw her face clearly. The flashback was so intense I could even smell the chalk in the room.

I know where I've buried those files. The other day I disinterred one on an ancient zip disc. I vaguely remembered that it was an intense piece. To my surprise, I discovered that it was also very funny in spots.

In the end, I did manage to fix the problem by studying it inside out, upside down. I knew I needed a tool that I didn't have, so I borrowed one from one of the rat's accomplices. I screwed up the nerve to ask her directly if she had anything I could use to defend myself. Apparently suffering from a bout of guilt, the woman decided to give me a copy of an e-mail that "la rata" had sent her. The e-mail offered proof positive not only of the rat's enormous hostility toward me but also of his concerted efforts over the years to thwart my prospects of being hired elsewhere, which is flagrantly illegal under federal law.

I made an appointment with the dean and showed him the document. I told him I had no interest in suing the university, that all I wanted was for him to make this illegal behavior stop. In my mind I was thinking,

"You get that rabid rat out of my life already!" But I spoke with the dean in a calm, cool voice. I wore my nicest suit. And I brought a witness. The dean assured me he would muzzle the rat. At that meeting, just before leaving, I also told him, quite politely, "I am sorry you made the bad decisions you made handling my tenure case; the university has invested a lot of money in my career, and it is unfortunate that it will not reap the benefits of that investment." Suffice it to say the man turned purple before I shook his hand and wished him luck.

He now works at another public university, as do the provost and vice provost who presided over that tenure case and appeal.

I exterminated the rat—at least from my career. Then I escaped.

Liberation

After that meeting with the dean, I applied far and wide for a new position. Like magic, the interview requests flooded my inbox and answering machine, including invitations for interviews for *tenured* positions at universities with much greater prestige than the one where I was denied tenure in its post-9/11 hysteria. This time I was determined to find, above all else, a healthy department—one that added up to much more than the sum of its parts—in a university that had an organized faculty backed by a national union, an active chapter that I could trust to guarantee recourse in case history repeated itself for me.

This was no small research project in itself. I was far more selective about my next tenure-track position than I had been when I went on the job market with my newly minted PhD. I also applied for a few jobs outside of academia, including one as a general manager of a public radio station (since I had solid credentials as a journalist as well), where I also made the short list. I withdrew applications at some public and private "ivies" after interviewing with them and intuiting bad vibes on the departmental horizon or discovering they were not unionized. In the end, I chose to accept a position in the English department at the University of Connecticut. Within a year, I was tenured in a much better department than the one from which I had escaped. My tenure case here was the slam dunk it was meant to be. My entire professional life has been, with a few swells, smooth sailing since then.

I am quite certain that my very best work is still ahead of me. Despite the concerted effort to demoralize, injure, libel, and harm me and tarnish my professional reputation, the experience I had being denied tenure made me stronger than ever. In fact, it liberated me. It did take awhile to recover, but what healed me in the end were my lifelong habits of thought, habits often deemed "radical," though I consider them simply smart and humanist: commitments to social justice, to the ethical and aesthetic analysis of cultural dynamics and cultural texts, to producing stories—be they in a fictional voice, in more traditional academic essay form, or in some hybrid form—by whatever literary means necessary. My tenure ordeal was a trial by fire. I survived it. My commitment to the humanities in its fullest expression was forged, like a sword, in that fire.

My move to Connecticut has also brought me into professional contact with an amazing group of colleagues inside the university as well as some phenomenal activists, artists, and organizers outside the university, among them Boricuas who, like me, know precisely what's at stake in the broader anticolonial movement for social justice in our nation and its communities stateside. Connecticut has the largest Boricua demographic per capita of any state in the Union. So I feel at home here in a way I haven't felt at home since living in Puerto Rico itself many moons ago.

Though this story ends well in its own way, I am also painfully aware of the stories that have not. Academic freedom has been and continues to be an endangered species in our post-9/11 era, which only compounds the risks that have always existed for the most vulnerable intellectuals in academe. In the past decade, I have closely followed the most egregious cases, hoping the victims stay strong, and lending moral support to junior scholars who have lost their battles and left academia for good as a result. In some of these cases, I also see the names of the perps who tried to destroy my career, members of this nomadic and barbaric tribe of public university administrators who migrate from state to state in search of larger six-figure salaries and fringe benefits. Once, in a very high profile case, I saw the name of "la rata" listed as an "outside expert" brought in to condemn a senior scholar in Ethnic Studies who was falsely accused of academic misconduct as retaliation for an essay he wrote on 9/11. In another high profile case involving a Nobel Peace Prize nominee, I saw the name of a high-level administrator I knew too well from my own ordeal.

What motivates these monsters?

The devil is in the details. If you study my own case closely and carefully enough, you'll find his marks in the sand. One day soon he will be dead, though. He's getting really old and really tired. And I'm going to dance a bugalú on his grave.

Identities

Tenure in the Contact Zone

Spanish Is Our Language, Too[1]

Angie Chabram
University of California, Davis

Promotion is advancement from one rank (in a specific title series) to a higher rank within the same academic title series (for example, from assistant professor to associate professor).

—Academic Personnel Manual, UC Davis.

In this chapter, tenure is not a generic rite of passage as is suggested in academic personnel manuals that decontextualize the process and homogenize the experiences, life histories, and social identities of professors who undergo this rigorous process everyday in vastly different ways across the nation. Rather, tenure is a phenomenon of what Mary Louise Pratt refers to as the "contact zone."[2] In this zone, the fate of a professor and the relationships between different ethnic, linguistic, and academic communities with different levels of access to power, knowledge and voice are negotiated through "long-term" and often "intractable" "unequal conflicts,"[3] contacts (*encuentros*), and ruptures (*desencuentros*).

This essay provides glimpses of these negotiations, which begin early in the lives of many assistant professors of color (most of whom are untenured) and continue well beyond tenure as these individuals negotiate points of entry and articulation and seek to redress long-standing social injustices. In this particular case, language and culture are at the heart of these negotiations—the site of contact and the arena of struggle and social transformation. They not only bridge rites of passage (including tenure) but also become the subjects of multiple contestations that link the academy to the community and alternative forms of study and pedagogy to mainstream universities and departments. Sometimes these contestations take people by surprise; other times they prompt an attitude of disbelief or anger. And at still other times, they prompt critical reflections on the place and context of language learning and the fate of minoritized cultural and ethnolinguistic communities in institutions of higher education. This is the case of the following essay, which is inspired by a paraphrase of combined verses from Olga García-Echeverría and Mary Louise Pratt:

> Aquí en esta historia mi lenguaje no se detiene. Cada nueva palabra/ Here my language remembers . . . those challenging times in a contact zone where cultures met, clashed and grappled with each other.
>
> —University of California, Davis. Motto: "Let there be light."

Sproul Hall. They say it's the tallest building in Yolo County

In the spring of 1990, it is transformed. Historically a center for language departments and study, it is now a center of loud protests. Aggrieved students and their allies stream into the gray building housing the Spanish department chanting, "Spanish is our language too, and if you don't like it the hell with you." Everyone is mesmerized by the event. Some voice the opinion that "No, this Chicana/o Latina/o protest can't be happening in Spanish; maybe in English, maybe in American history, but not Spanish." I am fully captivated by what I see: A total, living deconstruction of a Chicana/o nationalist imagination that urges us to "just get back to our roots (at the University of California at Davis) to live and breathe our Spanish mother tongue con orgullo y sabor."

As if it were that easy to do this in institutions of higher education. I remember the rude awakening I myself experienced decades earlier as an undergraduate at the University of California at Berkeley—that bastion of liberal ideology. Like many of the freshman in my cohort, I arrived in 1972 full of enthusiasm. Early on I knew I would immerse myself in my native Spanish expression, study Spanish, and help others unchain their tongues and expressive cultures. I was fully aware that Spanish was beginning to stake its claim as a majority language in the United States, particularly as the immigrant peoples of the Americas swelled the ranks of the native populations of the border states. And yet there at Davis I found a sharp divide between the academic and institutional construction of Spanish and the spoken language and cultural traditions of native Spanish speakers who were primarily from the greater Southwest and Mexico. These speakers not only were underrepresented on the inside of institutions of higher education there and everywhere but also most prominently represented only in Chicana/o Studies programs.

In many ways, the fault lines between community, the academy, and an extremely optimistic nationalist language ideology would be drawn around my institutional persona once I obtained a joint-faculty appointment in Spanish and Chicana/o Studies in the late 1980s. Because of the asymmetrical nature of my split appointment (80 percent Spanish, 20 percent Chicana/o Studies), I was only assigned one course in Chicana/o Studies and several courses in Spanish. I taught Chicana/o culture in Spanish, and I taught it in English in Chicana/o Studies. I also taught in the Spanish for native speakers program, and I developed a Chicana/o literature series (novel, theater, poetry). The composition of these classes was anywhere from 90 percent to 99 percent Chicana/o or Latina/o, although this group was underrepresented in the university and the Spanish curriculum at large.

Like many of the minority professors at my university, I did double time to build the curriculum in both units. Double meetings, double advising, and double service. It was not uncommon for me to stay at my office into the wee hours of the night. In my case, there were no teaching assistants available, no readers to help grade papers and exams, and very little technological and research support. To get an idea of the layers of work that I undertook at the start of my profession, it is necessary to understand that I was the first assistant professor housed in Chicana/o Studies, and, remember, I had a joint appointment. Although there were few affiliated faculty who were very active, there was only *one* other full-time faculty member housed in the program on a permanent basis at the time. Everything needed to be done there: we had to build the major, hire faculty, support student activities, and respond constructively to all of the obstacles that were consistently placed in our way. Perhaps most tellingly, we were housed in a temporary building and often shared our offices with students and lecturers.

We were devoted to promoting Chicana/o Studies and to recruiting and retaining students as well as building a national organization for Chicana/o Studies and for women from the working classes called Mujeres Activas en Letras y Cambio Social (Active Women in Letters and Social Change). We realized that we were often seen as a campus-wide repository for diversity. We also realized that notwithstanding this limited vision of our role in the larger university, and the hostility we often endured, ours was a historic mission that needed to be undertaken. We negotiated our path in the academy cognizant of the fact that our institutional site had emerged in a struggle against social and intellectual privilege. We were a small but empowered collective, and over the years we strengthened our program with the addition of several new faculty members who would help make the program the dynamic place it is today. Like our students, all of us were the first in our families to attend college. In the Spanish department, I was the only Chicana professor on the tenure track. From the moment I arrived, I was told that tensions had existed in the department with previous Chicana/o faculty members. The first few years, I was assigned primarily to lower-division courses and then later to a handful of upper-division courses. I was never assigned a graduate course and never encouraged to teach one. I soon learned that in the Spanish department I had the additional responsibility of raising general consciousness about the value of Chicana/o literature, culture, and history. There was also the expectation in both units (Spanish and Chicana/o Studies) that I should be a bridge person of sorts, the one who would negotiate numerous tricky curricular issues between these two departments, which shared some course offerings in their majors. Eventually, I would develop a memorandum of understanding in conjunction with the dean of letters and science and both departments to deal with the service overload that resulted from dual service commitments. I also made it a point to widely publicize my courses, develop lecture series, and create public recitations where students from Spanish could disseminate Chicana/o literature to the campus at large.

As time passed, it became evident to all involved that I had developed a strong rapport with the Chicana/o and Latina/o students on campus as well as other students from different backgrounds. In Spanish, my office was a hub of sorts—people formed long lines outside my office and often attended conferences with me on Chicana/o literature in addition to participating in collaborative research projects. I watched scores of them graduate with honors, attend graduate and law (professional) schools, and gain a strong sense of empowerment that enabled them to communicate with Spanish language communities all over the globe. I also witnessed their frustration with some Spanish classes and their indignation when they felt their native Spanish expression and linguistic capabilities were being devalued in a series of incidents in the department. I was troubled by what I heard but not surprised. From the moment I arrived, there were rumors about incidents, but they were often remanded to the private sphere or past history. One day, however, a group of students broke the silence: they spoke to me and took their complaints to the public sphere, offering testimonies to several newspapers (such as the *Davis Enterprise* and the *Sacramento Bee*) and television stations (Spanish and English) as well as the U.S. Department of Civil Rights, whose representatives came to campus to investigate complaints. The students could not understand why their native expressions were being maligned and not celebrated as positive "funds of knowledge"[4] or why their speaking abilities weren't factored into a general recognition of basic literacy and diversity.

According to the *Davis Enterprise*, on January 29, 1990 the students charged the Spanish department with treating them as "second-class citizens."[5] They concurred with the findings of a university task force, published in the *Davis Enterprise*, that took issue with an unjustified attitude among some in the Spanish department that "Castilian Spanish, as opposed to 'Mexican Spanish,' is the preferred regional variety."[6] In their own way, they reaffirmed Carlos Monsiváis's assertion that "from a cultural perspective, the mere assumption of 'speaking well' is suspicious because it does not tend to remit vivacity or idiomatic inventiveness but a petrifaction or immobility of a type of speech whose real vigor is 'rigor mortis.'"[7] In reality, the complaints spanned a broader terrain. As Lorena Natt explained in her story, "U.S. Probes Alleged UCD Hispanic Bias," "the emphasis of foreign language departments on classic literature and the use of the standard forms of language to the exclusion of contemporary forms of ethnic literature and dialectal varieties used by ethnolinguistic minority groups" were "clearly viewed by ... students as an attempt to invalidate their language and culture."[8]

To their great delight, students received strong support campus wide as they argued for a truly native form of language instruction that would consider their linguistic capital; bridge the chasm between native and nonnative classes and instructors, the academy, and the community; and help them establish valuable connections with people all over the world, including people in Spanish departments. As I reflected on their noteworthy aims, I was empowered by their courage, determination, and vision. In many ways, we were of a similar mindset, yet there were meaningful differences to be considered that stemmed in part from our different positions in the academy. I was a professor with professorial obligations and pressures, including an impending tenure case. I had my own concerns about the interplay between language, culture, and the curriculum over the long haul. Because I shared the students' racial and ethnic background, it was automatically assumed by some people that there was complete ideological conformity between myself, all of the students who offered a variety of suggestions, all of the larger Latina/o community, and all of the faculty members who supported change. Important nuances in thought around programs for reform were often erased within the public and private discourse to everyone's collective disadvantage.

At the broader institutional level, the scenario was highly disconcerting to me. I struggled against forms of institutional identity that would have me placed in the role of the token minority professor or in the role of the good model "citizen" (note the nationalistic tone) who should rubber stamp solutions that would not work for anyone (I didn't). I was also troubled by some of the implications of the curricular and ideological components of the prolonged debates. Understand, I was now in the professorial ranks, but in many ways I felt I had taken a step back in my professional and intellectual development since my "progressive" graduate school days, when the connections between language and power had been thoroughly investigated and lines had been drawn against cultural hegemony. Old battles that people didn't talk about anymore or assumed had been won in many parts of the world were surfacing all around me with regard to the public and institutional construction of the native speaker question. Foundational works in Chicana/o language such as *El Lenguaje de los Chicanos* and *Chicana/o Discourse* were largely unheard of. It was my job to introduce them, but truth be told, I was not the only one entrusted with this public charge. Colleagues from different campuses came to Davis and offered interviews to the newspapers, and a select group of students launched a hunger strike in support of Chicana/o issues in Spanish and a variety of other issues. Sympathetic professors from Spanish and Chicana/o Studies stood watch with the students who were not eating, and even Carlos Fuentes, the famous Mexican novelist of *Artemio Cruz*, who was visiting as a guest speaker, weighed in on the issue, offering all the cultural capital and heartfelt support of a Mexican brother from the South.

Meanwhile the campus student newspaper the *Aggie* kept the campus abreast on day-to-day developments, and the alternative voice, the *Third World Forum*, regularly published articles on language ideologies in Spanish departments in relation to histories of colonization in the Americas. Seeing the campus leap forward into an intensive process of language and ethnic consciousness was very rewarding for many professors and students from different departments who drew on the native speaker controversy as an important teachable moment. Generally speaking, the public dialogue moved from disbelief and outrage to a series of discussions about mandatory changes in pedagogy and the importance of Ethnic Studies. In my case, there were many productive and memorable moments, but the experience was also stressful because I was not only in demand but also untenured and highly visible. I did, however, have places of refuge: Chicana/o Studies became my sanctuary, Chicana/o cultural studies my new inspiration, and my extended familia and spouse became my anchors. There were, of course, the customary angry stares and scapegoating from the status quo contingency that at times made me want to run for a limpia or cleansing while at the university, but I maintained my position, even weighing in on the numerous proposals for reform.

In short, I supported the incorporation of Chicana/o literature so that it would be on par with Latin American and Spanish literature and linguistics, the hiring of a cadre of professors to teach the many genres of Chicana/o literature, and a curriculum of language teaching that would draw on students' strength and minimize "subtractive learning."[9] What was at stake here was educational equality and an end to the historic intellectual disparities that were evident in the underrepresentation of Chicana/o language and culture and literature in many Spanish departments throughout the nation. In Chicana/o Studies it also was also imperative to face up to externally generated charges of illegitimacy. It seemed as if Chicana/o Studies was constantly under attack by people who had no knowledge of its trajectory or possibilities. I wondered how people could so easily judge an emerging discipline with strong interdisciplinary foundations. Weren't we at a university that prided itself on the motto "Let there be light"? Wasn't knowing and actually being educated a necessary prerequisite for judgment? I also wondered how the playing field could be leveled when specialists in Chicana/o Studies weren't prominently included on the tenure and educational curriculum committees and in the higher ranks of the administration. I drew meaningful connections between what was going on in Spanish and Chicana/o Studies and wondered about what type of educational reforms would be required to change things on both fronts.

Although Chicana/o Studies was supportive, it was not without its own set of challenges. In the early years of its development, when I was appointed there, it was common knowledge that there was a legacy of nontenured but highly successful founding members of the program who went on to make great career strides in scholarship and administration. In the popular imagination, Chicana/o Studies was a revolving door—you came in, did your best, and left. Affected by the negativity that surrounded them, many people saw this as a sad but inevitable *fact* of life that I should accept, too. No way! As I presented myself for tenure in Chicana/o Studies (aware of the fact that I was the first split appointment to do so), I had to struggle against the mindset as well as a bit of anti-intellectualism that reared its head once in a while amid all of the heartfelt support and enthusiasm. I also had to fight a hostile mindset outside of Chicana/o Studies that devalued my area of study.

I remember one particularly painful experience in which Chicana/o literature was spoken about in a highly disparaging and demeaning way to me by a person of stature who would judge my tenure case. This person (an employee of the university) told me that "Chicana/o Literature was barrio crap." My training in social theory allowed me to see that pejorative language about Chicana/o literature carried vestiges of history, elitism, racialization, and class status. But it was Patricia Evans and her work on verbal abuse that allowed me to see that this degrading construction of my area of study and teaching incorporated all of the categories of verbal abuse, including withholding, defaming, defining, trivializing, harassing, blaming, berating, putting down, and name-calling. As the "Hidden Hurt" web page explains in reference to Evans' work, "Verbal abuse uses words (or silence) to gain and maintain control."[10] With this abuse, in one bold sweep the subject matter *and* professor could be unfavorably spoken, put down. There were implications that I'd think about more broadly speaking; if Chicana/o literature could be disparaged, then maybe it would continue to maintain a precarious representation in the curriculum and other fields would be more dominant. But let's face it, degrading words about your subject of study can be personal. In the workplace, verbal abuse can erase any pretense of neutrality and objectivity, destabilize young assistant professors who are vulnerable in their careers, and diminish them as well. As Evans says, "verbal abuse invades a person's inner world and self-definition," not only the outer one.[11]

In my case, I removed the chains on my tongue. I performed my own version of what bell hooks calls "talking back." No me rajé—I didn't back down. I am not bragging, just telling my truth. I demanded to be treated like an equal. I did not disavow or sugarcoat lived experiences and humiliations, nor did I keep silent. I gave testimony and sought out intellectual spaces that were supportive and affirmative. In the midst of the very public culture wars that were taking place on campus in newspapers and committees of different persuasions, my work helped me tremendously in my efforts to stay on track. So did academic conferences, the interviews I did with critics of Chicana/o literature, the social networks inside and outside of Chicana/o Studies, the support of cultural studies colleagues, and last but not least Zaré Dernersesian. Of tremendous importance to my tenure case were the outside tenure letters, which incorporated the opinions of specialists as well as the fact that I was evaluated in two departments and within a series of university venues. This offset whatever negativity came up.

At the end of a long year, I got the judgment—tenure! What a joyful experience. In many ways it was fitting that I celebrated my tenure in Los Angeles, my homeland, among close friends and familia. There was much to celebrate. I was the first woman to be tenured in my family at a major university and, like my mom, I had bucked tradition in my own way. I had forged a career path that was very uncommon for a Chicana Mexi-rican from my female-headed working-class background and neighborhood. But I had not done it alone. Aside from my familia, my community at the University of California at Davis had also won an important victory, as had the students who had viewed me as a mentor and sought inspiration from my career path. The people in my intellectual circle who supported me had also won, gaining an ally as well as a colleague. There were also material rewards that should not be overlooked in these hard times such as ongoing employment, health insurance, and retirement benefits.

And yet as I look back now (as a full professor), I realize that things did not go precisely as I had expected, notwithstanding my desire, convictions, and urgency to transfer to Chicana/o Studies full time. As I mentioned previously, in my case language had been a lifelong burning passion and a career path. As a youngster, I was very interested in unconventional forms of communication, including when Mom spoke Spanish to me (although she was fluent in English), and I answered in English (although I spoke and understood Spanish). It was a carefully orchestrated dance: we both knew that there was a bridge (of comprehension) between us whereby we both connected to both of the languages spoken by the other. But I wanted to speak more Spanish, to learn more vocabulary, to immerse myself in the culture and language of my forbearers from Mexico and Puerto Rico, and to become a Spanish teacher and professor. Although I met my goals—did a BA, MA, and PhD in Spanish; traveled to Mexico, Spain, and Puerto Rico; and taught Spanish in Spanish—my experiences in the contact zone meant that I would not be a professor of Spanish per se. My full-scale immersion into (Chicana/o) cultural studies helped me deal with this loss and see that in the global period, "old-fashioned" traditional institutional labels often didn't mean much. I found that in cultural studies, the authority of the monodiscipline was challenged as the margins came forward to engage intersecting problematics and arenas of knowledge. The possibility of teaching a bilingual curriculum gave me the needed link to my past and love of language. In the end, tenure was tenure. I had a chance to continue doing what I loved, and I felt a tremendous amount of freedom to venture into new areas of research, including feminism, ethnography, health studies, and cultural studies. Now as a full professor I see my experiences in Spanish as part of a larger social dynamic that brings together contested domestic and hemispheric histories, native and nonnative cultures, and dominant and alternative cultural and linguistic forms. For me, tenure forms one element within this complex social formation and my overall experience as a professor.

In many ways, the tenure process made me more aware than ever that everyday new Spanish-language experiences are being lived out in the world by people of different age groups, life circumstances, geopolitical locations, and educational venues across the nation and its multiethnic, global border zones. Their experiences are not uniform, and neither are their social positions, ideological investments, forms of expression, and possibilities for linguistic articulation in the public sphere. For this reason, it is imperative for educators and tenure reviewers alike to be cognizant of the different urgencies, languages, and cultural venues that frame Spanish in the contemporary global period and teach us much about Spanish language contexts and interactions, the different struggles of people to learn Spanish, and its vital connections to history and social life.

In the specific case of contemporary Chicana/o poetry, we can learn that "Spanish is a skill that we need to develop and hone like any other skill."[12] This process can begin at a young age for youngsters: "Spanish is a matter/of roling rrrrs/Clicking the tongue /And placing your hands/On your hips. . . . Of yelling, '¡Abuelia!' "[13] Here Spanish is also a matter of realizing that "the world is twice the size"[14] and discovering "that there is a world out there, a world with which we need to communicate."[15] For some high school youths, learning Spanish is a matter of private performance, pretending to be a popular icon.

As one youth in "Cantito" recounts, "Sometimes in my room, with the door locked, and the blinds drawn/I'd practice my broke-ass Spanish in the mirror, pretending I was/some suavesito big shot at Dodger stadium. . . . But most of the time I was Luis Miguel/because if his Spanish rolled out of his mouth like a broken wheelbarrow, who would care?"[16] Unfortunately, this youth's performances in Spanish class do not go as smoothly as his private ones at home.[17] He endures humiliation from his peers and his teacher, who assume that because he is Mexican (brown) he should know Spanish and speak fluently. Here readers can learn about the perils and harm done by linguistic profiling and about the alternative learning environments students themselves create.

Contemporary Chicana/o poetry also teaches us that in educational institutions Spanish is not always a place of subordination; it can also be a place of resistance. In the poem "Native Tongue" by Celeste Guzmán Mendoza, a Latina college student, who is repeatedly put down by a Professor X for not speaking her "native" tongue (Spanish instead of her Tex-Mex dialect[18]) and "not having a culture"[19] refuses to be silent. She complains to the administration about Professor X and recounts how she'd "paid to go to college" and "deserved better." Like the students in the protest that opens this chapter, she also resorted to activism by documenting her complaints to the dean and contributing to the production of a campus-wide video that explained "how offensive and disrespectful the native (Spanish) comment was."[20]

In "Lengualistic Algo," Spanish is not only the site of defense but also of (counter) attack and affirmation.[21] This poem takes the bull by the horns and forcefully talks back to the hegemonic language ideologies of purists in all locations who can't fathom that in the Chicana/o community "el español comes down/off its high horse . . . it learns to say pa' instead of para. . . . Orale!" Here the art of "code switching" is celebrated as is the act of "cruzando linguistic fronteras sin papeles."[22] In this alternative language paradigm, the value of language is its utilitarian function: "Aquí se usa lo que sirve/el rascuache/el mestizaje/las leftovers y lo yet-to-be born."[23] Yet this utilitarian function does not mean that the language itself lacks a symbolic, imaginative, or "human" dimension. Chicana/o language is personified many times over, actively interrogating those who would condemn it with this retort:

Hey! Ain't I a word?
Caigo/I fall from the hungry mouth of thousands
Salgo como balla (I exit like a bullet) de los barrios de Califas
Broto (I sprout) como lluvia en los desiertos de Arizona
Canto (I sing) mi tex-mex (next to) junto a Flaco Jiménez
And tell me, "Ain't I a word?"[24]

Alongside this rhetorical affirmation is an important acknowledgement that this vibrant, living language is still an unofficial, unrecognized language. As the poet explains, mainstream academics "ignore" Chicana/o language, and purists suggest that Chicana/o expression "contaminates" other languages. If this were not enough, in the poem the official standard bearers of words such as *Webster's* and *El Pequeño Larousse* dictionaries don't include Chicana/o language, while other official works disdain the language and even "spit" on it. If in this poem Chicana/o language carries a vivid memory of bleeding tongues and conquests, not one academy, dictionary, purist, or detractor can stop the flow of this language, which travels in many directions, moving, shifting, shedding, and being born anew.

Like Olga García Echeverria, Leticia Hernández-Linares suggests that Chicanas/os and Latinas/os need to own Spanglish as well as Spanish to show that assimilating into a homogenous monolingual culture is not the only way to succeed or find a voice.[25] However, even she recognizes that this ownership is not enough. We must also engage the complexities of how Latinas have been "constructed—marginalized, racialized and commodified" through language.[26]

Yet more is to be done if we are to change the language predicaments that Chicanas/os face in society, the academy, and with tenure. We need to advocate for a serious rendering of all forms of Chicana/o and Latina/o speech and to recognize that "we have a great many resources to call upon, including a standard variety Spanish."[27] We need to intervene in those tenure processes that reinscribe and project Eurocentric language ideologies and racial, class, and ethnic biases into the evaluation processes.

We need to understand that class- and race-based stereotypical negative valuations of Chicana/os in Spanish will only stop when they stop in K–12, when the youngest among us can speak without fear of recrimination or the necessity of self-censure. We need to really diversify the university and implement a zero-tolerance policy for instructors and administrators who demean Chicana/o and Latina/o language and culture or discriminate against and bully assistant professors and students who represent alternative ethnic, cultural, and linguistic traditions. Finally, we need to forge a path toward a better future that is evident in the curriculum and validates students' and professors' experiences and the tenure processes itself that "Spanish is truly one of our languages, too."

Notes

1. To Zaré Dernersesian, to my support team in cultural studies and to my students.

2. Pratt, "Arts of the Contact Zone."

3. Ibid.

4. This term is defined in the description of a book by the same name: "The concept of 'funds of knowledge' is based on a simple premise: people are competent and have knowledge, and their life experiences have given them that knowledge." González, Moll, and Amanti. *Funds of Knowledge.*

5. Sherwin, "Change Advised in the Spanish Curriculum."

6. Ibid. In her essay "Language Variation in the Spanish of the Southwest," Rosaura Sánchez makes an important point: "In a society characterized by stratification, language varieties are also stratified. Some are dominant, some subordinated." In Merino, Trueba, and Samaniego, *Language and Culture in Learning,* 76.

7. Monsiváis, "Prologue."

8. Natt, "U.S. Probes Alleged UCD Hispanic Bias," 2.

9. Valenzuela, "Subtractive Schooling: U.S.–Mexican Youth and the Politics of Caring."

10. Evans, "Books."

11. Evans, *Verbal Abuse Survivors Speak Out.*

12. Sánchez, "Language Variation in the Spanish of the Southwest," 80.

13. Soto, "Spanish," 2.

14. Ibid., 4.

15. Sánchez, "Language Variation in the Spanish of the Southwest," 80.

16. López, "Mi Cantito."

17. At school when asked to speak in class he is not only humiliated, "his tongue wouldn't work," "it was like it pulled a hamstring walking to the track meet" (López, "Mi Cantito," 25). As he recounts: "I knew Spanish-colored words but they were all like different colored marbles in the jar of my mouth and I couldn't pick out the right color" (López, "Mi Cantito," 25).

18. The blend of Spanish and English attributed to South Texas.

19. Guzmán Mendoza, "Native Tongue," 94.

20. Ibid., 91.

21. Sánchez, "Language Variation in the Spanish of the Southwest," 76.

22. Ibid., 23.

23. Ibid.

24. Ibid., 24.

25. Hernández-Linares, "Spanglish Superhighway, A Road Map of Bicultural Signs of Life," 85.

26. Ibid., 91.

27. Sánchez, "Language Variation in the Spanish of the Southwest," 80.

"Colored" Is the New Queer

Queer Faculty of Color in the Academy

Andreana Clay
San Francisco State University

June 26, 2015
Oakland, California

As I sit and finish this piece, the Supreme Court of the United States has just legalized same-sex marriage. In a 5–4 decision, written by Justice Anthony Kennedy, the Court stated the following: "No union is more profound than marriage, for it embodies the highest ideals of love, fidelity, devotion, sacrifice, and family. In forming a marital union, two people become something greater than once they were. As some of the petitioners in these cases demonstrate, marriage embodies a love that may endure even past death. It would misunderstand these men and women to say they disrespect the idea of marriage. Their plea is that they do respect it, respect it so deeply that they seek to find its fulfillment for themselves. Their hope is not to be condemned to live in loneliness, excluded from one of civilization's oldest institutions."[1]

It's a powerful statement on the eve of gay pride celebrations across the United States. Well played, SCOTUS. And it's a decision that I feel ambivalent about. It's not because it happened on the eve of "pride" celebrations, which were originally organized to recognize the 1969 Stonewall Riots in New York City, but are now simply elaborate parties replete with corporate sponsorships. No, my ambivalence comes from the reality that, on this same day, the first Black president, Barack Obama, delivered a eulogy for a Black, the pastor of a Southern Black church, whose roots lay in resistance and rebellion. Clementa Pinckney of the Emmanuel AME Church in Charleston, South Carolina, was murdered along with eight of his parishioners: the Rev. Sharonda Coleman-Singleton, Cynthia Hurd, Tywanza Sanders, Ethel Lance, Susie Jackson, Depayne Middleton-Doctor, the Rev. Daniel Simmons, and Myra Thompson. They were killed by a racist white gunman whose last words before he started shooting people were "I have to do this"—not a week before the Supreme Court announced its decision. So in this moment where I *might* feel joy I also feel sorrow. This dichotomy of joy and sorrow often structures the Black queer experience. This dichotomy of joy and sorrow also mirrors the personal or political or both and the experiences of life in the academy as a queer person of color. This may sound like an odd juxtaposition given that we tend to think of the academy as if it isolated and "ivory" at times but is still a bastion of liberalism and acceptance. However, the dichotomy of (false) hope about liberation in the form of once-denied rights being given and the ongoing violence and grief enacted on Black bodies in (safe) Black spaces (i.e., a Black church) is mapped on the bodies of queer faculty of color. It's a legacy that many of us carry—promise and loss—that informs our academic work, our political writing, and our personal lives.

Social scientists have long written about some of the negative experiences of LGB(TQ)[2] faculty even as queer theory was more broadly incorporated in the academy.[3] The increase in centers for lesbian and gay students on college campuses and the experiences of queer faculty mirrored the experiences and questions of the larger LGBTQ community and were rooted in questions of identity deployment,[4] coming out in the classroom,[5] and experiences on the job market as an "out" faculty member. These articles have served as training for those of us who study sexualities in various forms, shining a light both on the liberal discourse of the university campus and on the contradictions that many LGBTQ faculty face in this setting. For example, we face being thought of as specialized hires (sometimes too specialized) who don't really represent or understand the discipline they are hired into. Or we face being overburdened as *the* faculty member who is asked or expected to take on being a mentor to LGBTQ students, organizations, and hiring committees whether or not we're willing and whether or not this is work we can do well. And we face what it's like to be one of—if not the only—queer faculty in a department (or on campus) who is expected to come out at every instance in the name of diversity. Alternately, we face staying hidden as to not draw attention to ourselves. These challenges have not only become the building blocks for LGBTQ studies on identity and sexuality but also serve as a warning sign for those of us who identify as queer or transgender. They are a kind of handout for what we can expect once we leave the "freedom" of graduate school and enter the academy as full or adjunct faculty. This is the life of a queer faculty member.

One glaring omission from this body of work, however, is the experience of LGBTQ faculty of color. A quick search for academic articles related to the topic elicits a stunning zero number of entries focused on LGBTQ faculty of color. Rather, a combination of keyword searches brings up the experience of being tokenized and the similarity of being LGBTQ and "minorities" in the academy as if the two are separate categories without exploring how they might overlap. This is how it's often thought of on my campus, San Francisco State University, in a city long hailed as the "Gay Mecca." And this is why I started out with the dichotomy of same-sex marriage and murder, because this is the lens through which I see the (predominately straight, white, and male) academy and the (white and male) LGBTQ community beyond its walls. I jumped at the chance to write this chapter when asked by Tricia. Well, let me back up, I was *excited* to write this chapter because these are stories that are not told, that are overlooked, with many of us still expected to choose between "person of color" and "queer." I make this distinction because it also fits right within the overload and expectations that I outlined earlier, about not being able to say "no" to something because it is important, it feels dire, even if it probably isn't something I have time for given the other things I'm asked to do and feel the need to take on. I experience this in the departments[6] I teach and work in, where I am one of eight out, queer, tenure-track faculty in a department of thirteen but am also the only Black woman and one of two Black faculty. This may sound like progress and, in many ways, it is: I rarely hesitate to come out in my classrooms when I feel like it makes sense, and I hardly *ever* think about saying my partner is a woman—particularly when we also have a faculty profile wall in the hallway of my department with pictures of us to join the other "husbands" and "wives" of my queer comrades. Yet, in spite of the outness of our faculty, we regularly meet to discuss anonymous student evaluations that call my out gay colleagues "faggots," chastise my white lesbian colleagues for being "intimidating," or any of us for "favoring queer students in the classroom." Yes, this happens in what is deemed one of the queerest cities in the country, whose Black population, because of steady gentrification and displacement, has dropped from 11 percent to 4 percent in the last two decades. And *this* dichotomy— Black displacement in America's Gay Mecca—profoundly shapes my experience on and off campus and throughout academia. It's working to balance this dichotomy that links me with a long history of experiences among LGBTQ faculty of color in the United States in and out of academia.

This essay evolved out of informal discussions with a small group of queer faculty of color. Tricia invited queer faculty of color to reflect on our experiences in the academy. Many people wanted to participate but told us they couldn't, citing the reality of "really wanting to" and "Thank you for asking, but I'm overburdened (or sick) in this moment." I could have, perhaps *should* have, said the same. We asked faculty to reflect on questions based on the general conversations Tricia and I have noted about the environments that queer faculty of color face. Some responded in writing, some were more comfortable talking, and others sent e-mails. Another important site this essay draws on is the blogosphere, which has emerged as a space for faculty of color and LGBTQ faculty to write about our experiences. They are too distinct to summarize in broad terms, but they show what I discuss at the beginning of this essay—how queer faculty of color write about their experiences in and out of the ivory tower.[7]

Still, this is not and does not purport to be a representative discussion. Rather, this is a small glimpse into our experiences, one that I hope will be a catalyst for many more because many of us work in silence, which contributes to the already isolating and sometimes hazardous experience of being faculty of color in a white- (and male-) dominated space. This is a topic, or series of topics, that requires its own anthology devoted to queer faculty of color. What is important about this essay and conversation is that it tries to capture the experiences that many of us talk about informally and adds to the discourse on queer visibility inside and outside the academy.

Further Down the Yellow Brick Road:
Rac(e)ing/Quee(r)ing the Academy

The prompt for this discussion was a re-reading of "In the Merry Old Land of Oz: Rac(e)ing, Quee(r)ing the Academy," E. Patrick Johnson's candid essay on being a Black gay man at a primarily white institution in the early stages of his career.[8] For many of us, Johnson is best known for his influential role as editor of *Black Queer Studies* (*BQS*), co-edited with Mae G. Henderson (2005). The essays in *BQS* and the anthology itself have allowed many of us to work within the frame of "queer of color critique," as well as providing a literal and theoretical space for the intersections of race (Blackness) and sexuality (queerness). "Oz" drew on some of the themes raised in *BQS*, including Johnson's personal narrative. The candidness with which he speaks about the racism in his first tenure-track position is one that many of us experience—silently, or, at least, not with a larger (read *white*) audience. In many ways, his piece is a breath of fresh air: putting to print for a wider (whiter) audience the experience of LGBTQ faculty of color, but it's also an excruciatingly painful read *because* of that everyday experience. For instance, in the section "Keep the Nigger-Boy Running Part III: One More River to Cross," Johnson describes one of numerous, inappropriate actions from a male, senior colleague: "A senior colleague, with a repulsive personality, apparently needs to work out his own sexuality issues through me, the department's resident Black faggot. He does so by trying to bait me while I'm standing at the copier. He places his latest book in my face (the cover is a picture of Greg Louganis in a Speedo diving into a pool) and chants, 'Isn't that hot? Wouldn't you like to taste that?' He further shows his affection by groping me in the department office, feeling he is allowed to do this because the LGBT student group has written, 'Hug a Queer Today' on the sidewalk."⁹

Although this may seem like an extreme example, one that many imagine could never happen, Johnson pinpoints an ongoing experience for LGBTQ faculty regardless of race. The baits or threats, the intimidation and sexual harassment have been recounted by queer white faculty in the aforementioned studies. However, the intersection of race and sexuality makes this interaction particularly charged. The powerful position (and positioning) of the senior colleague is reminiscent of the interactions that Anita Hill recounted with (now) Supreme Court Justice Clarence Thomas, whom she worked for when he was the head of the Equal Employment Opportunities Commission. In this instance, even though Thomas and Hill were both African American, working together toward equity, it became painfully clear during his hearing and her trial that his discomfort with his own sexuality and race were targeted at a colleague who others might assume was an ally.

The assumption revealed by the Thomas hearings was that sexual harassment doesn't happen in professional, equitable, middle-class spaces and certainly not by professional, equitable, middle-class men. And it is the assumption of equality—that a PhD and academic position somehow level the playing field—that permeates relationships between junior and senior faculty. It's one that allows this kind of harassment to continue in much the same ways that sexual harassment between men and women in the workplace continues to thrive: those who are harassed are questioned more than they are believed, and it's on top of the many other challenges one must face as a member of a marginalized group in academia. It's important to consider the stakes in this unequal relationship between colleagues who might seem like equals. Later in the essay, Johnson discusses how this senior colleague evaluates his teaching and that his assessment is used in a reappointment letter that Johnson describes as "venomous and explicit in its bigotry, especially in the way it discussed how my preoccupation with race, class, gender and sexuality, 'may become mechanical and obscure equally urgent questions about other textual and cultural complexities.'"[10]

The charged intersection of race and sexuality that Johnson faced is especially clear in his recounting of his experience with a student newspaper. While he makes clear that many of his students were intellectually interesting and wonderful to teach, some—particularly those who wrote for the conservative student newspaper—saw him as a "lurking, animalistic sex machine."[11] After answering questions about his social life as a Black queer man with a candor he immediately regretted, he not only found his comments luridly presented but a year later he was also mocked by the conservative student paper with the "Bones Thugs N' Harmony" award for his liberal ideas. The picture that accompanied the "award" was a send up of the Oscar statue. According to Johnson, the picture "in profile showed a man holding his penis" and the plaque read: "The Macho Man Johnson knows all the tools of his trade. His equipment, we hear, is not only big, but also very powerful. And he's not afraid to flaunt it. But, we'll take his word for it. Here's to the chocophile in us all."[12] The students received a "talking to" from the president of the university.

The struggles and humiliations Johnson lays bare are not enough somehow to deter us from the path we have set ourselves on, one that is many times intertwined and inseparable from personal and political struggles. Johnson writes in his closing paragraph of his "cautionary tale": "As a Black, gay, southern, feminist, revolutionary, my presence in the academy is bolstered by a legacy of poor, queer, little colored boys who challenged what it meant to be a professor despite tripping on and being hit by the yellow bricks on that stony road. The academy is full of folk who uphold the virtues of the most pernicious forms of sexism, racism, classism, and homophobia. Although I'm not so naïve to think

I'll soon see the end of this reign of terror, I am fierce enough to know the 'schooling' I received in the projects, to which I owe my PhD in how to read and write, is the only weapon this little colored boy needs to run on."[13]

The tools and skills we have as queer faculty of color, are ones, interestingly, that many of us have honed over a lifetime and that began, as Johnson describes, "in the projects" or at home on the margins.

I know, it sounds like a battleground. But how, one might ask, can the privileged, erudite world of academia be a battleground? Not everyone's experience can be or is like Johnson's, right? It's funny you should ask, with "you" also being the ever present "prove it" voice in my head, ready to pounce on any false claims and any bit of imposter syndrome present. Frankly, the answer is mixed. In the twenty years since Johnson began his position at Amherst, the college on which the essay is based, many things have changed and . . . stayed the same. Since that time, which was roughly the same time the studies on LGBTQ faculty were first written, those of us who have entered the academy have experienced dangers similar to those Johnson outlined, while at other times it feels equally like one of the safer spaces that we've encountered. In the remaining pages, I include some of the voices from queer faculty of color who agreed to engage this topic.

Ain't No Thang: Twenty-First Century "Freedoms"

The informal discussion I've had with queer faculty of color demonstrates a surprising level of difference from the experiences that Johnson recounts in his essay, some of which I've highlighted here. In some ways, the academy seems to have followed the trajectory of popular culture and discourse: visibility, acceptance, and "equality." As Eric Grollman, Assistant Professor of Sociology at University of Richmond and editor of the blog Conditionally Accepted, states in his contribution to this conversation: "I think much is the same as Johnson's early experiences, though there have been some improvements. The changes in university policies and, to a lesser extent, campus culture are undeniably signs of progress for LGBTQ people. However, I continue to feel the sense of invisibility he experienced, the sense that sexuality (both as my personal identity and my area of research) is an after-thought at the university. I would say I haven't faced the same level of outright hostility he has faced; instead, heterosexuality-as-the-norm remains in place, including the pressure to be cisgender (i.e., be gender-conforming in appearance)."

At the same time, things have barely changed in our everyday interactions on campus. For instance, I rarely write about my academic experiences on my blog, queerblackfeminist, but in a blog post dated September 12, 2012, I wrote specifically about the impossibility of separating popular culture from everyday life. The topic was Chris Brown's misogyny and history of domestic violence, which shows up frequently on my blog. I argued that it was difficult to separate his individual acts from the misogynist culture that women—particularly Black women—face, even when we set up intentional communities that are queer, feminist, and Black:

> I'm Black, a woman, sometimes read as queer and I look like I look: light skinned, freckles, dressed like a person of my generation— which at my university sometimes means that I look much younger than other professors (even though I may not be). And I'm treated, apparently, like others think a young freckled face Black woman with a natural should be treated. Here are some highlights: first day of class and a young, African American man that I have never met shares his experience working with youth and says, "You know they are doing things that I never did when I was their age . . . like, excuse my language, eat pussy." First. day. Next day: meeting with colleagues on campus to talk about my department (I am acting [department] chair this semester, so I'm meeting a lot of new folks), all are more senior than I am and, at one point, an older, white man I haven't met before says something about another female colleague who is older and more senior than he is and he refers to her as a girl, twice. Girl. Like emphasis on the g. Another day: I'm looking into buying a new computer and, after I say exactly what I want, the male [staff person on campus] winks at me and says "Sure, but maybe you should consider this computer (a different brand) it's better and you can do all the work you want to do on it." Another wink. Not the computer I asked for. Not the computer I researched for months beforehand. And I'm not mad at the individual men I've pointed to here, really. These are just daily recounts of the last two weeks. I have others. I'll have more the next time I post. And it may not be a big deal to folks. I can work through these things, I do. And I don't mean to literally compare them to the bruises, broken bones,

and memories worked onto the bodies of women who have been abused. But living in a culture that communicates the hatred of and disregard for women in these small, sometimes subtle ways leaves me feeling bruised, traumatized, and broken.

For many of us from marginalized groups, campus life is no different than the everyday experiences outside the university. Although we have attained three letters behind our names—something that is granted to few people of color each year[14]—that isn't reflected in our day-to-day interactions, even on campus. And I'm not arguing for a special distinction, but for some semblance of acknowledgement and respect—something my male, white, and heterosexual colleagues rarely need to think about. As other women of color have noted, I am rarely called "Dr." in the class, unless I ask to be. Otherwise, I am referred to as "Ms." or, as is the climate on my campus, by my first name. In spite of the visibility of queer people and the embrace, at least at the level of popular culture, of people of color, the academy remains alienating to many of us, a place where we sometimes *become* alien. As Grollman suggests, "the culture feels dominated by extremely wealthy white people—a dynamic that adds to my sense of alienation and impostorism. Frankly, interacting with such people feels like interacting with people from a foreign country, except it seems that I'm the foreigner. I worry that my middle-class background fails me in some of these intangible ways, perhaps even pieces of cultural capital that would help advance my career even further."

Like Johnson, many of us from working-class and poor backgrounds often experience the academy—both as students and professionals—as a place unlike any other we've known or been trained in. The majority of us in this conversation identified strongly with our working-class or working-poor backgrounds and noted the ways that the intersections of race and class made the university particularly alienating. And, as Grollman points out, that often extends to queer faculty of color who were raised middle class.

The intersections of race and class, and the structures of racism and classism, are what queer people of color kept coming back to in these conversations. Whereas the dominant discussions of LGBTQ faculty experiences focus on the continuing importance of being "out" in the classroom as a model for LGBTQ students, for queer faculty of color the experience is more complicated. As Grollman states, "I am, without a doubt, out as queer on the job. However, I've been consumed with ensuring that my queerness does not make colleagues or students uncomfortable, for fear that it will result in professional consequences (e.g., tenure denial, poor course evaluations, claims of sexual violence). When I teach, I am most likely in a suit, knowing well that gender nonconformity is read by others as a sign of being gay. I typically wait until later in the semester, sometimes after course evaluations have been submitted, to formally come out to my class. In a way, I feel technically out: everyone knows, but, essentially, I try to help them forget on a daily basis."

The discourse of queer visibility assumes that the only identity that matters in the classroom and on campus is a queer identity. This identity takes center stage, becomes the one that is necessary to identify as and fight for. Interestingly, as Shawn Trivette, writing about his experience as a guest author on Grollman's blog, sees it, as "part of [his] role as an educator is offering support and empowerment to students, particularly marginalized students." He goes on to center this experience on LGBTQ students, who, he states, "are in many ways a marginalized population; self-disclosure is a way of offering encouragement to these students by providing a successful role model who is in some way 'like them.'" And his logic very much follows the narrative of academic research on LGBTQ faculty: providing mentorship and visibility for one's students. More important, as queer faculty, this is seen as inextricably linked to the position of educator itself. However, this narrative is interrupted, sometimes inverted, in the case of Grollman, who, while out as queer, speaks to the necessity of adhering to expectations around gender and, implicitly, race.

Some of us adamantly push back on this narrative as we assert a critical queer politic. As Roshanak Kheshti, an associate professor in Ethnic Studies at the University of California, San Diego, describes it when asked about the necessity of "coming out" on campus,

> because of the subject matter that I research and teach—which is media, sexuality, gender, and race—I've never found it necessary to disclose, to engage in some sort of speech act where I have to disclose my sexuality. Almost everything I teach is based in critical theory, so it's coming from a place of critical and analytical rethinking; therefore, I've never had to do that sort of coming out. I have had to come out to students in ways that I found to be very awk-

ward. For instance, I was asked to be a faculty sponsor for a lesbian sorority, which I found shocking because of the subject matter that I teach, which is both critical and queer. And I did have to come out to a group of lesbian students as someone who really could not support this sort of fee-based organization that was so apolitical. I'm finding that as LGBTQ becomes absorbed into the institution, the spaces for students and faculty are becoming more mainstream and center, instead of left. So I find myself having to come out as not mainstream and center.

As Kheshti describes, the stakes for many of us, which are rooted in going against the norm, have much more to do with articulating a political identity incongruent with increasing homonormativity. And they are stakes that often emerge from our experiences as outsiders as people of color less than our experiences being queer. For instance, many of the pieces that I have written that have an explicit queer focus come from and often privilege a working-class Black background.[15] I noticed this in a recent blogpost on the death of Leslie Feinberg in November 2014. I set out to write a piece about the influence she/zie had on me as a queer dyke who read *Stone Butch Blues* immediately when it came out on the heels of my own coming out in 1993. But there was something else about her/hir writing that moved me, which I didn't understand until I sat down to write:

> I read *Stone Butch Blues* as I was coming out of college, a site that both liberated me and ripped me apart. I was liberated by figuring out, after sitting in a Black feminist professor's classroom, what I wanted to do with my life—feeling seen and heard for the first time. Ripped apart because that experience moved me so far away from my working poor/working class roots. From my working class family, a family of railroad workers, transcriptionists, nurses, and factory workers. Most of whom were or have been ripped apart by a "globalized economy" that has so little regard for (working) people. All throughout college, I pushed myself further and further away from my family, from my "past." I couldn't reconcile working class, poor, and college. It didn't make sense to me. . . . [In *Stone Butch Blues*] I picked up on every detail, every line about working class life. The things I missed. The things that haunted me. That comforted me. The things I longed for but couldn't communicate, couldn't discuss because there was no solidarity, no interest in blue-collar life.

As Kheshti describes and as I recount in this blogpost, many things have changed for out queer faculty of color since Johnson wrote his piece, and the intersections of race and class complicate the discussions of LGBTQ life in the academy. Interestingly, class rather than queer identity was a link between many of our stories about academic life—trying to fit in and conform to gender expectations that are imbued with race (white) and class (middle-class) norms on university campuses. And although almost all of the faculty included in this conversation were familiar with and sometimes trained in feminist of color theory and queer of color critique, discussions of intersectionality are largely absent from campus life. These norms have crept more and more into LGBTQ discourse. For instance, a recent study on campus climate from Western Washington University conducted by the LGBT Advisory Council (2012) failed to include LGBTQ faculty of color in their study, stating, "Unfortunately, this project only gathered data on the needs of LGBT [sic] faculty and not faculty who are members of minority ethnic and racial groups."[16] The erasure of a queer of color faculty and the difficulties for the research team to understand an intersectional experience was evident from the beginning of the study when the author identified those who are both LGBT and racial and ethnic minorities to be "superminorities" who were underrepresented in the city of Bellingham, Washington, and the campus itself.

Marlon Bailey, an associate professor in Gender and Women Studies at Indiana University speaks to this categorization of "super minorities" for faculty whose marginalization is marked by race and sexuality, albeit in a more nuanced way than the study. As he explains, he and other Black faculty must engage in race labor, a super duty, one might assume, to reconcile the racism embedded in (and often, ignored) in interactions where sexuality takes precedence: "LGBTQ faculty are supported if they are white. However, I am the only openly Black gay man on the faculty, at least in the College of Arts and Sciences, and my experiences with IU and my colleagues have not been particularly supportive not only due to simultaneous racism and homophobia but also because I am not legible to my colleagues and my students as an out Black gay man, who works on and is committed to Black LGBTQ communities."

The "race labor" necessary to become legible in the setting as a Black gay man working on Black communities is the necessary work of queer faculty of color, specifically in Sexuality Studies departments and, increasingly, on campuses where diversity is a code word for LGBTQ, without feeling the need to address race or racism. Often, as Bailey later described, it is up to faculty of color to conduct this extra labor not only for ourselves but also for incoming faculty of color who may be overlooked because of their racial or ethnic background. Search committees might think, "We already have X number of faculty of color, why do we need more?" Moreover, once faculty are hired in Gender and Women's Studies or Ethnic Studies departments, the understanding of intersectionality is often lacking. As Bailey describes:

> My colleagues in GS, and this is so typical in the field of Gender and Women's Studies, refused to deal with race, both in terms of their white privilege and what it means to be a person of color at IU. Out of the four department chairs I had while there, only one understood and took seriously the profound and convergent racism and homophobia that I experienced on a daily basis, especially with undergraduate students. The real experiences of LGBTQ people of color at IU, for my colleagues is merely abstract at worst and theoretical at best; neither accounts for the material and tangible micro aggressions and violence we experience in these spaces. The courses that I taught in AAADS [African American and African Diaspora Studies] on sexuality, which had more Black students, those classes were often dogged by homophobic students, who didn't seem to be able to accept the need to engage gender and sexuality in a Black Studies class, even though they enrolled in a class called "Gender and Sexuality in Black America." Some of the students were homophobic which impacted how they engaged the material and me.... Most importantly, the students had never had an openly Black gay male professor before, so they really didn't know how to deal with me.

Bailey's experiences relate directly back to the challenges that Johnson wrote about and experienced decades earlier. However, they also highlight a significant difference in terms of "progress" in disciplines sometimes viewed as progressive because of their title and presumed content while there is an inability on the part of faculty and students to reconcile the intersections of race, gender, and sexuality. This inability to reconcile a queer of color experience is one that many of us continue to grapple with both personally and politically in academic settings. Kheshti brings this up again in her discussion of class, which she must confront over and over again on a campus that values, even prides itself, on being attentive to needs of LGBTQ faculty, staff, and students. As she states:

> so, the ways in which I sought a place for myself in the academy very much mirrored the way that Patrick wrote about it in his piece. I did not see any models or archetypes that I could imagine myself as, other than, of course, the queer people of color and, as an undergrad, the white feminists that trained me . . . therefore, I had to accept my identity as an interloper, which made, essentially, my very, very interdisciplinary scholarship just kind of in keeping with the general position that I felt I occupy, given the accumulation of identities that I carry around with me . . . there have been lots of moments of incongruence and discontinuity when it comes to reconciling my class background with the class background of many of my colleagues that have been at UCSD forever. . . . Like, sometimes I'll interact with a dean and it'll feel like an out of body experience because I'll feel like I'm not entitled to be in that space or I'm an interloper in that space.

Kheshti's experience of being or feeling like an interloper on her university campus is similar to the position that I described in the beginning of this essay: between same-sex marriage and Black death. It means not fitting into the joys of one, white space, and not being recognized for grieving the trauma of another. That is the ongoing experience, you know, on top of fulfilling what we were "hired for": teaching, research, and service.

There is much more to say. I have only provided a brief glimpse, not necessarily of the challenges, but rather of the everyday experiences of queer faculty of color. And, as rushed as it felt to write this and as ill equipped as I felt to write about a "general" experience of queer people of color experience in the academy, I was excited to be asked to relay *something* to try to fill this particular void. Moreover, in the short period of writing and engaging with other faculty, some who couldn't even participate because of time constraints, it has been extremely rewarding to remember and hear—and reaffirm my experience. What we know somewhere to be true: we know, as the opening paragraph shows us, how to celebrate a sliver or representation of queer life—same-sex marriage— an acceptable reflection of the dominant white, middle-class culture, but we continue to fail to reconcile race and class. How that sits on our bodies as queer faculty of color is something we continue daily to wrestle with.

Notes

1. *Obergefell v. Hodges.*

2. Although Tricia invited LGBTQ faculty of color to share their experiences, the stories of transgender faculty are just now emerging. I say "queer" in a very specific way—as in people who identified as queer, gay, or bi but not as trans.

3. D'Emilio, "The Campus Environment for Gay and Lesbian Life," 16–19. See Taylor and Raeburn, "Identity Politics as High-Risk Activism"; See Gamson and Moone, "The Sociology of Sexualities."

4. Bernstein, "Celebration and Suppression."

5. Russ et al., "Coming Out in the Classroom."

6. I was hired to teach in the Sociology department, but many of the faculty hired in that program teach in Sexuality Studies. We have merged administratively, and I am currently chair of both the department and the program.

7. Crystal Fleming (http://awareofawareness.com/), Andreana Clay (http:/ /queerblackfeminist.blogspot.com/), Sista Outsider (http://sistaoutsider.com /), Abigail Sewell (http://www.abigailasewell.blogspot.com/), Kortney Ziegler (http://blackademic.com/), Raul Pacheco-Vega (http://www.raulpacheco.org /blog/), D.A.T.T. (http://decolonizeallthethings.com/), and "Gay prof" (http:/ /centerofgravitas.blogspot.com/).

8. Johnson, "In the Merry Old Land of OZ."

9. Ibid., 97.

10. Ibid., 99.

11. Ibid., 100.

12. Ibid., 101.

13. Ibid., 103.

14. A 2013 *Inside Higher Ed* report shows that, of the 52,000 PhD's awarded in the United States that year, roughly 5,200 went to Black and Latino graduates while 13,000 were awarded to Asian Americans. No other groups were listed, nor were distinctions made about discipline or ethnicity within groups.

15. Clay, "Intergenerational Yearnings and Other 'Acts of Perversion.'"

16. Dozier, "The Experiences of LGBT Faculty at Western Washington University," 1.

Manifestos

Performative Testimony and the Practice of Dismissal

Jane Chin Davidson and Deepa S. Reddy

California State University, San Bernardino and University of Houston

Unacknowledged, invisible, ignored, made irrelevant—we all know what it means to be dismissed. But dismissal in the workplace is a practice that has traditionally kept the glass ceiling in place, even as laws prevent discrimination based on gender and race.[1] For faculty members of Women's Studies, the circumstances of the workplace are inexplicably complex, even more so than the mystification of the tenure process that bypasses the transparency of normative labor laws. The threat of being fired is a condition of dismissal, but its associated form of exclusion and subordination tends to work invisibly through tacit judgments of the worker that undermine rather than condemn overtly. Dismissal then is an act of silencing that is in itself a silent act. Through the combined experiences spoken as a partnership between two Women's Studies professors, this essay seeks to review the continuing practice of dismissal as an unacknowledged, habituated, and customary act in the collegiate workplace—the space that ultimately represents the institution of education and the State.

Rather than addressing dismissal as an insular problem of "women's relationships," this paper seeks to reconcile our personal participation in the community called "Women's Studies" with the larger institutional order of the academy, the university, and the state. It's critical to acknowledge from the outset that Women's Studies has outgrown its status as an activist political fringe in the university. But the current problem returns to questions long addressed in the particular history of the institutional silencing of "women's voice." The landmark event we consider was the public dismissal of Anita Hill's testimony in the 1991 Supreme Court confirmation hearing of Clarence Thomas. Hill's most significant contribution to civil rights was exposing the institutionalized obscuring of the political interests of women of color through the act of discrediting speech and negating their testimonies. The response by

Kimberlé Crenshaw in her study on how women of color were subordinated by both feminist and antiracism discourses developed into the current discursive strategy known as *intersectional critique*,[2] and the issues Crenshaw critiques can be reviewed through an update of the function of the performative speech act that affects the social contract for academic labor and the state. In the aftermath of Hill's testimony before the Senate, Thomas's performative counterpart appears to be his continuing use of silence—having refrained from contributing to oral arguments since February 22, 2006, he broke his silence with a joke in court on January 14, 2013, creating a controversy.[3] The aim of this essay is, therefore, to conceive of "dismissal through silence" as a practice that expands the meaning of the "speech act" beyond J. L. Austin's conception of "doing things with words."[4] How does personal dismissal relate to the silence of a functionary of the State, whose nonspeech is perceived as complicit with dominant forms of authority? Whatever the message, spoken or unspoken, interpretation is incumbent on the "ear of the other" as articulated by Jacques Derrida, whose reading of Nietzsche's *On the Future of Our Educational Institutions* (1872) draws a line from the university to the state.[5] But it is the communal ear that should be made distinct among cultures, movements, constituencies, fraternities, and even our partnership.

An investigation into the practice of dismissing through silencing in Women's Studies exposes a kind of tyranny—the attempt to delimit contestations made by minority women in Women's Studies is a subordination of voice, speech, and naming. Patricia Matthew challenges this tyranny by creating a textual space for their unwritten experiences. In the concerted effort, biographical telling is one objective of this essay; the other is in the greater theoretical inquiry into race and institutional silencing. Rather than viewing the problem as simply a "women's" problem, the aim of this essay is to reconceive of Women's Studies within its new role in the matrix of the academy and the state. Derrida's analysis on the state functionary is useful here, as is Gayatri Chakravorty Spivak's theory on the speech of the subaltern. Crenshaw's intersectional critique, however, brings together the recent critical dynamic of race in the United States at the institutional level.

Dismissal means so much more when acknowledging the way in which fraternal majorities still rule in the academy, where race is still determined by negative stereotypes. Within the historical formation of feminism, which was a celebrated unity and advocacy by and for white women, the "addition" of nonwhite women to Women's Studies occurs around negative concepts of the Other.[6] But rather than creating a forum for cultural subjectivity, this essay takes seriously Crenshaw's demarginalizing critique by focusing on dismissal as a negative determination premised on the female, nonwhite status. Through a reading of Derrida's exposure of how speech and interpretation are integral to the power of education and the state, this essay asserts that the legislated authority of the silencing of nonwhite women in Women's Studies reflects the greater condition of dismissal in the courts as it is in the classroom—the greater impact on the social contract of the academy can be viewed legislatively by the silencing of ethnic studies in Arizona.[7] These issues of race were addressed early in the development of Women's Studies by feminists such as Wendy Brown and Biddy Martin, but the return on their efforts seem now to have vanished. The question posed by this paper is whether Women's Studies should be viewed as fully incorporated into the state institution. If it should, then the demise of the original activist community is confirmed along with its objective of dismantling patriarchal structures.

On the Future of Our Educational Institutions

Women's Studies emerged more than thirty-five years ago as the "project of institutionalizing," according to Wendy Brown, with the objective of transforming "curriculum, method, field, major, or bachelor of arts" during the "profoundly important political moment in which women's movements challenged the ubiquitous misogyny, masculinism, and sexism in academic research, curricula, canons, and pedagogies."[8] The practice of dismissal was always distinguished by the denial of women's representation in the perception that an *entire segment of the population* could not contribute intellectually—could not teach, write, or speak at all. The establishment of a powerful Women's Studies advocacy led the way to statistical changes in the institution. In 1969, four out of five faculty members were men; today, the ratio is approaching 50 percent.[9] Almost half of all teachers in higher education are now women. Some of us entered the academy at a time when Women's Studies provided an opening for multiculturalist discourses, since we ourselves embody this diversity. Between the two of us, we have taught and resided in a variety of places, among them England, South Africa, Toronto, California, Michigan, and Texas. In recounting our faculty experiences among the different places we have taught, the teaching experience is vastly different but inherently the same—in some schools, Women's Studies is still considered provocative, as if time stood still, while in others the demographics among white faculty hires have not changed at all. Our globalist departures followed after the curricula of multiculturalism, when global courses began to show a distinct edge in schools since they facilitated cultural understandings and enabled taking stock of different groups and different needs and contributions to American life. "Diversity" was both a niche and an across-the-board requirement that eventually proved the success of the institutionalization of woman's studies; unquestionably, Women's Studies became a value-adding extension intellectually, professionally, and bureaucratically. The latter would have the most profound effect.

But by the end of the 1990s, the contradiction of the term *women's studies* was made transparent by the internal crisis within historical feminism. The self-critique of Women's Studies was focused primarily on what Brown describes as the "superordination of white women within Women's Studies [as] secured by the primacy and purity of the category gender," resulting in a type of "guilt that cannot be undone by any amount of courses, readings, and new hires focused on women of color."[10] Explained further by Biddy Martin, the self-definition from the outset entailed a habituated language marked by "exclusions with the sexual, racial, ethnic, and, to a lesser extent, class differences which are obfuscated by uncritical invocations of an internally consistent category of 'woman.'"[11] Categorization united women in the coalitions of the 1970s, and while the 1990s self-critique implicated our older white colleagues, we as women of color would also witness the unproductive, unfair browbeating of this generation by those who were overenthusiastic about "correcting" the racial disparity.

For the most part, the problem is generational. Recent efforts by younger faculty who wanted to introduce more conversations about theory and gender would fail in the face of the heavily experiential framework established by those who came before us. Larger programs dominated, and the traditional centers of power prevailed. Critiques failed. Efforts at dialogue failed. Junior colleagues of color left Women's Studies feeling like it offered them no safe havens, little camaraderie, and only few possibilities for intellectual growth. The older generation of feminists whose indefatigable commitment to the core principles of early "women's lib" resisted the shift toward the destabilized definition of "woman" and theories of gender construction. Many were only partially accepting of us younger women and women of color; those who were searching for more integrative approaches were alienated by faculty (of all colors) interested in protecting and cordoning off their turf in Women's Studies. Their reasons were both ideological and pragmatic in scope.

At times, we felt that academic politics were on par, as usual, and all our generational, ideological, experiential, and other fissures existed within that framework. But at other moments, the dismissals were crystal clear. In one example, our senior colleagues were praising us for two years of service in the program bringing a Women's Studies degree into existence and reestablishing a biannual conference called "Women's Studies Week." The name of the conference was deliberately changed from "Women's Week" in order to affirm and consolidate a Women's Studies professorship funded by a single donor. We had invited bell hooks to speak on campus to confirm the scholarly transition. The endowment represented major progress in the development of Women's Studies. The name change was important since it signaled a commitment to efforts at critical reading, more innovative use of theory, and the inclusion of theories from all sources, not just Women's Studies. (The title was actually a compromise, since "Gender Studies" would've been ideal.) But to our dismay, the event soon reverted back to its older title, "Women's Week," and this slight, this disjuncture, represented the enormous gulf, an entire crevasse, between the existing program and the attempt to create a space of genuine interdisciplinary dialogue. What we had instead, what we were trapped in, was our own separate feminist politics. For us, the younger generation, the construction of the subject was important for articulating our form of identity politics, one in which the "woman" signifier was under investigation just as the essentialist concept of race of Asianness, was also being questioned. Those members who were instrumental in reverting back to the old name were surprised at our discontent since they were unable to grasp what it meant to change the title.

The solipsism of issues haunting Women's Studies for the last thirty or so years can be viewed by the persistent attempts to reevaluate the "future of Women's Studies," as exemplified by the 1997 special issue of *Differences: A Journal of Feminist Cultural Studies* entitled "Women's

Studies on the Edge." When Joan Wallach Scott published the 2008 edited book of the same title ten years later, the lack of progress was conspicuous: in fact, the problems seemed worse. Scott emphasized the "outmoded political position" of Women's Studies in the loss of radicalism, activism, and "critical purchase" while disparaging the "ongoing difficulties of articulating Women's Studies with ethnic, queer, and race studies."[12] Problems today appear anachronistic as nonwhite female professors are still not taken seriously in Women's Studies departments. Andrea Smith's tenure denial by her Women's Studies peers at the University of Michigan, for instance, puts into question the rejection of women of color, even if they publish prodigiously and are hailed by their students as excellent teachers. Of course, the arbitrary nature of tenure becomes the alibi, the assumed reason, since candidates are known to have failed as much as they have succeeded when judged according to similar outputs in research, teaching, and service. So, is it our imagination when it seems like only women of color are fired or given low scores in the tenure review? We have witnessed the latter and noticed how certain faculty members had published much less and yet were promoted to chairs and administrative positions. The judgment of job performance is the purported task, but everyone knows it is the person of the candidate that is ultimately evaluated. It would be difficult to articulate the affective, emotion-based and subjective events that occur before a dismissal's final outcome. One can never know what the actual reasons are for why colleagues would deny tenure and the presumptions by which accomplishments are overlooked and underrecognized. Unlike any other labor relations, dismissal in the academy is a complete vote of no confidence; the professor loses her ability to be counted or fully represented by the tenured constituency. She has not simply lost her job; she is barred from the particular Women's Studies community that was supposed to support her. This is a disruption of a community in a world where community is supposed to be sacred.

Given the history of institutional advocacy in Women's Studies, dismissal within ranks presents a conflicted set of circumstances. A grassroots organization that united to empower women has become integrated into the education system and is now part of the state apparatus, which inevitably leads to contradictory political conditions. And still, the banding of women under the signifier of gender has been affected by the signifier of race in ways that have not been addressed. Whereas the former is a community created from coalitions, the latter is assigned to different people based on their "nonwhite" status. A racially inscribed group of women, marked by what Hall describes as the "floating signifier" of race, is vastly different from a community that bands together under the distinction of "woman."[13]

The dynamics of these power relations work in the collective unconscious in a particular way. Only someone who is dismissed because of both race and gender can speak of a particular experience. But how is one to articulate, attest to, or make a case of showing efforts that go unacknowledged by a dominant majority? The impossibility of knowing bias can only be matched by the difficulty of expressing the sense of being made to feel irrelevant after working ardently on behalf of Women's Studies, spending a great amount of time producing events and organizing Women's Studies projects, obtaining funding, and then spending copious hours managing them for the greater good of the association. Is it just our imagination when later we are summarily dismissed when we ask for individual support from Women's Studies—to ask for the use of the funding we obtained?

This dismissal happens through a discriminatory use of "governance" where the community called "Women's Studies" functions as the State. For example, we have seen our nonwhite colleagues request the use of funds to support an extension of a Women's Studies project only to find that new rules were suddenly put in place that disallowed the use of funds in this specific way. At the next meeting, a hearing was requested to bring up the issue that was too hastily dismissed. By then, simply raising the issue was perceived as a threat, and people got upset. Our colleagues (who were untenured) were charged with "unethical behavior" by (tenured) ranking members of the group, and the reasons given were that bringing up the issue in public instead of addressing it in private was injurious to the group's leadership. So, instead of discussing and resolving the problem out in the open, the matter was sent up the chain of authority to university administration. There the accusations were embellished further and charges were made that surreptitious inquiries about the group's finances were tantamount to theft. Anyone who lives in a "raced" body knows the meaning of such accusations. As Homi K. Bhabha explains, "race becomes the ineradicable sign of *negative difference.* . . . We always already know that blacks are licentious, Asiatics duplicitous."[14] Among the overwhelming majority of white members of Women's Studies, one has only to ask if such accusations could be so easily made by white tenured female professors against white female untenured professors.

Workplaces are fraught with such experiences. How is the problem different in Women's Studies? Even if the old "woman's lib" unifier no longer applies, we are still under the illusion that feminist advocacy continues to unite us as a political party. But if we accept the evolution of Women's Studies as an academic development, then we need to understand that it now follows the traditions of an institutional fraternity inextricable from the State. The acknowledgment of the conventional rules, established by the heteronormative rather than by gender identity, would provide a different perspective for viewing the problem. That is, dismissal within Women's Studies is both a refusal of recognition and the subjection to a fraternal norm (under the definition of fraternal as the long tradition of a *paternal* structure of institutional brotherhood). If indeed one does not belong to the coalition because of the nonwhite classification, then one is outside of a social collective regulated by a priori fraternal unconscious. And not to be taken into account by one's colleagues is a problem of recognition, as Butler explains: "If I understand myself to be conferring recognition on you, for instance, then I take seriously that the recognition comes from me. But in the moment that I realize that the terms by which I confer recognition are not mine alone, that I did not singlehandedly make them, then I am, as it were, dispossessed by the language that I offer. In a sense, I submit to a norm of recognition when I offer recognition to you, so that I am both subjected to that norm and the agency of its use."[15]

Accordingly, dismissal is not merely top-down, not something enacted by the privileged and directed overtly against women of color. Institutional and multicultural politics are far too complex for such reductions. The invisible practice of dismissal is far more insidious and found in actions that are left unexamined and therefore far more powerful since the practice is integral to relationships between faculty peers, administrators, especially within the norm and the hierarchy of authority in the committee-specific framework. Those of us identified as females of color could explain what it means to submit to the power of the majority by quietly obeying, keeping one's head down, and not making waves. We see how those members are often rewarded for their silence. This sort of response or strategy can be viewed as a type of *self-dismissal*, if indeed the goal is to gain relevance in the academy and recognition of efforts and accomplishments. This is a normative role for women of color in Women's Studies, and as we shall see, the prescriptive model is premised on the "unquestioning state functionary." Of course, this type of behavior as a minority is not statistically measurable, so the notion that university faculty and administration have entirely transformed to meet the diversifying demographics of college campuses is not accurate. Women of color are still the superminority. In the 2009 survey of all academic-ranking teachers of degree-granting institutions, 60,162 of the 89,906 members were white, with almost exactly half—29,490—counted as women; 9,161 teachers were Asian, the largest minority, but only 3,748 of them were women. The statistics for gender are better for the 3,404 African American female teachers out of 5,949 Black members in total and the 2,092 of 4,304 Hispanic teachers who were female.[16] Whereas progress is lacking for hiring nonwhite female faculty, equality has been achieved for white female faculty, which thereby constitutes the majority norm of the academy.

The Impossibility of Intersectionality

The problems within Women's Studies could be resolved by using Crenshaw's intersectional critique to take into account intersecting critiques of race, sex, and class and thereby acknowledge difference. Crenshaw explains that her objective was to develop specifically "a Black feminist criticism because it sets forth a problematic consequence of the tendency to treat race and gender as mutually exclusive categories of experience and analysis."[17] The tendency today is to leave out the word *demarginalize* from Crenshaw's stated aim of "demarginalizing the intersection of race and sex." Crenshaw's influential critique is associated with the double discriminations of Anita Hill, based on intersectional interests (as Black and female) that are never acknowledged, spoken, or addressed since they are dismissed by the secondary mainstream of white feminism and male race critics. If indeed the majority norm of Women's Studies is mainstream white feminism, then what would demarginalizing race look like in Women's Studies? In its intersectional self-critique, would Women's Studies not place precedence on the unequal representation of nonwhite women faculty in the academy?

To invoke the "intersectional" today presumes the coexistence of race and gender but does not acknowledge the need to address and develop the complexity of issues that are considered mutually exclusive to one or the other. For instance, feminists may have been sincere in heeding Crenshaw's warning: "Neither Black liberationist politics nor feminist theory can ignore the intersectional experiences of those whom the movements claim as their respective constituents."[18] But the ability to make this claim for a cohesive constituency among gendered or Black communities is not at all the same as it was in the 1980s. The clear sense of identity through which Crenshaw defined her revelations would be difficult to restage today. The presumed activist coalitions underlying the cohesive groupings of the past are no longer recognizable, which is why our efforts to update feminist theory in Women's Studies were so important to us. Due largely to the influence of Butler's performance of identity, extending to discourses of histories of sexuality and the floating signifier of race, the idea of "community" is now defined in localized terms based on contingencies, performatives, and specific locations of culture. Gender difference and racial difference are never static—the meaning of gender, sexuality, or race is never permanent. The major change in recognizing a community of "women" is that identification is interpreted differently by the person being viewed and by the person doing the viewing—even when both are of the same gender or race. As women who have lived under this type of subjection, the experience that we interpret as dismissal might be generally understood as simple oversight by other women, as the unintentional failure to take our supplications seriously. How can we take our own issues seriously when the so-called Women's Studies community does not appear to hear or to understand them? This is precisely why dismissal works as a form of subjection.

There is an ideology of dismissal, and Spivak was the first to address it in "Can the Subaltern Speak?" Her groundbreaking 1988 essay argued for the "muted subject of the subaltern woman" who was silenced by none other than the poststructuralist intellectual elite, the diagnosticians of power and desire, ascribed to the "radical criticism coming out of the West."[19] Spivak exposes the elite's efforts to preserve the sovereign subject, and in her project of "measuring silences, if necessary—into the object of investigation," her aim was to "give the subaltern a voice in history."[20] More than simply a question of representation, Spivak was confronting the "immense problem of the consciousness of the woman as subaltern," and her famous citing of white men "saving brown women from brown men" shows how the muting of subjectivity proves the documentary absence of a community that cannot account for itself.[21] The subaltern unable to "write" her own desire and interest is the premise of her absent history, and this problem is closely connected to the aims of Matthew's project in giving voice to the written and unwritten experiences of brown women in Women's Studies. The reproduction of power is given to "the domination of the ruling class 'in and by words' [par la parole]," according to Spivak, who invokes Althusser's structuralism on behalf of the process of accumulating knowledge.[22] In serving the labor of the intellectual institution, words comprise the instruments of material production. Spivak's problem is similar to ours in that given the opportunity to "write" about our own dismissals, *the task requires a confirmation of absence.* We can only attest to the sense of being ignored, the neglect of our contributions when we present them, only to find that they are oddly included later when no one remembers who should be credited. Bringing it up only makes us feel ridiculous.

Spivak's reminder of the ideology of state institutions is equally important for Women's Studies since one of the main assertions of this essay is that Women's Studies is now officially (intellectually, professionally, and bureaucratically) part of the state education system. When Derrida published his study on "'academic freedom,' the ear, and autobiography" as part of his project in reading Nietzsche's *On the Future of Our Educational Institutions*, he viewed the unpublished series of lectures as "a modern critique of the cultural machinery of the State and of the educational system that was, even in yesterday's industrial society, a fundamental part of the State apparatus."[23] Nietzsche is biographical in tone when he distinguishes the institutional and generational difference by which philosopher-teachers and students interact intellectually and academically. Derrida concludes that in serving the state, the education system exerts tremendous power through the notion of academic freedom.

The primary problem that Derrida was wrestling with was the fact that "the only teaching institution that ever succeeded in taking as its model the teaching of Nietzsche on teaching will have been a Nazi one."[24] Derrida's own youthful years were marked by the Vichy disenfranchisement of Jewish people in Algeria when he was stripped of his French citizenship and was expelled from school. As such, Derrida's study of the relationship between biography and the performatives in *Otobiographies* resonates deeply as a personal reference to the conformity of education to the State. He implicates the collaboration of the *Gymnasium*, raising the question as to how Nietzsche, the most influential philosopher for today's (poststructuralist) analysis of desire and power, could be interpreted for the advancement of the public polity of Jewish Holocaust. Nietzsche himself had warned that the "concept of politics will have merged entirely with a war of spirits: all power structures of the old society will have been exploded—all of them are based on lies: there will be wars the like of which have never yet been seen on earth."[25] While spoken in the same words, the philosopher was heard by the Nazi regime to say something completely opposite. Derrida defines the "destinational structure" of hearing that allows for "double interpretation and the so-called perversion of the text."[26] He asserts that the functioning "ear of the other" determines whose voice is being heard, and his inquiry implicating the power of the listener is inseparable from Spivak's question about the subjugation of the subaltern's speech. If Spivak's aim was to measure the silence of the "poor, black, female" subaltern, then Derrida's was to interrogate the deafness toward Nietzsche's exhortations by the antisemitic members of the *Gymnasium* who were serving the state. Throughout his essay, Derrida invokes the dialectic of the "dead paternal language" of history and the law that is distinguished from the "language of the living feminine against death, against the dead."[27] Significantly, the performative hearing of the subaltern's living language is required if she can be given a voice in history.

But the related argument posed by this paper is that the act of silencing is a racialized performative such that through the concept of academic freedom, the self-imposed silence of the docile and unquestioning members of the German university would enable the most heinous crimes against the Jewish as the racialized Other. Derrida determines that "the autonomy of the university, as well as of its student and professor inhabitants, is a ruse of the State, 'the most perfect ethical organism' (this is Nietzsche quoting Hegel)" and this ruse of academic freedom actually "conceals and disguises itself in the form of laissez-faire."[28] Universities only appear to act independently—state administrators only seem to refrain from interfering with teachers. The most effective regulatory power is self-surveillance, which is inherent in the type of person who fits the institutional profile. Derrida describes the way in which the "State wants to attract docile and unquestioning functionaries to itself. It does so by means of strict controls and rigorous constraints which these functionaries believe they apply to themselves in an act of total autonomy."[29] In this way, the practice of self-surveillance and self-silencing became the most dangerous form of dismissal when exemplified by the German cause of discriminating against the race of Jewish people.

THE IDEAL IN EDUCATION is premised on doing the very opposite of silent compromise, and after World War II, today's academic should very well be able to speak up when discerning the danger of racial division. While we note the stark differences between Derrida's time and our own, it is important to note that universities functioning as institutions of the state have silenced voices (Steven Salaita at the University of Illinois-Urbana), cut or withheld funding to Ethnic Studies departments (San Francisco State University), and effectively dismantled tenure (University of Wisconsin), and so we ask questions. What exactly can we say (and who do we say it to) if *not* to Women's Studies when we see other women of color being denied tenure for no apparent reason outside of their skin color? And when the institution is ostentatiously *not* diverse, what can we say or do, outside of trying to wield influence in search committees—if we get the opportunity? Derrida explains that the ruse of intellectual autonomy is one that authorizes complicity to hate and prejudice, simply through compliance with the "objective" laissez-faire doctrine. When academics become "unquestioning functionaries" of the institution rather than doing the work of the intellectual, the practice of noninterference authorizes the subjugation of others.[30] And we have all seen the silent, docile woman of color whose self-imposed silence in Women's Studies makes her look invisible. Those who are teachers and leaders should be the ones who stand up to injustice; but even in the highest American court, the leaders who administer justice fall short of their responsibilities. The prime example that correlates to institutional activism and silencing in Women's Studies can be found in the 1991 Hill–Thomas event. In reviewing the aftermath, the perpetual power of the state (that oversees the university and by extension Women's Studies) makes apparent the impossibility of intersectionality in the institution. It would be fair to say, however, that Hill gave voice to a great number of women when she educated the nation about what constitutes a hostile work environment in regards to being sexually degraded by one's boss. The dismissal of Hill's biographical testimony was made clear, however, when Thomas was confirmed as a Supreme Court justice.

Once Women's Studies had "arrived" as a "legitimate" constituency of academia, its activist role was relinquished by its institutionalization.

The idea that women have achieved equal status tends to eliminate the urgent need for activism in the workplace. The biographical assertion of the nonwhite female subject proves the deception of this assumption, which is the point of our dialogic expression presented in the first part of this essay. But rather than view the problem as a segregated "women's" problem, the aim is to connect to Derrida's juxtapositions of biography and performative iterations in order to reconceive of Women's Studies in the matrix of the academy and the state. Once Women's Studies is completely indiscernible from the educational institution, does it not bear the signature of the state and its inherent dangers of repression? And as such, should the activist in Women's Studies rethink the role and function of her or his participation—what should women of color do in Women's Studies? The role of leadership and that of the teacher would make this an ethical issue on behalf of the general effort toward social justice.

DERRIDA'S OWN *BIOGRAPHÈMES* recounted elsewhere as "de-citizenships, ex-inclusions, blacklistings, doors slammed in your face" underlie his message in *The Ear of the Other*, giving a subjective example for how Nietzsche's teachings could be so easily misconstrued by ordinary people in Germany.[31] Derrida's citation of Nietzsche's semiautobiographical voice in *On the Future of Our Educational Institutions* proposes a signature event that constitutes a performative that is significant for a constituency— the greater speech act that institutes the "force of the law." Likewise, Thomas's sole oral contribution to the public discourse consists of a conspicuous silence, which can be viewed as a form of self-dismissal. According to Adam Liptak writing in 2013 for the *New York Times*, Thomas's silence is remarkable in relation to the history of the court since "it has been more than 40 years since a justice went an entire term, much less seven years without saying a word at oral arguments."[32] As the second African American associate justice in the history of the Supreme Court to be confirmed, Thomas's impact on giving minority populations a voice in the legislative process is characterized by voicelessness. But others such as Michael McGough from the *Los Angeles Times* argue that "Thomas has remained silent all these years to confound his critics" because he has been outspoken in *published comments* that are "endlessly informative about his jurisprudence (sometimes scarily so)."[33] In fact, Thomas's written dissent for the Court's landmark Alabama case on same-sex marriage came well in advance of the court hearing in February 2015, signaling to the public that, against his opinion, the Court was poised to recognize the constitutional right of same-sex marriage.[34] In this way, staying mute as an oral contribution during the hearing serves to punctuate Thomas's ultraconservative vote.

AS AN EXEMPLARY CASE in the public spotlight, Thomas's performative of silence is a correlative to what's expected of nonwhite members of Women's Studies today. The role of docility in the disguise of autonomy appears to be the very role that the judge serves, befitting Derrida's profile of the functionary of the State. Outside of the written text, Derrida was invested in the speech act in which the "very emergence of justice and law, the founding justifying moment that institutes law implies a performative force, which is always an interpretative force."[35] As legislative practice, the law must be delivered through the spoken word for debate to occur. The activity must be differentiated from actions "in the service of force, its docile instrument, servile and thus [thought to be] exterior to the dominant power."[36] The practice of silence is therefore Thomas's performance of a "speech act" that is actually in service to dominant power.

Thomas recently made news when he spoke for the first time, breaking his silence in court. The occasion garnering significant press coverage consisted of a few seconds when he was making a joke. On top of the insignificance of his comments, most newspapers reported the "mystery" in regard to what he actually said since his remark—"Well—he did not" was a fragment recorded in the court transcript because it was inaudible overall.[37] Liptak compiles the various reasons that Thomas articulated throughout the years for "his general taciturnity." "He said, for instance, that he is self-conscious about the way he speaks and has recalled being teased about the dialect he grew up speaking in rural Georgia. In his 2007 memoir, 'My Grandfather's Son,' he wrote that he never asked questions in college or law school and that he was intimidated by some of his fellow students. At other times, he has said that he is silent out of simple courtesy. He has also complained about the difficulty of getting a word in edgewise on an exceptionally voluble bench."[38]

Liptak's characterization of Thomas as a judge who dismissed his own voice out of fear and self-retribution biographically contradicts the character of one who could rise to the highest civic profession based on the demands of oral debate. What Thomas performs on the public stage, however, is his apparent ability to fulfill the cause of a political majority through practicing a quiet obeisance, keeping his head down, and causing no audible approval or dissent. Whether or not Thomas exemplifies Derrida's "unquestioning functionary," his strategy of self-dismissal enables a powerful outcome: the Supreme Court justice title for a Black male affects the balance of the conservative vote. This model for self-dismissal ensures success for anyone submitting to the power of the majority. By not making waves, nonwhite women in white Women's Studies can attain a similar position in the program, unlike those who speak up when injustices are committed.

In contrast, Hill's courage in speaking out was rendered ineffective by the Senate, but according to *Time* magazine writer Jill Smolowe, Hill's testimony had a profound effect on the public discourse as well as on women coming forth in cases of workplace sexual harassment. One year after her testimony, the Equal Employment Opportunity Commission (EEOC) recorded 50 percent more sexual harassment filings than the year before, although only 5 percent of the 40 to 65 percent of female workers who initiated a claim actually filed a complaint.[39] The act of dismissing Hill's witness of workplace discrimination actually ended the self-silencing of others. This was an original aim of feminist intersectionality, the paradigmatic model for Women's Studies.

Moreover, when Thomas made a rare statement in 2013 with a joke, it was all the more meaningful because it was an underhanded criticism of the academy, revealing his anxiety toward the highest fraternal order to which he belonged. The court hearing that day was a determination on whether it was constitutional for defendant Jonathan Edward Boyer, an indigent man charged with murder, to wait five years for a trial in Louisiana because the State lacked funds during the economic recession to pay the two lawyers appointed to represent him.[40] Since Louisiana requires two lawyers to defend death penalty cases (in the original charge), the joke referred to the qualifications of the two lawyers handling the case. Apparently, Justice Sonia Sotomayor had questioned why the prosecutor at the lectern, Carla S. Sigler of Louisiana's Calcasieu Parish, had described one of the defense attorneys Christine Lehmann, a Yale graduate, as a "very impressive attorney." Liptak explains Thomas's response to Sigler: "Although the transcription is incomplete, some people in the courtroom understood him to say, in a joshing tone, that a law degree from Yale could actually be proof of incompetence or ineffectiveness."[41] It is well known that Thomas is unappreciative of his alma mater. After graduating from Yale Law School, he blamed his affirmative action status for flagging his judicial career.[42] In essence, Thomas broke his silence to excoriate one of the law schools that since 1941 admits exclusive membership to the Supreme Court bench. It would seem that Thomas could not accept his own legitimacy in the Ivy League fraternity, serving as a reminder of the academic realm of Harvard, Yale, and Columbia that actually constitutes the power of the state.[43] The fact that a descendent of slaves growing up in the extreme poverty of Pin Point, Georgia, could rise up to become appointed by George H. W. Bush, was in all likelihood affected by the fact that both he and the president were both Yale graduates.

Silence appears to be a form of protection from the authorizing State—its constituents either toe the line or risk the consequence of speaking out under the denial that no real harm comes to dismissing the living voice of the discriminated. Here the racial subordination of Derrida's Jewish community parallels the injustices endured by Thomas as characterized by a legacy of poverty after slavery. To end racial discrimination of any kind requires that a majority population speak up on behalf of the oppressed. One would hope that the actions of a Supreme Court justice could affect the continuing discriminations that are brought to the highest court. But in her essay "Burning Acts: Injurious Speech," Butler reveals the way in which the Supreme Court overturned convictions of race-hate crimes was really a form of dismissing acts of violence through the trumping of "freedom of speech" over the "hate speech" law—confirming Derrida's argument about the ruse of academic freedom.[44] The seminal 1990 case involves a white teenager who placed a burning cross in the front yard of a Black family's residence, which subsequently led to his conviction under the hate-speech ordinance passed by the St. Paul City Council. The Supreme Court overturned the ruling based on the logic that the burning of the cross is protected as a type of First Amendment speech.

The conclusion is that the tyranny of dismissing through silencing is a racialized performative that has broad and severe implications for women of color. The foreclosing of the living speech act in the recent elimination of the voice given to a Mexican American history also functions on behalf of perpetuating what Derrida describes as the dead paternal language of the law. Arizona's House Bill 2281 enacted in 2010 follows the same dismissive logic by forbidding a public school program that "is designed primarily for pupils of a particular ethnic group" based on the idea that "ethnic solidarity" is a dangerous threat to "the treatment of pupils as individuals."[45] One can imagine that this very example of "linguistic discipline" promoted as a protection of "individual freedom" personifies not only the rhetoric that dispelled Jewish history from German education but also enabled teachers and students to think themselves more "free" in doing so.

THE ORIGINAL ACTIVISM OF woman's studies was invested in challenging the paternalistic law. The institutionalization of Women's Studies therefore contributes to a totality of silencing of women of color—in the courts, in education, and as a day-to-day effectiveness in her teaching institution. And while we as teachers might not have overt examples that are mutual to HB 2281's disruptions to curricular development nor were we discouraged from building coalitions among racially marked members of Women's Studies, the divide and conquer of the tyranny of dismissal would surely have such an effect. Our experience sees only the cordoning off of woman's studies, in which our acceptance was always within set limits. This surely can also be understood as a form of silent dismissal. Our contributions were always nothing less and certainly nothing more—in other words, what would it mean, really mean, to think of Women's Studies as core not just to its own curriculum but to all programs' curricula? What would it mean to conceive of all classes as sensitive to and aware of the politics of gender, race, class, and sexuality? What would it mean to use "women's studies" as a framework to rethink the promise of a liberal arts education? We could never get to such questions and would always lock on the point that certain courses just couldn't be said to have Women's Studies content. As a reminder of the dictates of the state institution, the very ways that allowed our major to come into existence and provided easy rationale for growth and survival would actually make the ideal curriculum impossible.

In truth, the individual categories for identity can never be fully integrated nor separated no matter what the intersectional theory suggests. On that basis, as well as the fact that "nonwhite" remains the impossibility of Women's Studies, its institutionalization is now indubitably complete. We must remind ourselves that nonwhite as a negative stereotype in Women's Studies follows the continuing norm and logic of the greater social unconscious, which has nothing to do with actual American communities. The disparity of experiences between the Hispanic person being identified and the one doing the identifying can be viewed by the enforcement of the other half of the 2010 legislation, Arizona HB 2162, the "new misdemeanor offense for the willful failure to complete or carry an immigrant registration document." This mandate presents a clear-cut case of dismissing a subject who is constituted solely by language as differentiated from recognizing the embodied subject who performs her own identity. Through the arc of her work on subject formation, Butler addressed discursive identities and those that are performed. Butler's theory of the performance of gender undertook the embodied rituals, the individual sociality, and specific gestures that can also reveal the constitution of cultural difference. But her later inquiry into the effects of naming and interpellation imposed by language acknowledges the arbitrary regulation of the sexual or racial stereotype through the linguistic performance. Critics of Butler's theories on the discursive production of identity suggest that she reduces the subject to a mere product of language who lacks agency; but isn't this is precisely the work of dismissal, especially the objective of the HB 2162 and 2281 stereotype? Those who identify the subject according to the preconditions created by language would circumscribe the Mexican woman to the interpellation of the criminal status, although immigration laws—for Asian Americans especially—in the United States have always been predicated on discrimination and the fraternal norm. The opposite of subjection through language is the embodied material "self"—the true "speech" of the subaltern requires the embodied response of the interpreter.

Brown articulates the paradox in which "marked subjects are created through very different kinds of powers—not just different powers. That is, subjects of gender, class, nationality, race, sexuality, and so forth, are created through different histories, different mechanisms and sites of power, different discursive formations, different regulatory schemes."[46] At the same time, people are not "fabricated as subjects in discrete units by these various powers"—as living subjects, it is impossible to "extract the race from gender, or the gender from sexuality." Still, Brown suggests that the powers of subject formation "neither constitute links in a chain nor overlapping spheres of oppression; they are not 'intersectional' in their formation."[47] As women of color, our experiences emerge from relations in history among different cultural systems. But the way in which we are treated is completely contingent on investment in the "nonwhite" intersection, which has become another kind of stereotype.

If Women's Studies has indeed become fully integrated as a university institution, the question of its critical relevance should be at the forefront of the next round of self-evaluation. Scott came to the conclusion that the power of feminism was always attributed to interrogating, disrupting, and denunciating all forms of oppression, which she reiterated as the "practice of critique." Accordingly, she promoted feminist critique as the major imperative practice for the perpetuation of Women's Studies rather than defending and protecting an unchanging feminist orthodoxy. The only way that woman's studies could remain relevant was to openly self-scrutinize within its own objectives, ideals, and advocacy. Such a stated strategy acknowledges and dispels the idea that feminism could remain united ideologically under the signifier of "gender," which would ultimately disfigure the "woman" in Women's Studies.

Notes

1. We use the word "race" with the understanding that race is a social construct; we also understand that this social construct carries consequences and privileges with it.

2. Crenshaw, "Mapping the Margins."

3. See Liptak, "Justice Clarence Thomas Breaks His Silence."

4. Austin, *How To Do Things with Words.*

5. Derrida, *Otobiographies.*

6. "Nonwhite" does not logically represent an entire community, and through the work of Judith Butler, this essay acknowledges the cultural contingencies—the particularities and locations of culture—that make impossible a cohesive Asian experience. (Our own life experiences as two Asians from separate parts of the world, for example, are vastly different.)

7. See Arizona's House Bill 2281.

8. Brown, "The Impossibility of Women's Studies," 83.

9. Finkelstein, "Diversification in the Academic Workforce," S142.

10. Brown, "The Impossibility of Women's Studies," 93.

11. Martin, "Success and Its Failures."

12. Scott, *Women's Studies on the Edge,* 8, cover.

13. Hall, *Race, the Floating Signifier.*

14. Bhabha, *The Location of Culture,* 108.

15. Butler, "Giving an Account of Oneself," 22.

16. U.S. Department of Education, Winter 2009–10, compiled by University of Washington, MLIS candidate, Camille S. Davidson.

17. Crenshaw, "Demarginalizing the Intersection of Race and Sex," 57.

18. Ibid., 72.

19. Spivak, "Can the Subaltern Speak?" 66.

20. Ibid., 92.

21. Ibid.

22. Ibid., 68.

23. Derrida, *Otobiographies,* 33.

24. Ibid., 24.

25. Quoted by Derrida, *Otobiographies*, 32.

26. Ibid., 32–33.

27. Ibid., 21.

28. Ibid., 33.

29. Ibid., 33.

30. This in in the context of our discussion, and speaking overgenerally, the treatment of nonwhites by the whites in Women's Studies.

31. Cixous, *Portrait of Jacques Derrida as a Young Jewish Saint*, 5.

32. Crenshaw, "Mapping the Margins."

33. McGough, "Justice Clarence Thomas' Silence."

34. Liptak, "Justice Thomas's Dissent."

35. Derrida, "Force of Law," 13.

36. Ibid.

37. Cohen, "Speak, Clarence, Speak!"

38. Ibid.

39. Smolowe, "Anita Hill's Legacy."

40. See Manning, "Sulphur Slaying Case."

41. See note 2.

42. See Toobin, "Clarence Thomas Speaks."

43. Writing for *Time* magazine (May 8, 2014), in "The Most Popular Law Schools of Supreme Court Justices," Kiran Dhillon reveals that Harvard, Yale, and Columbia produced the most Supreme Court Justices—fifteen, six, and two, respectively. Before 1941, justices did not always obtain law degrees.

44. Butler, "Burning Acts."

45. Taken from Arizona's House Bill 2281.

46. Brown, "The Impossibility of Women's Studies," 86.

47. Ibid.

Talking Tenure

Don't be safe. Because there is no safety there anyway

Sarita Echavez See
University of California, Davis

It's easier to talk than write about the experience of going through the fundamentally humiliating and disciplinary process of tenure evaluation. Part of the problem is semantic: the rhetoric of evaluation and assessment implies that the process is fair, transparent, and meritocratic. But even the briefest description of practically any institution's tenure procedures and policies to nonacademic professionals elicits expressions of dismay and bewilderment. It's unfathomable to professionals outside of academia that tenure candidates receive little to no feedback or explanation about the outcome of their application for tenure, whether it's negative or positive. It's shocking to them that tenure candidates, with their jobs and livelihoods on the line, typically have no opportunity to substantively respond to negative appraisals of their work. Tenure candidates cannot attend their own tenure meetings and cannot defend their own record before their colleagues. Lawyers raise their eyebrows and mutter something about *habeas corpus*. When I explained my own experience at the University of Michigan to my brother, who has worked in investment banking (which has a reputation for cutthroat competitiveness) and the fast-paced Internet industry for more than a decade, I couldn't get through to him until I compared tenure and the academic profession to the formation of guilds. Then his brow cleared. He nodded, adding that, from what he knew of the history of the rise of guilds in Western Europe, they were created to protect specialists from the democratizing effects of industrialization and mass production by creating an elite, exclusive, and exclusionary organization.

In my own tenure case, I went through a double or parallel tenure application because I was hired as an assistant professor in two departments, a joint appointment housed in the program in American Culture and the English department but actualized by the larger vision and persistence of the faculty and students in Asian/Pacific Islander American

(A/PIA) Studies, a nonbudgeted unit.[1] In the years and months leading up to tenure, I was told repeatedly that I was a shoo-in for tenure. I'll not easily forget the backhanded compliments I received from a depressing array of colleagues—senior white women and men and senior and un-tenured non-American men of color. Their confidence in me came out of a mix of encouragement and resentment: there was no way I wouldn't get tenure because academics of color like me who work on minoritized cultures benefit from some kind of race card. Indeed, such compliments would come my way even after I was denied tenure in the English department but received a unanimous positive vote in American Culture. As I was scrambling to figure out how to make plan B or plan C work so that I could continue to keep up with my mortgage and graduate student loan payments, a senior white woman colleague assured me just days after I'd heard about the English department's vote that I would sail away from Michigan and "go on to become a diva somewhere else." The envy and resentment in her voice were unmistakable. I also talked on the phone with one of my white colleagues in English who was going up for tenure at the same time and had received a positive vote.[2] To this day I still am shocked by the memory of that mournful voice coming over the telephone line lamenting how horrible this whole situation was for the *department's* morale.

What are the origins of these twisted forms of resentment and hostility? Would it be absurd and disrespectful of me to invoke Native American and First Nations scholars' analyses of white settler colonial pathology? Of U.S. Ethnic Studies scholars' analyses of white supremacy? In other words, are white academics structurally positioned to express their anxiety about the illegality of settler presence and occupation and their resentment of the incursion of non-Native and Native colored bodies only through expressions of sympathy, encouragement, and care?

Looking Down the Barrel of Joblessness

Though everyone around me was utterly shocked when the English department's negative vote came down, I had made sure I applied for more than twenty jobs the year I went up for tenure. Just in case. I was a finalist for jobs at two other campuses that year, but those ultimately went nowhere. Apparently, my candidacy had become the occasion for major disputes to break out among the faculty, and I began to feel like a mobile disaster zone. My only comforting thought was that I had done my very best during those campus visits, projecting as well as feeling a newfound if ironic confidence in my work even as I was undergoing the process of getting fired.

The departmental votes were announced midway through the fall term, and the college decisions were announced midway through the spring term. Nearly half a year after I was told that I would go off and become a diva somewhere else, I heard that the English department's negative decision had been overturned by the College of Literature, Science, and the Arts, apparently an unprecedented event in the history of the department. Instead, American Culture's positive vote had been upheld by the college. There was a week of confusion when no one seemed to know whether my appointment had been moved entirely into American Culture or had remained a joint appointment in English and American Culture. I received two formal letters of confirmation from the college, one that stated that I was tenured in American Culture followed by another one much later stating that I was tenured in both American Culture and English. I didn't pause to think about it much at the time, but a tiny thought crossed my mind that it might be awkward in the future to walk back into English department meetings after a little more than a third of my senior colleagues had voted me down. Indeed they had to meet and vote on my case *twice*. A positive tenure decision in that department requires a supermajority of two-thirds of the voting tenured faculty, and I was told that I'd missed the supermajority by a handful. After reviewing my case, the college had notified the department that it was going to overturn the decision but, before doing so, it apparently gave the department a chance to hold a second meeting about my case. According to the department chair, at that second meeting several concerns were voiced about the repercussions of the administration's overruling, including the possible negative impact on the department's reputation on campus. They voted again, this time whether or not to fight the administration's decision. They voted not to do anything, and the vote was not unanimous. That's how I got tenure in that department.

At the time, I didn't think at all about what it would mean in the future to be a member of the faculty with the burden of that kind of microhistory—the only tenure case in the English department's history to be overturned by the administration, as far as I know. There were only two pieces of information that I could absorb. I still had a job. At the same time, I heard that four friends and colleagues in Women's Studies, American Culture, Native Studies, Latino/a Studies, History, and English—all of them had joint appointments—had been fired. This was devastating news, especially after I already had lost three friends and colleagues in Psychology, African American Studies, Art History, and American Culture who had been fired over the previous two years. It couldn't be a coincidence that all of the firings were coming out of my small circle of friends. The same month that I heard that the college had upheld my tenure, I attended an unprecedented and vibrant gathering of twenty-nine Filipino and Filipino American Studies scholars organized by Martin Manalansan and Augusto Espiritu at the University of Illinois, Urbana-Champagne (UIUC), a conference entitled "Philippine Palimpsests: Filipino Studies in the 21st Century." To date, out of the nineteen scholars who have gone through the tenure process from that group at UIUC, eight were denied tenure, one voluntarily resigned before coming up for tenure, and one was denied full promotion to full professor. Of those eight negative tenure cases, five retained their jobs because the negative decisions were overruled at some point in the process. The negative promotion decision also was overruled, and the rank of full professor was achieved. But the reality is that more than a third of our community of scholars have experienced and faced concrete hostility. This has been nothing less than an assault on an intellectual community.

Because I was hired as a joint assistant professor in two budgeted departments (English and American Culture) and as core faculty in the nonbudgeted unit A/PIA Studies, I knew that I'd be working at least twice as hard as most of my colleagues. I also took up an appointment in yet another nonbudgeted unit, the Center for Southeast Asian Studies. Those of us who work in fields such as Ethnic Studies, LBGTQ Studies, and Women's Studies that are associated with identitarian politics know full well that we're signing on for endless hours of unpaid, unrecognized mentoring, community building, and program building. But we do it because it's the most enriching if challenging part of what we do. Corny as it may sound, it's also a way of giving back and ensuring that the politics of reciprocity and mutual obligation that founded such areas of study and social movements live on. When I started my job at Michigan, I half suspected there might be repercussions when I turned down a few invitations to dinner parties at senior colleagues' houses and instead turned up at various student organizations' spoken word and poetry readings, hip-hop dance performances, undergraduate thesis celebrations, and Mr. and Miss A/PIA contests. I didn't fully realize that passing on these invites (what Dionne Bensonsmith calls elsewhere in the collection "soft service") meant missing out on the power wielded by the university's social economy. For the longest time, I didn't know that I was not part of the social economy that underwrites the university. I only found out that I was not being invited to play basketball with senior male colleagues or attend clothing and jewelry swaps organized by senior women colleagues when I found out that my untenured white colleagues typically were receiving such invitations. But I was—and remain to this day—sure and confident in the knowledge that there is a high cost that accompanies the privileges of such guild membership, privileges that people of color and not just white people can access and enjoy. To put it crudely, the research suffers. Thought diminishes. Creativity wanes. There is an intellectual rigor that comes along with the attempt to refuse to participate in the aspirational search for respectability and social mobility in academia—the attempt to not be safe.

I ADMIT THAT I didn't know just how hard I'd have to work as soon as I heard that I might be out of a job. When I was feeling especially angry and frustrated during that horrible year of going up for "tenure," I would calculate the value and time savings of sheer ignorance. Neither of the two white colleagues in the English department who were going through tenure at the same time had to figure out ways to address every graduate student mentee's concerns about the stability and future of his or her field exam or dissertation committee, figure out the pros and cons of hiring a lawyer, put together the materials for an appeal or a lawsuit, and attend lengthy meetings in person and on the phone to strategize about individual as well as collective responses to the tenure crisis, As my friend Hiram Pérez puts it, "It takes a lot of work to get fired."

It seems impossible to come through the process intact or unscarred whether one is retained or fired. As I've gotten more emotional distance over the years from the experience of going through tenure, I've begun to realize that, more often than not, my colleagues who went through tenure without a hitch—white colleagues and colleagues of color, LGBTQ colleagues, and heterosexual colleagues—have not been able to move on with their lives and their research and publishing programs. If they haven't lapsed into quite shocking modes of complacency and habits of passivity, so many seem driven by conflicting feelings of indebtedness to and anger at the institution, continuing dependence on the judgment of others—often or especially those with no expertise in their fields—for the conferral of legitimacy on their work, and panic about the ensuing intellectual paralysis and inability to publish beyond the first book.

But the tenure process also can engender moments of possibility and banditry. The student-organized March 2008 conference "Campus Lockdown: Women of Color Negotiating the Academic Industrial Complex" at the University of Michigan was a temporal and political rupture wherein students seized the space and resources of the university and used them for purposes alternate to those of the academic industrial complex.

In the wake of the staggering number of high-profile[3] and lesser-known negative tenure decisions for professors of color at the University of Michigan, a group of graduate students of color went into action. They galvanized undergraduate students, lecturers, and assistant professors so that we would have the space and time for genuine education at the university. Despite the compressed timeline that we all were dealing with, these students did an extraordinary amount of research on tenure at higher education institutions and coauthored a six-page pamphlet, "Talking Tenure," distributed at the Campus Lockdown conference, and this essay's title is very much a symptom of my attempt in this essay to pay tribute to their work. These students drew on a range of skills: organizing, political strategy, and fundraising skills acquired before graduate school typically from community-based or nonprofit jobs; research and teaching methods that they were learning within and across disciplines in graduate school; and trade union organizing skills associated with their crucial positioning as graduate student instructors who were members of the second oldest graduate student union in the country. Speakers included Piya Chatterjee, Angela Davis, Ruthie Gilmore, Fred Moten, Audra Simpson, and Haunani Kay Trask.

It's hard to communicate what happened at the conference, and what I saw, heard, and felt. The intense focus of the audience members throughout the day, some of whom bused in from as far as New York City. The cheers that broke out when Angela Davis Skyped in and smiled. The silence when Fred Moten said, "Don't be safe. There is no safety in being safe anyway." The laughter at the graduate students' dramatic parody of life in the academy, an original play that they wrote and acted so as to fulfill the funding requirements for one of the many grants and sponsorships they got their hands on.

As I waited for news about whether the English department's decision to deny tenure would be upheld or overruled and about whether some of my dearest friends would be fired or not, I was privileged to experience the collective commitment to *thought* in an imperial university and country made stupid by its own commitment to what I can only take to be white settler colonial rage, the intense resentment generated by the buried knowledge that white presence in the academy is not a result of meritocratic achievement but rather a history of illegitimate incursion and occupation. Campus Lockdown provided a space and framework for the critique of the university as an ideological entity, one that has become committed to tutelage rather than literacy, what one Southern California organization recently dubbed "Learning, Not Schooling: Beyond the Academic Industrial Complex." Campus Lockdown instead created the conditions for the analysis of future objects that we cannot see now.[4] For me, it simply made it possible to live on. I gained clarity about my vocation as a teacher and a writer-scholar. I understood that I must find ways to insist on the importance of the continued struggle for creativity and thought in the university if we are to thrive and not merely survive. And I remain fueled by a deep sense of utter gratitude to the students and colleagues who saw us all through.

It remains excruciatingly painful to write about that experience governed as it is by what Andy Smith half-jokingly calls the "post-traumatic tenure syndrome." So instead of trying to write more, I have transcribed two radio pieces that I did with the Portland-based radio show "APA Compass" on KBOO community radio. Right after the Campus Lockdown conference, Asian Pacific American (APA) Compass member Marie Lo asked whether I'd like to contribute an "Angry APA Minute" to their show, and I found myself wanting to talk about the past and present of education as a means of colonization, making connections between what my colleagues and I were undergoing and the history of the United States policy of "benevolent assimilation" in the Philippines. Then in the wake of yet another series of shocking negative tenure decisions at the University of Southern California, Marie asked to interview me about the "Race, Tenure, and the University" September 2010 public forum at USC that I helped organize. Here they are, for the written record: "Benevolent Assimilation in the Twenty-First Century" and the radio segment for "APA Compass," KBOO Community Radio, March 2008.

Every Filipino in the American academy has a gift. That gift is the knowledge that education was and is the most powerful weapon of American colonialism in the Philippines. It is that gift that allows me to understand the insidiousness of the tenure system for women of color in the university today. Let me put it plainly: tenure means total unaccountability. With tenure, you get to do anything you want. And that begets not freedom but forms of irresponsibility, apathy and racism that consolidate rather than trouble the relationship between power and knowledge. So what I want to remember is what Fred Moten said at the recent Campus Lockdown conference here at the University of Michigan: "Don't be safe. Because there is no safety there anyway." And all I have to do is remember my own father's and grandfather's attempts at safety. All I have to remember is my Cantonese-speaking father who took a government scholarship as a ticket out of the ghetto, as a ticket to Singapore's elite English-speaking bureaucracy. This was a bureaucracy that would reward him and reward him yet mark him ultimately as a Chinaman from Chinatown. All I have to do is remember my Filipino grandfather who was houseboy to an American university president in Kansas, in the heartland, in the Midwest, where I now work. This was a system that would reward and reward him as he worked his way to a bachelor's degree at the University of Kansas and then a master's degree at the University of Michigan, where I now work. All I have to remember is that he insisted to his children—my mother—that the only two things in life that anyone and everyone would desire is to get an education and to become an American. Which is really not two things but one very dangerous thing. So I remember my legacy: the paternalism at the heart of this patrilineal legacy, and in so doing I refuse to do honor to the reproduction of colonial knowledge that is at the heart of this legacy. I refuse to belong to the house of the American university even as I work in it. For I recognize its rewards for what they are. Tenure is nothing but a bribe. A form of bribery that is, after all is said and done, benevolent assimilation in the twenty-first century. This is Sarita Echavez See, and this has been my "Angry APA Minute."

"Race, Tenure and the University"

Interview by Marie Lo, APA Compass,
KBOO Community Radio, September 2010

Introductory segment:

Sarita Echavez See (excerpt from interview): From what I see is happening is that the larger cultural moment is being reflected and worked out in the university. And in some ways the university is not an ivory tower. It's not isolated from the United States and from the larger political moment. It actually reflects really quite clearly what's going on nationally.

Marie Lo: That was Dr. Sarita See, a professor of Asian/Pacific Islander American Studies at the University of Michigan. In addition to her groundbreaking work on Filipino American art and performance, she has been an active organizer for change within the university system. As Dr. See points out, higher education is not just where students go to acquire knowledge. It is also where what counts as legitimate knowledge is itself debated. Academic tenure is supposed to offer scholars the freedom to develop innovative and perhaps controversial research without fear of losing their jobs. But for many faculty of color working in the areas of U.S. Ethnic Studies, their radical scholarship often makes them vulnerable to being denied tenure in the first place. There have been a number of recent high-profile tenure cases such as Professor Don Nakanishi in the University of California Los Angeles and Professor Jane Iwamura from the University of Southern California, who is currently in the midst of appealing her university's negative tenure decision. Dr. See is one of the organizers of an upcoming forum called "Race, Tenure, and the University" to be held at USC. And she talked to APA Compass about some of the systemic obstacles that faculty of color face and what the lack of tenured faculty of color means for higher education and beyond. Thank you for agreeing to talk to us today. And my first question is: For our audiences who may not really know about the tenure process, can you talk about that a little bit?

Sarita Echavez See: The tenure process that I'm more familiar with is for a research university wherein you get a job as an assistant professor and for the first four or five years or so, depending on your institution, you are expected to publish articles and/or a book based on your research and also start to establish a reputation for yourself as a scholar and as a teacher not only on your own campus but nationally or even internationally. And then typically in the final year you're getting evaluated for up to a year, sometimes even longer, by your colleagues at the departmental level and then at the upper administrative level who are evaluating whether or not basically they will award the candidate tenure. Which is to say, a permanent position in the university. I mean, tenure basically means it's harder to fire you, as one of my colleagues put it. And so one way to look at tenure is that it's supposed to secure a position for the scholar who then should be free to pursue research and teaching with more freedom of speech. So that's kind of the promise typically associated with tenure. The other side of this—and this is unfortunately what we've been witnessing more and more and especially in certain fields like Ethnic Studies, Women's Studies, Queer Studies—is that tenure is not so much a path to greater freedom for scholars but rather a hazing process, whereby you actually get into a country club or a fraternity. And the standards for evaluating faculty are pretty much just as random as any kind of fraternity or sorority. Or perhaps not even random but based on immaterial things like whether or not you're perceived to fit in or to be a troublemaker. That's kind of in a nutshell, from my vantage, what tenure means.

ML: And then this dovetails into another question: What are the stakes for retaining faculty of color?

SS: A number of things are really at stake and these are high stakes. For the fields that particular faculty of color tend to represent, that is, like for example Asian American Studies, Pacific Islander Studies, Latino Studies, Chicano/a Studies, Native American Studies, Arab American Studies, those interdisciplinary fields first of all have a commitment—a historical commitment—from the 1960s on in the United States to making their research and their findings and their scholarship relevant and accountable to the communities who are—who form—the subject of scholarly study. So that's a really important thing. These are standards of accountability that make certain fields really different from other, say, more traditional or more conventional modes of scholarship.

And I think that's actually a real threat to the university. Anything that's going to call for a certain dissolution of the border between what is academic work and what is, say, activist or community work? I think that is potentially very threatening. The other thing that's at stake is that, generally speaking, to my mind, fields like Asian American Studies and other U.S. Ethnic Studies prepare students better for life and work in a polyethnic, polycultural country, society, and world. If students are not prepared for that, I think that's a real disservice to our students and it's also a real disservice, generally speaking, to the kinds of options that students can have after they graduate. So what I do see as a more and more intensified assault on Ethnic Studies and Asian American Studies, for example, is connected to the shrinking of options generally speaking for young Americans today.

ML: Then in terms of these kinds of shrinking options, in terms of the fact that there are Ethnic Studies programs, there are Asian American Studies programs, so what exactly is happening within the institution? I mean faculty are being hired, but then they're not being retained.

SS: That's a great question. That's also a huge question because it really does depend on the different institution and the different region or location where the university or college or community college is located. But just to give the University of Michigan as one example, a number of faculty of color were actually hired about ten to twelve [or] thirteen years ago under a different president, under a very interesting administration who really were, looking back now, really committed to fostering the development of certain fields that, like I said, would prepare University of Michigan students for the realities of what the United States looks like today and in the future. And in that interim, what happened is a series of events that also got reflected within the institution, within the university. That is to say, the series of lawsuits and legal cases that were striking down affirmative action. I mean . . . political backlash against the kinds of advances that were made in what we can say was the multicultural movement of the 1980s into the 1990s or so. So from what I see happening is that the larger cultural moment is being reflected and being worked out in the university.

ML: That actually brings me to the particular case of Professor
   Jane Iwamura of University of Southern California. And you
   have been really involved in publicizing her recent tenure denial
   and also trying to connect her case with the larger and systemic
   tenure denials of other faculty of color both at USC and beyond.
   Can you talk a little bit more about her case?

SS: Well, I can't actually talk in a lot of detail about what happened
   within the institution of the University of Southern California
   because it's a complete black box. And I should note that USC
   is a private university. So unlike many public universities where
   tenure cases are a matter of documentation and records, private
   universities really don't have that kind of accountability to the
   public. So that's actually one of the larger problems. These major decisions impacting an individual's whole career are made
   behind closed doors and without any kind of argumentation in
   any kind of public sense. But in terms of the particulars of Professor Iwamura's research and teaching and service record, what does
   connect Professor Iwamura's case to those other cases that have
   received a lot of attention and also cases that have not received that
   much attention is that it's not a question of whether or not she's
   qualified or not. From what I see of her record, Professor Iwamura
   is almost overqualified for this position. She is the cofounder of a
   really important emergent subfield in Asian American Studies, that
   is, Asian American religion. We're not talking about somebody
   who has once again just sort of, you know, made the grade. This
   is somebody who, like a number of other cases mostly women of
   color faculty who have been denied tenure, we're talking about
   the cream of the cream. Professor Iwamura has a BA as well as her
   PhD from the University of California. She also has a theology
   master's degree from Harvard. Her wonderful monograph, a book-
   length study called *Virtual Orientalism* (Oxford University Press), is
   coming out this December. Her record's actually stunning. She got
   pretty much the *highest* award—teaching, service, research achievement award—that USC gives to junior professors. This kind of case
   we've seen. We've seen a number of these cases. Not just qualified—to my mind, *over*qualified.

ML: So I'm going to ask you for your assessment. You have these
   fantastic scholars. Why does the university not make an effort to
   retain them?

SS: Right. Just to mention yet again: the university is really not an isolated space. It really kind of reflects the political conflicts and tensions and rifts as well as alliances that we find in the everyday world. So that's one way to think about the university. It's a place, a site, of debate and conflict. Which is what it should be actually! Everybody's work—Professor Iwamura's work—should be debated. However, this is not a question of a debate on an even playing field. This is a question of who's going to be allowed to continue their work, to pursue work that, from the vantage of certain scholars who are either indifferent to or hostile to the kinds of emergent, new ways of studying, for example, the ways in which Asian Americans practice religion or what kinds of relationships Asian Americans have with notions of the sacred. Nobody else is doing this. And so what I do see Professor Iwamura and others who are doing this kind of truly new, original scholarship, which is what the university should be committed to supporting in the first place. What I see them doing is actually coming up with new methodologies, new theories, new structures, new ways of thinking about these objects of analysis.

ML: I'd like you to talk a little bit about this upcoming forum that is taking place on September 22 at USC that you've become very involved in.

SS: There's going to be a really exciting public forum, "Race, Tenure, and the University." It's going to feature a number of really exciting professors: Denise da Silva is associate professor of Ethnic Studies at UC San Diego, and she published this groundbreaking book called *Toward a Global Idea of Race.* Jim Lee is the new chair of Asian American Studies at UC Irvine and his book is called *Urban Triage* on literature by writers of color. Andrea Smith is a particularly well-known Native feminist scholar and activist and cofounder of *Incite! Women of Color against Domestic Violence*, and she teaches at UC Riverside. And finally, Cynthia Young is associate professor of English and African and African Diasporic Studies at Boston College, and her work is on African American radical social movements. So these are a number of speakers with lots of different takes on the politics of the university and the connection between scholarship and the world. And there's also going to be a number of graduate students and undergraduate students at USC who are going to be involved that day as well. So we're hoping that this public forum will instigate a number of conversations and productive debates about the structural biases that we've been talking about. And hopefully will simply raise the level of discourse about these issues.

Notes

1. The term *nonbudgeted unit* refers to programs or entities on campus that usually have neither a substantial budget nor regular or staff to support their events, programming, mentoring, and other activities. To my mind, it is deplorable but not atypical for interdisciplinary entities such as Asian/Pacific Islander American Studies to be starved of resources even as they serve as crucial nodes of intellectual, political, and mentoring activities.

2. Four assistant professors came up for tenure in English that year, two women of color—including myself—and two white professors, and the two white professors received positive votes and the two women of color professors received negative votes.

3. See Appendix A: Campus Lockdown and the *"Talking Tenure"* newsletter.

4. I am riffing here on one of Theodore Gonzalvez's wonderful comments at the aforementioned March 2008 "Philippine Palimpsests" conference about the kind of futurist, anticipatory attitude we should have toward our objects of analysis.

Hierarchies

Still Eating in the Kitchen

The Marginalization of African American Faculty in Majority White Academic Governance

Carmen V. Harris
University of South Carolina–Upstate

> I, too, sing America.
>
> I am the darker brother.
> They send me to eat in the kitchen
> When company comes,
> But I laugh,
> And eat well,
> And grow strong.
>
> Tomorrow,
> I'll be at the table
> When company comes.
> Nobody'll dare
> Say to me,
> "Eat in the kitchen,"
> Then.
>
> Besides,
> They'll see how beautiful I am
> And be ashamed—
>
> I, too, am America.
> —Langston Hughes, "I, Too."

I was the last American-born person of color to be hired in my division: that was in 1997. Since then, the division has devolved into departments, but the statement holds true. I am a historian by trade. I am the third in a series of African Americans to have taught on a tenure line in history, and the first to get tenure. Since that time, we have only invited three candidates of color to campus for employment visits in my department. I received my master's and doctoral degree from different institutions. As a result, I have twenty graduate courses in history—far more than most PhD's. My major field is United States history and my research merges multiple historical subdisciplines (Southern, public policy, African American, agricultural, gender) in various ways. I have received graduate fellowships, was a Ford Foundation postdoctoral fellow, and recently won an award for an article published in a journal.

I teach at a public liberal arts university in the South, which was founded at the end of the civil rights struggle. It's only twenty-five miles from where I was born and grew up. The institution, therefore, does not have a history of institutionalized segregation. However, my experience here has led me to question whether a lack of such a history sufficiently immunizes such institutions from replicating the systems of power that were present in institutions in this state that were historically white before 1964. When I arrived here, the relationships I developed in my department led me to feel that this was a place where I could develop professionally and thrive even without a critical mass of African Americans. There seemed to be more African Americans on campus when I arrived than are here now. From my perspective, African American faculty have less visibility on campus. The easy answer, of course, is racism—plain and simple. However, this is an academic community. People don't use the "N" word, nor do they seem consciously prejudiced against faculty or students of color. Had it not been for my research on intersections of Southern racial ideology and public policy, I may have convinced myself that I worked in a community of closeted racists. However, through that research I came to recognize that the dearth of African American faculty was the consequence of processes that are presumably race-neutral but in the hands of frail humanity result in a bureaucracy that produces racist outcomes.

The concept of "bureaucratic racism" transcends disciplinary and geographic boundaries. It is typically applied to the relationships of people of color to the apparatus of the state. In particular, it deals with the ways in which states encode race into law to control access to resources and rights.[1] I have found the concept useful to my analysis of the relationship of African Americans to the United States Cooperative Extension—both as workers and as clients. In this paper, *bureaucratic* from *bureaucracy* is the dominant part of the concept. Bureaucracy is manifested in systems of institutional organization aimed at establishing policy ostensibly on objective, apolitical bases without reference to distinguishing traits such as class, race, or gender. The presumptive outcome of such structural planning is that equity can be achieved by removing subjective variables from the equation. However, I have found that such bureaucratic systems hold the potential to operate in discriminatory—racist—fashions. This racism is not a conscious outgrowth of bureaucratic planning, but rather it is often an unanticipated consequence of policies framed during less diverse times and whose subsequent modifications have failed to keep pace with the evolution of societal norms. Even when society evolves in ways that more consciously recognize diversity, bureaucratic policies are often slow to catch up—if they ever do. As bureaucracy is supposedly rooted in objectivity, the need for modification is not always recognized.

Bureaucratic racism has touched my life through the process of faculty governance, which is part of a "joint effort" of institutional administration in which the influence of various stakeholders—faculty, students, administration—varies, depending on the particular policy. There is a presumption that my interests converge with those of my white colleagues in all respects as part of the faculty collective. By asserting the rights of stakeholders through a collective identity, what gets overlooked is the reality that these groups are composed of persons who hold different perspectives rooted in their personal and professional identities and histories. As a result, what is perceived to be neutral is, in practice, an extension of professional identities and histories.

Faculty governance includes the power to determine who will become part of the body through the process of academic searches. Therefore, it serves as a barrier to entry to an institution, and it manages opportunities not just for existing faculty but also for potential new hires by establishing criteria and procedures for recruitment, hiring, advancing, and terminating members. Therefore, in my opinion, it is essential that governance be consciously inclusive beyond the standard "minorities and women are encouraged to apply" language in advertisements to ensure that the door to academia is open to people of color.

The historical roots of faculty governance, the font of most current policies and practices, limit inclusivity because opening the doors to academia may seem sufficient to "traditional" academics. I argue that it is not. Faculty governance took form in an era when persons of color—and white women for that matter—were not a visible part of white-male-dominated institutions. It was from these institutions that the earliest faculty advocacy organizations drew their founding members. Charters and bylaws were largely color and gender blind because the white male experience was the default standard. While some headway has been made to encourage diversification of faculty in updated statements, faculty governance at the institutional level has not been sufficiently reinvented in ways that acknowledge that traditional rules and regulations were not crafted to encourage diversity and that there is a need to consciously take account of race and other "diverse" factors in policy. Perhaps revisions have not occurred because they require a rethinking of how the faculty collective envisions itself. Positions on the rights and responsibilities of faculty are written in presumptively authentic, universal language. However, rules and regulations are interpreted by individuals.

This is evident in documents such as the Statement on Governance of Colleges and Universities from the American Association of University Professors (AAUP) and American Council on Education (ACE), which was first crafted in 1966 during the civil rights era. Portions of this statement reaffirm pre-civil rights standards with references to statements on academic freedom from 1940 and procedural standards for dismissal in 1958.[2] The 1966 statement asserts the importance of collective faculty participation in various activities of institutional life. However, it is silent on the importance of racial diversity in shared governance. That the document, written a mere two years after Title VII of the Civil Rights Act was in place, makes no mention of the importance for governance to be racially inclusive is somewhat surprising and somewhat not. This document reflects the belief (hope?) that academia could produce a model of collective rule that transcended discrimination in the wider world. However, the document also reflects the compromises needed to establish unanimity between two competing arbiters of academic governance.[3] While it is certainly understandable that the AAUP and ACE aim to promote a collective voice, it was disappointing to see these institutions fail to take the lead in emphasizing diversity in shared governance in a nation grappling with an increasingly diverse society. The AAUP/ACE statements assert the primacy of faculty in matters related to "faculty status" such as "appointments, reappointments, decisions not to reappoint, promotions, the granting of tenure, and dismissal." These statements demonstrate a respect for the right of faculties to craft policies that best reflect their institutional culture. However, experience on the ground, in the daily governance practices, demonstrates that university faculties are not immune to conscious and subconscious forces that create insider privileged groups and outsider marginalized groups within the faculty collective. Issues such as what is valid scholarship, what subjects are "important" (in the social and behavioral sciences), and what types of service are valued are areas of contested power between the marginalized and those in the center. In my experience, when minority faculty joined my institution, the questions were not revisited to determine whether established answers were sufficiently inclusive.

The AAUP has taken note of the issue of diversity, faculty governance, and minority faculty in what, in my opinion, is an atomized fashion. A standing committee on historically Black colleges and universities (HBCUs) and scholars of color exists at the national level. The committee focuses more heavily on governance and its blind spots at HBCUs. Affirmative action and diversity are addressed through white papers and opinion pieces, but a forceful policy statement is lacking. The AAUP is "engaging in a multi-year effort to consult with historically Black institutions about academic freedom and shared governance, to strengthen academic programs, and raise the stature of these institutions among colleges and universities."[4] There is no evidence, however, that similar attention is given to these issues where minority faculty are in the employ of non-HBCU schools. In addition, the AAUP website includes a table containing a survey of data on HBCU faculty's opinion on faculty governance. "Shared Governance, Junior Faculty, and HBCUs," an article written by Beverly Guy-Sheftall in 2006, addresses the issue of minority faculty participation but within an academic setting in which African Americans are dominant. In 2000, a "how-to" on diversifying faculty was published that addressed the supposed barriers that existed to making faculties diverse. A paper presented by AAUP counsel Ann Springer and Charlotte Westerhaus, Vice President for Diversity and Inclusion for the National College Athletic Association (NCAA), from 2006 on diversifying faculty is also posted.[5] Also on the site is an AAUP/ACE extended white paper published on diversity ten years ago. The white paper reflects the dissonance between expressed beliefs—that diversity matters—and real world practice—that it's often overlooked in faculty governance. While these publications all address important issues affecting African American faculty, they do not address the issue of the importance of direct and active voice for African Americans—and other minority faculty—on matters relating to the governance in nonminority colleges and universities. In the absence of overtly established principles of inclusion, when the faculty acts in its role in governance it should take care to ensure that policies enacted do not inadvertently disadvantage some sectors of the faculty. African American faculty are often "left in the kitchen." The power they lack to influence policies—no matter how benignly they were crafted—consigns them to the margins and holds the potential to disrupt their professional lives.

My personal frustration confronting the governance policies at my own institution reminded me of the poem by Langston Hughes that precedes this essay. Hughes wrote the poem in 1924 when he found himself stranded in Genoa, Italy. Broke and without a passport after his wallet was stolen, Hughes was part of a collective—the citizenry of the United States—that seemingly did not acknowledge his membership or his right to expect that his institution would provide him support. Hughes's poem expanded on Walt Whitman's celebration of the common white men and women of America in "I Hear America Singing" published in 1867. At a faculty senate meeting at which I unsuccessfully attempted to point out the pitfalls of proposed administrative revisions in the faculty manual for marginalized faculty, I felt as if my membership in the general collective was irrelevant as was my expectation that my colleagues would give my concerns due consideration. I had been attempting to voice my concerns regarding a chapter on the process of administrative review in several different meetings only to be thwarted by my lack of familiarity with *Robert's Rules of Order*—a deficiency I have since corrected—which were established to promote orderly conduct of meetings. However, I began to feel that its purpose was to use bureaucracy to stifle discord through parliamentary procedure. The committee in charge of revision had not provided opportunities for faculty to meet with the committee in informal (non-*Robert's*) forums in which concerns could be expressed and discussed. After having my concerns postponed at a general faculty meeting because I was out of order (outside the collective), the senate was my last hope of raising a discussion about the review policy. The faculty manual, I had learned from personal experience, was so subjective that it held the potential to adversely impact marginalized persons disproportionately through restrictions on appeal. I recognized that what had happened in my case could happen to *any* faculty member—regardless of race—who did not have strong allies (most of the senior faculty are white). I believed the modifications to these procedures that I wanted to propose would be beneficial to the collective. With the exception of three foreign nationals who were of color, everyone in the senate was white. I pleaded for a no vote. I invoked the concept of bureaucratic racism. Perhaps *racism* isn't a wise word to use in a room full of white folks who likely are not conscious of the complexities of race, but I did it anyway. I got nowhere. In other words, I felt as if I had no place in the conversation. I felt I had been sent to the kitchen.

Why was I at the senate? Why didn't I volunteer to serve on the committee if the aspect of governance was so important to me? I did volunteer. I was the first to volunteer. At the moment I volunteered, I was asked if I wanted to chair it—but I declined because I knew I would be unable to devote the amount of time that chairing would require. I lived in a town twenty-five miles away and I had school-aged children. My husband worked as an academic dean in another town about twenty miles from where I worked but also forty miles from my home. The school day ended at 3:30, and while sometimes I could have friends back me up, I didn't want to impede the progress of such an important committee because of my life challenges. But I fully expected that I would serve and would, when necessary, communicate electronically in helping to draft a manual. I believed that the changes I advocated for would not only enable marginalized faculty without powerful allies to fend for themselves but also ultimately empower the entire faculty. To my surprise, I wasn't appointed to the committee. Neither was any other African American member of the faculty, nor was any member of the faculty who was of color invited to work on the committee.

As quoted in the AAUP/ACE statement, the faculty's role in management of the institutional professoriate regarding "appointments, reappointments, decisions not to reappoint, promotions, the granting of tenure, and dismissal" demonstrates the vital role that faculty governance plays in hiring and retaining diverse faculty. On matters that are crucial to the establishment for criteria for job security and professional advancement, African Americans were frozen out. I raised my concerns regarding the lack of minority representation to the chair of the faculty—he suggested I brought up race too much—and to our chief institutional officer, who took a laissez-faire approach that this was a faculty matter, although he annually publishes a letter in which he announces that he is primarily responsible for diversity matters and an inclusive workplace. The main mechanism for registering comments on these chapters was an online response box in which comments could be left for members of the committee. However, this was not a message board or a blog, and therefore I have no idea where those messages went or who read them after I clicked "submit." My concern that the policies in question might

Racial Demographics by Percentage in Spartanburg County

	White*	Black	Hispanic/Latino
State of South Carolina	63.9	27.8	5.4
Spartanburg County	69	21	6.4
Institution: Students	56.6	27.1	4.9
Institution: Faculty	71.5	6.7	3.62

Sources: 2014 U.S. Census Quick Facts; South Carolina Commission on Higher Education Document Catalog

*Not Hispanic or Latino

have a disparate impact on protected groups, endanger their equal opportunities to advance, and might thereby expose the university to adverse legal actions were not, in my opinion, given due deliberation.

This episode is part of a larger pattern, and I reference it as a preface to my discussion of other episodes of bureaucratic racism in my institution. While the new faculty manual has yet to be adopted, governance under the current faculty manual illuminates the already problematic exclusion of minority faculty from governance—even when policies explicitly require their participation. Before I go further, however, a demographic profile of the institution in question will help establish the context in which these episodes have occurred. The place where I work is in Spartanburg, South Carolina. It is only in the racial distribution of faculty that the institution does not reflect the society generally.

The variance between the demographic of African American faculty to state, county, and student African American populations is the most seriously out of line. Only one department on campus has more than one African American tenured or on tenure track (it has two). Six of our departments and schools have one tenure-track African American faculty member, and four have none. Clearly these numbers offer one reason why African Americans might remain in the academic kitchen in this instance: there are not enough of them to go around. For African Americans to be present at all the important "tables" when consequential decisions are made, an extraordinary service burden would have to be imposed on them that would not be required of white faculty. The literature is replete with studies that illustrate how excessive service obligations imposed or accepted by minority faculty have the long-term effect of stifling their professional advancement and limiting their future prospects.[6,7] To be sure, some colleges and universities have thoughtful action plans for addressing this issue. However, the lack of African American participation—or in some cases their conscious exclusion from the committees that speak to the leadership on behalf of the faculty—exacerbates the problem.

Using actual cases from my own institution, I will elaborate on these points. These are real events. When events do not directly involve me, I have taken pains to conceal identities. I also hope that I do not appear to have shown up here to gripe. I decided to present this paper as a way of dealing intellectually with a problem that has been professionally daunting to me as an African American scholar. I hope I can successfully strike that balance by linking these anecdotes to the concept of bureaucratic racism without seeming shrill.

Our institution is part of a university system with two levels of governance. Both the local faculty manual and some systemwide policies dictate procedures. While this system has established practices to ensure diverse inclusion in matters of governance, local documents have not reinforced these policies. Examples of that breakdown between a system that encourages diversity and a local campus whose hiring practices appear out of line with that policy suggest how bureaucratic racism in faculty governance can marginalize and exclude faculty of color.

Imagine yourself for a moment as the only faculty of color in a department. Elections are being held for a representative to the promotion and tenure committee. This committee is one of the most important on any campus. Rather than the floor being opened for volunteers, it is announced that a candidate has volunteered for the position, but it is also noted that nominations would be accepted from the floor. I nominated myself. Thereafter ensued one of the most awkward moments of my professional life. A junior faculty member started calling on others who were tenured, saying, "I recall you saying that you wanted to serve." The person even suggested that we should fight to have a person who was expected to receive tenure but had not yet received it serve on the committee. "We need someone on the committee who will fight for our people," the person said. Clearly, my colleague did not believe that I was capable of filling that role. After several minutes of white colleagues failing to make eye contact with me, I withdrew my name. But I have not forgotten the humiliation and shame I felt as I realized that I was not accorded the same respect as the whites in my department. It would be bad enough, in my opinion, if this were the only instance of marginalization, but it has not been. African American faculty have not only been excluded from positions in which they could play a role in the evaluation of the quality of others but also have been disadvantaged in applying for leadership positions that are subject to faculty governance.

The AAUP 1966 statement reads, "The selection of academic deans and other chief academic officers should be the responsibility of the president with the advice of, and in consultation with, the appropriate faculty."[8] The university system policy on searches for all academic administrators requires that "search committees must be representative of the University community's diversity as it relates to race, gender, and tenure status whenever possible and practical." This has not been the case at our institution in recent history. In a recent search for a unit dean, no faculty of color from the unit served on the committee. A slate of candidates was assembled by department chairs who were all white and, with one exception, male. It was a slate created in their own racial image. Every member of this slate was approved by the overwhelmingly white faculty except for one, leaving one slot open. Both an African American full professor and a white male were nominated from the floor, and the slot was given to the white nominee. There was minority representation after it was pointed out to a senior academic officer that there were no members of color on the committee. However, all the members of color were from outside the unit. Such committee members tend to defer to the unit consensus. Faculty of color within the unit, who would work for the new officer, had no role in the selection process. They had no knowledge of what went on in the interviews. While they could ask questions in the candidate forums, they could only offer insights in the form of feedback on instruments distributed after each presentation. Regardless of the caliber of the successful candidate, a form of bureaucratic racism was revealed when no minority faculty members in the unit were granted the most intimate access to the candidate because it was not explicitly required in the local procedures. For faculty of color in the unit, it is imperative that we know that senior administrators know that we are here and understand our issues—particularly when those administrators are newcomers to the institution. It is of paramount importance that when senior administrators make decisions that affect the entire collective, they do not rely on the historical memory of the "usual suspects" to establish priorities. History and precedent are not always wise policy. *Plessy v. Ferguson* was a precedent, but one that resulted in the marginalization of African Americans from American life. That marginalization continues to reverberate all the way to the academy in ways that are not immediately clear to those within the system. The incidents at my institution, those I have already recounted and others I share in what follows, show that the application of selectivity and precedent has reinforced the marginalization of African American faculty. Indeed, in my opinion, it is selectivity with impunity that—more than any other factor—pushes African Americans into institutional kitchens.

Selectivity may be operative in other areas of academic life that impinge on minority participation in faculty governance. I could probably count on my hands, perhaps just one hand, the number of African American faculty candidates who have been invited on campus visits in my thirteen years at my institution. In recent addresses to the faculty, our chief institutional officer lamented the low numbers of African American faculty. He has appointed an individual to take lead on addressing this problem; however, without resources it is questionable whether anything substantive can be done to correct the dearth of African American faculty. Our state budget is in crisis. Diversity is seen as a luxury instead of as crucial part of the institution's long-term plans.

So what can be done? Even in hard financial times, a collegial working environment can go a long way toward diversifying faculty and creating a critical mass of faculty of color who can assume governance responsibilities. One of the greatest tools for recruiting minority faculty is existing minority faculty who are satisfied. When faculty of color feel valued and included, they are more likely to be forceful ambassadors for the institution and may contribute positively to minority faculty recruitment and retention. Conversely, when faculties of color do not feel valued, it may be manifested through attrition. Just recently, we lost a well-qualified African American woman as two different departments dithered over who would evaluate her for tenure. The chair of the department into which she was originally hired was so disciplinary bound (at least in her case) and so discouraging about her chances for achieving tenure that she sought and successfully attained employment elsewhere. She came to the institution with a strong record of achievement. When she announced her resignation, the institution's efforts to "match" the offer were, in my personal opinion, half-hearted and clearly—given her decision to depart—too little, too late.

Bold leadership in both faculty and administration is required to increase the number of African American faculty to critical numbers. Senior leadership exacerbates instances of bureaucratic racism by standing behind faculty decisions to "respect" faculty collective prerogatives even when there is clear evidence that these prerogatives are disproportionally damaging to the opportunities and morale of minority faculty. Their passivity reinforces the idea that conscious considerations of diversity have no place in governance of the faculty collective.

Faculty of color also contribute to the problem. I can attest, from personal experience, to the physical and psychological costs of entering the "trenches." Manifestations of stress as physical ailments and depression, ostracism, and being branded as a malcontent are all powerful disincentives to speak out. Therefore, as a means of personal survival and to avoid isolation, faculty of color sometimes retreat into silence, which does not necessarily alleviate the physical and psychological strains. Bureaucratic racism thrives in such uncontested environments.

FACULTY GOVERNANCE AND faculty diversity are intertwined. Springer and Westerhaus state that a homogenous faculty not only fails to represent the diversity of views and experiences crucial to a broad education but also leaves an institution vulnerable to damaging discrimination lawsuits.[9] Such lawsuits are both expensive for the institution and damaging to faculty resources and morale. Having a diverse faculty limits such claims, both by students and faculty, and an easily observable commitment to diversity by the institution and the faculty in both policies and hires provides a strong defense to claims of discrimination. A diverse faculty, especially one that has bought into good diversity policies and commitments of the institution, is also less likely to engage in the kind of discriminatory activity that creates legal liability for the institution.

While the Springer and Westerhaus article focuses on the legal benefits of diversity, I believe other components of their argument provide compelling justification for faculty diversity as a means to improve shared governance. Diversity in points of view and in curricula follow the inclusion of minority faculty—particularly in areas outside the hard sciences. Participation of faculty of color in meaningful ways on important institutional committees holds the potential for positive impact on morale as regularized interaction with faculty of color by the majority faculty may engender greater understanding of the obstacles faculty of color face and may result in the crafting of policies that are inclusive and equitable. It should also contribute to respect for the abilities of such minority faculty.

Contrary to the notion posited by collective statements by academic advocacy bodies such as the AAUP and ACE, a monolithic faculty mindset does not exist. Practices of shared governance should not merely focus on faculty sharing governance with other groups of stakeholders. It should also focus on the sharing of governance opportunities between subgroups within the faculty collective to ensure diverse participation. This can only be achieved when the wall between the kitchen and the table is removed and faculty of color are given a seat at the table.

Notes

1. See, for example, Jaimes, "American Racism."

2. AAUP, "Statement on Government of Colleges and Universities."

3. When I presented this paper at the 2010 AAUP conference on governance, Larry Gerber, chair of the organization's Committee on College and University Governance, said the statement was a compromise between the two organizations and would be very difficult to amend to the satisfaction of both groups.

4. AAUP, "National AAUP Committees"; AAUP, "The Historically Black Colleges and Universities"; ACE/AAUP, "Does Diversity Make a Difference?"; and AAUP, "Resources on Minority Serving Institutions."

5. AAUP, "Shared Governance, Junior Faculty, and HBCUs"; AAUP, "Faculty Governance at Historically Black Colleges and Universities"; AAUP, "How to Diversify the Faculty"; ACE/AAUP, "Does Diversity Make a Difference?"

6. University of South Carolina Upstate, "Common Data Set."

7. See Aguirre, "Women and Minority Faculty in the Academic Workplace"; Cox, "Women of Color Faculty at the University of Michigan"; Griffin and Reddick, "Surveillance and Sacrifice"; and MacLean, "Participation in a Professional Association's Annual National Conference." For campus policies, see University of Missouri–Kansas City, "Selected Recommendations for Supporting Women and Minority Faculty," and Indiana University–Bloomington, "Tenure Guide."

8. AAUP, "Statement on Government of Colleges and Universities."

9. AAUP, "How to Diversify Faculty."

Contingent Diversity, Contingent Faculty

Or, Musings of a Lowly Adjunct

Wilson Santos
Full Sail University

Editor's note—Before the story of Medieval History Ph.D. Melissa Bruninga-Matteau was featured in the Chronicle of Higher Education[1] *and we learned that PhDs could be on food stamps, before the number 70 percent became perhaps the most ubiquitous number in conversations about the makeup of the professoriate,[2] and before Adjunct Walkout Day (February 2015), I knew the question of how the contingent crisis is experienced by faculty of color needed to be part of this volume. Trying to learn more about the issue was difficult, though the AAUP's 2010 report offered important figures and recommended best practices for ensuring some kind of equitable workplace for the most vulnerable members of the faculty. In 2011, I wrote the following on the companion blog to this anthology:*

> *It is impossible to talk about the practices and issues related to race and tenure in any meaningful way without considering how much universities rely on contingent faculty to prop up their educational missions. Women and faculty of color are disproportionally clustered in contingent positions, and the majority of tenured faculty spend at least part of their careers in contingent positions—as adjunct or part-time faculty, visiting professors, postdoctoral fellows and, of course, as teaching assistants.*

This chapter offers perspectives from three adjunct faculty of color with varying relationships to the academy: a full PhD, a doctoral candidate, and Wilson Santos as he was deciding whether to continue graduate work beyond his master's degree.

I asked Santos to write about his experiences, and this essay reflects how he came to understand the exploitative nature of adjunct culture. He asked the kinds of questions whose answers at the time he wrote this essay were only of interest to those most affected by the contingent economic model. Santos is a former graduate student, and when I asked him to write for this anthology, he was my colleague, teaching in Montclair State University's first-year writing program. Occupy Wall Street had hit its stride, and Wilson told me about visit-

ing Zucotti Park. We talked about the 1 percent without really discussing the vast inequities in the system of higher education. He was at a crossroads, trying to decide whether or not to pursue an MFA, experimenting with different narrative voices in his writing, and looking at the academy with clearer eyes, especially at a time when "Occupy" was on the lips of many workers. Wilson presented me with a complete essay with facts and figures, and a critical but evenhanded assessment of how tenured faculty like myself are complicit in this system so long as we say nothing. I had been reading about faculty members like Dionne Bensonsmith and talking to colleagues from around the country about the experiences of contingent faculty, including a doctoral student whose identity I am protecting so that her candor doesn't cost her her job. With Wilson's permission I have included their stories here.

Bensonsmith was interviewed for the student-run Claremont Port Side *after her class at Scripps College realized that she was on a short-term contract. The doctoral candidate (Candidate X) was preparing to defend a dissertation written in anthropology at an Ivy League institution when I asked her to share her adjunct experience in a major U.S. city. This essay reflects not only the facts and figures Wilson found as he reflected on his experiences but also the shifts and struggles that are the daily routine of contingent faculty. Whereas the other contributors in this collection could report promotions and publications over the course of this project, those who write in this essay have moved from job to job, trying to make their work matter without any of the institutional support tenure-line and tenured faculty take for granted. Each narrative turns on understanding the degree to which adjunct culture curtails professional and personal goals.*

Contingent faculty across the country have made gains in some ways—more are unionizing, and more are gaining ground in the effort to participate in departmental governance. National institutions like the Modern Language Association have been challenged to address this issue more substantively than they have in the past. Despite these gains, the underlying dysfunction that adjunct culture reveals still has not been addressed in any material way. The three stories here show what is at stake and what it costs to be part of higher education without the stability and institutional support that all faculty require and deserve.

Recently, a former professor I took classes with as an undergraduate passed me along the hallway of one of our university's newest high-tech academic buildings. Surprised to see me, he asked, "Hey Wilson. What ya doing here?" Happy to see his familiar face, I gleefully responded, "I'm teaching here now. As an adjunct." As he walked away, he chuckled and shot back, "Great for you. Now you're really being exploited." We both laughed it off. "Yeah. Exactly," I agreed, without having given his comment much prior thought. His tone did not offend me. I knew he was more sincere than sarcastic. Since he is a self-described Marxist, it came as no surprise to find him in solidarity with the lowly adjuncts. At the time, I was wearing a slick black jacket and red T-shirt with an image of Marx printed on the chest, a black bar covering his eyes and underneath written, "the working man is a sucka." The irony of his remark juxtaposed against the apparent statement I was making with my red T-shirt did not elude me. Instead, it got me thinking, "Does he know something I only casually thought of before?" I began to ask questions.

What do you mean I'm being exploited?

I certainly don't feel exploited. Nor do I feel oppressed by my supervisors in the first-year writing program. I don't feel the crack of the whip at my back. In fact, the treatment here has been absolutely cordial and very supportive. Everyone in the department seems to be in solidarity with one main focus in mind—to educate students. Overall, the students have also been very receptive to my teaching style. Based on the overwhelmingly positive student evaluations at the end of each semester, and dare I say, the 100-percent positive comments on ratemyprofessor, students seem to think favorably of me. It's a good feeling to receive e-mails from students saying, "I just wanted to write this e-mail to thank you not only for teaching me how to set up an argument, or cite sources, but also for helping to know that I can do anything I truly work hard for. You have made a huge impact on all of us and for that you have become my favorite teacher at MSU." My experience as a teacher has been really quite amazing. So what did he mean, "Now you're really being exploited" when I love my work and always look forward to teaching my classes?

In a political science class titled "Race, Gender, and Welfare State Politics" that Dionne Bensonsmith was teaching, she decided to include her own experience in the class's discussion about contingent faculty. Bensonsmith has a PhD in Political Science from the Maxwell School of Citizenship and Public Affairs at Syracuse, a degree she earned while working full-time in different administrative positions. She's used to multitasking, perhaps more than other doctoral candidates, but conducting a job for a full-time position while teaching that semester (Spring 2012) had proven especially difficult. So during a lecture on the structure of contingent labor she decided to explain to her students her own experience as a contingent worker—recognizing that, at first glance, she seemed the very opposite of one. In addition to wanting to provide an explanation for the juggling act she was managing she explains that it was "hard to teach that class and not be angry about what's going on in higher education." Her explanation about the experiences of some 70 percent of faculty teaching in higher education resulted in an article about the issue written for Claremont Port Side, *an online publication run by students.*

Despite my sunny attitude, I know there is a sharp distinction between the gratifications of teaching versus the poor working conditions lowly adjuncts endure. For one, the pay is very low. According to a 2004 report by the American Federation of Teachers (AFT), "Across all institutional types, the average part-time/adjunct faculty member earned an annual base salary of $9,745 in 2003–04, or $2,758 per course. In comparison, full-time faculty members earned an average annual salary of $58,306, or $11,051 per course."[3] The report went on to note, "Part-time faculty members at two-year community colleges, four-year comprehensive colleges and public research universities earn between $5,200 and $16,000 less per course than do full-time tenured/tenure-track faculty members."[4] Since the publication of this study in 2004, a more recent 2010 AFT survey of part-time adjunct faculty shows that these numbers have remained relatively the same or have only seen moderate increases for both part-time and full-time faculty.[5] All of this while administrators' and college presidents' salaries have gone up dramatically. But let's not even go there yet. So why is there such a large discrepancy between adjunct pay and full-time tenured and tenure-track pay, especially when many adjunct faculty have PhDs? First, we must acknowledge two points here. First, tenured professors do more than just teach. Nonetheless, looking closely at this staggering difference in pay for service (even given the additional service requirements of full-time faculty) makes the system seem quite unjustifiable and even exploitative. The terms *livable wages* and *fair compensation* keep coming to mind.

According to the Claremont Port Side, *Bensonsmith makes $7,000 per class with extra compensation for advising student theses. Her annual salary is around $30,000 per year, a large portion of which goes to paying her health insurance. For non–tenure-track professors who teach part time—fewer than four courses—health benefits are not guaranteed by Scripps. In comparison, an article in the February 2012 issue of the* Port Side *found that Scripps's highest-paid professor makes a base salary of $142,939. Bensonsmith told student* *reporter Jean Larsen, "I have a PhD but . . . I make the same amount of money as a friend with a high school diploma. We have reached a very perverted point in the system."*[6]

Before my encounter in the hallway, I knew that financially I was struggling to meet my bills every month. I didn't need a Marxist to point that out to me. I knew I was making more money when I was freelancing as a graphic designer and hustling on the weekends to get DJ gigs at clubs and lounges. I knew I had taken a dramatic cut in pay, but I had convinced myself that this was a necessary sacrifice in order to gain experience for a more permanent position in the future. But for how long can an individual sacrifice? And what guarantees does one have at the end? Advancement opportunities for adjunct faculty are nearly nil, and the retention rate is very low—a factor that probably makes it easier for institutions to exploit contingent faculty. It's hard to organize academic nomads. In a 2008 study conducted at Colorado Mountain College, researchers found that more than 30 percent of adjuncts only stay five semesters or less, while another 20 percent stay fewer than ten semesters. Sixty percent of respondents answered that they work as adjuncts because they love teaching and another 55 percent because they love working with students; only 18 percent cited the money as a retention factor.[7] The 2010 AFT survey demonstrates that these figures are consistent with the national trend.[8] The Colorado study also notes the high costs associated with the need to recruit and hire new adjuncts every semester and recommends reasonable steps toward retaining and assimilating adjuncts into permanent positions. But the road to moving up from part-time to a full-time, nontenured position can generally take several years, if it happens at all, and when one does get such a position, contracts at public institutions in New Jersey, for instance, are usually state mandated and can only last three years. As an adjunct, one must ask, "What is the likelihood of gaining a full-time, permanent position? And how long will it take?" The answers to these questions are bleak. And depressing. It is up to individuals to determine how long they can sacrifice, keep their eyes on the prize, and still remain motivated one semester after another. And so I ask myself the bigger question, "How much longer can I afford to be an adjunct?"

As long as I'm still physically and mentally healthy and I can cover my bills from month to month, I can probably sustain myself for a few more semesters. But that really depends on whether I'm physically healthy. The truth is, the situation is so precarious that I feel I'm just a car accident away from total ruin. It only takes one small accident or physical illness to prevent me from working, totally destroying my ability to provide for my family. At most institutions, adjuncts don't have benefits. We don't have health insurance. There's no workman's comp waiting to sustain us while we recover from an injury. And so I walk through life very carefully, trying to avoid the slightest risk to my health and body. It's come to the point where I'm considering wearing a motorcycle helmet to drive my car or just to cross the streets of New York City. Already I look both ways four times before I cross. But what happens when one is physically incapacitated or succumbs to those common happenings of life like a bad cavity that has become infected and is painful enough to require a root canal? Recently, I had just this situation. And yes, you guessed it: adjuncts don't have dental plans either. So what happens to the poor when they don't have dental plans or can't afford the $1,400 cash for a root canal? The toothless poor are not all crackheads as often assumed; they just can't afford to keep their teeth. After enduring the pain for over a year, I came close to losing one of my own recently, but was lucky enough to scramble together the cash for a root canal. These are the hard truths and tough decisions one must make as a low-income earner. Why should an educated individual, charged with the all-important task of educating America's youth, who in turn pay outrageously high tuition rates for their education, have to make such decisions? That professor in the hallway is really starting to make sense now.

Doctoral Candidate X talks about another kind of vulnerability. Working as an adjunct in a university system with satellite campuses means that she is often juggling the paperwork of different paychecks. One semester, several years ago, she missed paperwork that would have informed her that she wasn't being paid the correct amount. The result is that the university owes her $18,000, but because she didn't file the claim in time, technically the university doesn't have to pay. If she raises a fuss, she risks being seen as a troublemaker. She also risks being exposed because she is currently teaching at multiple satellite campuses, something she's not supposed to do. She fears drawing attention to herself, being found out, and losing all of her income. She says bitterly, "I'm owed all of this money, but since I didn't get the paperwork on time, I can't fight for it without risking my job."

But Why are There so Many Adjuncts?

If being an adjunct is such a horrible job, why are there so many? At first glance, the answer is simple: because people need work and graduate students preparing for teaching careers can benefit from developing and teaching their own courses.

Doctoral Candidate X explains that when she started working on her doctorate in anthropology, she also started as an adjunct instructor in English at two other schools while also serving as a teaching assistant in her home department. She explains that at one institution she has been "allowed to write and develop [her] own course and [has] taught it for the past four years." At the other school where she teaches, she reports having "received invaluable mentorship from senior faculty members—who have assisted in both course development and job searches." Bensonsmith did not start off on the contingent track, though her path to Scripps included diversity fellowships that offer valuable research time for new PhD's but may ultimately hinder their tenure-track job prospects. As part of a concerted effort to increase diversity in its faculty and curriculum, Grinnell College hired thirteen faculty of color. Bensonsmith was one of those faculty members. After four years, when it became clear that the college and Bensonsmith weren't a good fit, she decided to leave. The term fit is as vague as the notion of collegial, but it can be the deciding factor in personnel decisions, and faculty who are in contingent positions are the most vulnerable. In addition to facing obstacles of introducing what to Grinnell was a new and emerging field in political science (public policy) to a department that was open to the new field in theory but not in practice, and the typical negative student evaluations that people of color often contend with, Bensonsmith was isolated in a small Midwestern town. Bensonsmith describes an ethos familiar to anyone who has been affiliated with selective liberal arts colleges and the pressure of what she aptly labels "soft service." Soft service is not the service institutions rely on to run (student advisement, personnel hiring and evaluation, special event planning), but the social expectations one must adhere to in order to be considered collegial: attending christenings, throwing showers, participating in potlucks, and students expecting baked cookies before evaluations.

Of course, the contingency model is deeply embedded in colleges and universities across the country. Most current data show contingency faculty, which consists of mainly adjuncts, make up an average of 70 to 75 percent of college instructors nationwide. At some institutions, the number is much higher. At Colorado Mountain College (CMC), for instance, "According to data taken from the CMC payroll system, individuals in an adjunct role represent 85–87 percent of the total CMC faculty during the academic year. This includes all individuals paid through an adjunct faculty account number."[9] This figure closely reflects what one would typically find at a community college. This also represents a dramatic increase in adjunct instructors up from around 30 to 35 percent in the late 1970s. Over the past forty years, colleges and universities have reversed the faculty makeup from a majority tenured pool to a majority adjunct pool. Tenured professors are quickly becoming an endangered species while the current system slowly replaces tenured professors with an army of adjuncts with low pay and no benefits. Given this discouraging trend, what motivation is there for a prospective professor to seek permanency within the university? And why have so many professors consequently settled neatly and quietly into their roles as lowly adjuncts?

This last question prompts me to consider Dr. Martin Luther King Jr.'s assertion that oppressed people typically deal with their oppression in three characteristic ways; the most popular stance is acquiescence. King argued that too often the oppressed resign themselves to their oppression and ultimately become conditioned to it, therefore accepting exploitation as a normal way of life. He argued, "To accept passively an unjust system is to cooperate with that system; thereby the oppressed become as evil as the oppressor. Noncooperation with evil is as much a moral obligation as is cooperation with good."[10] Such is the case with adjuncts and tenured faculty, who by virtue of their silence and cooperation with an unjust system have enabled such a system to thrive and create the current hostile working environment for the majority of college instructors. If the decline of tenure continues as we have seen in the past decades, then we may very well see the end of tenure outright in another 30 to 40 years. What does this mean for the integrity of the college professor and the students they teach? Ultimately, who pays the price?

Without a doubt, the students are the ones who bear the final burden of this devaluation of instruction as the primary goal of the university. As the university moves toward a corporate model, the instruction of students becomes a secondary focus. While registering for classes, students frequently ask me, "What courses are you teaching next semester, Professor?" Regretfully, I respond, "I don't know if I'll even be here." As an undergraduate, I recall taking two, sometimes three courses with professors I found best fit my needs. I developed close student–teacher relationships with many of them. They served as mentors and role models and counseled me on future plans. As an adjunct, I don't have the capability of doing the same for my students. When a Latino student recently told me, "You've changed my life. I'll never be able to see things the same again," it was discouraging to know that I could have done more for him and countless others had we been given the chance to develop that student–teacher relationship I once enjoyed. This revolving-door adjunct culture does little to encourage instructors to engage with students beyond merely the one class they encounter each other in. It also forces the best professors to look for financial security outside the university. A good quality teacher, who is keenly aware he or she is a good quality teacher, is unlikely to settle for a low pay scale knowing adequate livable wages can be secured somewhere else, even if it means changing professions.

After her contract ends, Bensonsmith discusses leaving the academy. She doesn't want to be a pure researcher, but she has a sharp eye on her prospects. Like many other PhDs seeking the increasingly elusive tenure-track position, she can see colleges and universities shifting away from tenure-track models and towards short-term contracts. Sometimes they come with alluring titles like "Teaching Fellowships," but the end result is similar—an unstable professoriate. As she points out, "The people who are hurt really are the students," and to the student reporter she explains, "You're going to suffer for it. I'm going to leave and you're going to want a recommendation, you're going to want to keep ties." The student reporter gets it and explains: "Students benefit from secure faculty who no longer have to spend time job-hunting, who put down roots in the community and who can afford to invest extra time in students."[11]

I can actually see the progress most students make from the time they first enter my classroom until finals. Because I am a Latino man, teaching in a department that is mostly dominated by white women (I am the only Latino man from a group of nearly seventy instructors in my department with only one other Black male), students of color are particularly drawn to me and benefit most from my presence in the classroom. But my current financial situation probably won't allow me to return next semester, depriving many students—but more specifically, students of color—from having access to a positive role model.

I've already had to make that tough decision once.

While teaching at Essex County College in Newark, New Jersey, I found myself in an all-too familiar environment, where 95 percent of my students were Black and Latino. Because I graduated from East Side High School in Paterson, New Jersey (remember the movie *Lean on Me?*), I knew firsthand the miseducation these students typically enter the college with and the lack of role models present in many of their lives. I knew that these types of students would reap the most benefit by having me as their instructor, and I really wanted to help them. Regrettably, I could not afford to return there after only one semester. If the pay scale at a four-year college seems low based on the figures I cited, then the deplorable wages at this community college, which fall way lower than the national average, are really quite depressing. By way of comparison, at Montclair State University where I currently teach, a part-time adjunct earns $3,600 per course, with a maximum number of courses they can teach capped at only two per semester. At Essex County College, a part-time adjunct earns $1,800 per class. Sad, right? But wait, it gets worse. When one factors in class sizes and class time, the gap between pay dramatically increases. At Montclair State University, a typical writing class is capped at nineteen students, with courses meeting twice a week for a total of 2.5 hours. At Essex County, writing courses are listed with a maximum of thirty students, but enrollment easily ends up with thirty-eight to forty students, with classes that meet three hours a week. A basic calculation of these comparative figures shows that a professor at the county college is essentially expected to work twice as hard for half the pay, ending with compensation that is equivalent to 25 percent that of an adjunct at a state university.

This staggering difference also cuts right through racial lines, since there are more African American and Latino teachers working at community colleges, while, as I already noted, the opposite seems to be true of four-year colleges. Let's compare Essex County College with Montclair State University, for instance. According to the fall 2010 "Annual Institutional Profile Report," at Montclair State University there were 383 full-time (tenured and nontenured) white professors on record compared to only seventy-one Black and Latinos combined.[12] While at Essex County College, fifty-eight full-time professors were white and fifty-seven were Black and Latino, an even fifty-fifty split. The data on adjunct hires by race are nearly impossible to find. Neither school keeps track of the racial characteristics of its part-time faculty, which makes up the majority at both schools—62 percent at Montclair State and 82 percent at Essex County. This is clearly a result of the transient nature of contingent faculty. They simply can't keep track of the majority of their faculty because the retention rates for part-time faculty are very low. Most adjuncts only stay on a few semesters at any given school. The 2010 AFT survey, however, shows that 84 percent of adjuncts are white, but only 4 percent are African Americans, 3 percent Hispanics, and 2 percent Asians.[13] It's a really sad feeling to know that there is little room within the system that allows me and countless other good teachers a path toward stable and permanent employment doing what we love. Based on the data I just presented, which is the national trend, I will likely be marginalized along with other teachers of color and relegated to teaching at a community college for much lower wages. Under the current system, adjuncts, students, and even tenured professors suffer since their numbers continually dwindle as a result.

Over the years, there have been many well-intentioned moves to improve the conditions of adjuncts by trying to award them fair compensation and adequate benefits for the important service they provide. Organizations such as the American Federation of Teachers, the American Association of University Professors, and the Association of American Colleges and Universities have all stressed the need to further assimilate contingency faculty within the college community. Other, more vocal activist organizations devoted solely to advocating on behalf of contingency faculty—the Coalition of Contingent Academic Labor and the New Faculty Majority (NFM) come to mind—have been at the forefront of the battle for equality. Maria Maisto, NFM's board president, claims, "While attempts to 'integrate' faculty more effectively into the life of the institution have become more commonplace, institutions making these efforts have largely ignored bread-and-butter issues like salary, benefits, access to due process, academic freedom, job security, and professional advancement."[14] All of these efforts appear to be too little, too late. Although the conversation is being had, is conversation enough to bring about change? This system of exploitation has become so deeply entrenched within universities that it will take a vocal army of adjuncts to fight the righteous fight but with little chance of ever being victorious against the corporate machine that has become the university. In her article "Adjunct Leaders Consider Strategies to Force Change," Colleen Flaherty claims the plight of the adjunct "isn't getting the traction it deserves at the institutional level." According to Flaherty, "Matt

Williams, the vice president of the New Faculty Majority, agreed, calling lack of public awareness of the adjunct issue the biggest obstacle to fixing it."[15] So how do we bring about more public awareness? Perhaps more unionizing efforts like those being pushed by NFM or its current attempts to recruit student organizations that are "sympathetic to the quality-of-life issues" plaguing adjuncts. Or maybe we simply need some concrete action, like some 1960s-style mass protests spread across campuses. Unfortunately, the majority of adjuncts are either unaware of their exploitation—like I was—or have basically resigned themselves to an unjust system they feel powerless to change. The system has succeeded with its public relations campaign, convincing us and the public at large that these cuts to faculty salary are necessary in order to deal with budget woes, that the price of doing the business of education requires sacrifices from all sides, including yearly increases in tuition. With a close scrutiny of this business model, one quickly sees the obvious discrepancies. The numbers just don't add up.

If Tuition Goes Up Every Year, Where Does All the Money Go?

A peculiar thing has happened to the university. To deal with budget problems, universities have been "forced" to save money by cutting services—mostly by replacing full-time faculty with contingency faculty. While the number of full-time tenured professors has gradually decreased over the past forty years, data show that tuition has steadily increased. According to a study by Vance Fried, published on the American Enterprise Institute website, "Over the past two decades, the cost of a college education has risen dramatically. Tuition and fees have increased at twice the rate of inflation, rising more quickly than market goods or services and outstripping the growth in family incomes."[16] But if tuition keeps going up and teacher salaries keep going down, then where is the money going? Certainly, it is not being invested in instructional programs; if it were, we would be looking at an increase in teacher salaries, not a decrease. In fact, the opposite is true. As noted by Richard Vedder, professor of economics at Ohio University, "Data from the National Center for Education Statistics show that most colleges (but not community or liberal-arts colleges) have reduced the share of resources devoted to undergraduate teaching, spending more on other things—research, administration, student services (luxurious recreational and student centers), athletics, etc. Only about twenty-one cents of each new inflation-adjusted dollar per student since 1976 actually went for 'instruction.'"[17] The university has, in essence, lost sight of its main focus—namely, the education of its students. By putting more resources toward sports programs, recreation centers that rival huge chains like L.A. Fitness, modern student centers, cafes, manicured lawns, inflated administration salaries, and aggressive PR and marketing campaigns, the university has shifted from being a bastion of knowledge and learning to what Mark Edmundson calls a "retirement spread for the young." In his essay "On the Uses of a Liberal Education," Edmundson notes how college catalogs in the late sixties "were austere affairs full of professors' credentials and course descriptions," while today, most admissions offices operate more like marketing departments, highlighting all the bells and whistles that come with a student's tuition while deemphasizing genuine education.[18] I recently asked my own students what their experience was like when touring the campus during new student orientation, and all responded that they were shown the modern recreation center, the twenty-four-hour on-campus diner, the numerous fraternities and sororities they could join, the great sports teams, and, yes, even the fact that we have a Starbucks on campus. None were taken to the library or an actual lecture class in progress, nor did they have a chance to meet or even speak to a professor to get an idea of what education at the university is essentially like. The focus of the orientation was instead on how much fun they could have. At some public colleges, only 25 to 35 percent of student tuition fees actually go toward faculty salaries, while some private institutions spend a deplorable 13 to 15 percent on instructional services. Clearly, most of the money from tuition fees and state funding at public colleges is being diverted from what should be the primary mission of an institution of higher learning and toward noninstructional fluff.

And while colleges have cut faculty salaries by virtue of eliminating most full-time faculty positions, administration and college president salaries have continued to climb. In her recent *New York Times* article, Tamar Lewin points out that in "the decade from 1999–2000 to 2009–10, average presidential pay at the [fifty] wealthiest universities increased by 75 percent, to $876,792, while professorial pay increased 14 percent, to $179, 970."[19] These increases were simultaneous with reductions in the number of full-time faculty, their ranks now filling with more than 70 percent part-timers who earn an average of only $9,000 to $14,000 per year. It's also worth noting, according to a review of federal tax records

(2008–2009) by the *Chronicle of Higher Education* that presidents of more than thirty private colleges earned well over $1 million in compensation, with the top salary going as high as $4,786,830 to the former president of Touro College, Bernard Lander.[20] I'm not "hating on" Mr. Lander or the million-dollar presidents or administrators earning six figures, but after following the money trail and discovering the decentralization and commoditization of college as a corporate institution, the exploitation of the lowly adjunct really becomes quite apparent. Why isn't the money trickling down to where it matters most—student instructional services? Students and parents either don't realize or don't care that their yearly tuition increases are not buying knowledge, only prestige. In fact, on the first day of class, I usually ask my students as they introduce themselves, why are they in college? Most students answer, "To get a degree," while maybe, if I'm lucky, one might say, "to learn and be educated." There is a distinction to be made between being educated and earning a degree. Clearly, there is a disconnect between what should be the role of the university and what the university actually represents, which has become a mere extension of consumer pop culture, selling degrees as products to eager student customers.

"Will I Have to Go Back on the Food Stamp Line?"

Here I am, a colored man, holding a master's degree, teaching at one of the top public colleges in the state of New Jersey, possibly heading back to the food stamp line to join countless other people of color seeking public assistance. As a child, I grew up on welfare. Being one of eight children raised by a Dominican immigrant mother with a third-grade education and an absent father who came and went at his leisure, my family relied on social services for sustenance. I remember being embarrassed to shop at the local bodega in the Bronx, with the colorful paper money the city issued us in booklets. I vowed then at a young age that when I grew up I would be self-sufficient and never rely on welfare. For most of my life I've kept that vow. That is, until I decided to return to school to earn a master's degree. Sounds ironic? That's because it is.

Before returning to school thirteen years after earning a BA, I carved a modest living mostly as an artist, making decent money as a graphic designer or producing music and spoken-word songs that earned me royalties and licensing fees, promoting parties in New York City clubs, and traveling around the world doing DJ gigs. Although I had no health insurance or other benefits that come with working in the mainstream, I was self-reliant and independent. During the last semester as a graduate student, I found myself very tight for money. Since I am a single father, raising a son, now seven years old, I could not afford to go without food and health insurance. I felt like Will Smith in *The Pursuit of Happyness*. Putting my personal pride aside, I went on the food stamp line and was awarded assistance for six months, with the option of renewing after that period. That assistance helped me get through graduate school, but I didn't return after the six months to renew.

Today, I find myself facing a similar decision. I'm tight for money. Do I have to go back on the food stamp line? The answer is probably yes, although I'm trying desperately to avoid that. But maybe for at least another six months until I find something more stable. I keep returning to the question, "Can I really afford to work as an adjunct and for how much longer?" The sad reality is that, like most adjuncts, I really love teaching. I love going to work week after week, and I know the students benefit from me being there. Some might argue that a master's degree no longer holds much value, that an adjunct should not get paid what a tenured professor does. This might be true. But one thing is clear: students in large part do not distinguish between adjunct, part-time, assistant, associate, or tenure-track or full-time tenured professor. They never notice the difference, nor do they really care, as long as the professor is doing his or her job by engaging them in the classroom. It should also be noted that if adjuncts do indeed offer less value, then why has the university placed so many instruction hours in the hands of adjuncts? (For example, across its twenty-four campuses, City University of New York employs approximately 10,500 adjuncts, compared to only 6,700 full-time faculty.[21]) The basic answer is that colleges fill their ranks with adjuncts simply to save money, as I have already asserted. But the truth is that adjuncts do offer tremendous value to the student's learning, and they'd offer even more if they could only be treated equally and granted respectable livable wages and benefits. How can anyone be expected to make a living earning $14,000 a year with no benefits and little room for advancement? It's just not humanly possible in America, and it should be considered morally reprehensible by the entire academic community—from students to university presidents.

In theory, I could probably avoid returning to the food stamp line again in the future if only I went back to get a PhD to increase the likelihood of landing a full-time gig at some college or university. But when one reads stories of other graduates and PhDs such as Dr. Tony Yang, Melissa Bruninga-Matteau, Elliot Stegall, and Kisha Hawkins-Sledge—all standing on the food stamp line while working as adjuncts at multiple colleges—or considers the fact that current trends point toward a hostile environment and accelerated declines in full-time hires, then suddenly the prospect of going for a postgrad education looks more like a five-year risk rather than a five-year investment.[22] The truth is, there is little chance I will continue as an adjunct much longer unless some dramatic changes come to the now exploitative system. But the likelihood of that is as good as me winning the Mega Millions—1 in 176 million.

Doctoral Candidate X, close to defending her dissertation, is hopeful: "I plan on being an adjunct until I defend my dissertation, which will hopefully be this year. I have not had a negative experience in being a part-time employee, but I view older colleagues who have been Adjuncts for twenty to thirty years with a sense of dread. Partly because in many ways they have, to quote Wordsworth, "given [their] hearts away" to a place that pays them very little and is now threatening to take away their health insurance. Youth has a way of allowing us to forget the necessity of health insurance, but as we age it becomes ever more important, which leaves many in a vulnerable position. In short, I do not want to wake up twenty years from now and still be an adjunct."

Running into that professor in the hallway was a wake-up call. He was one of the professors during my first semester who I could say was instrumental in changing my life forever. I recall telling him then the same thing one of my own students told me recently: "I will never see things the same way again." Here we are, seventeen years later, now colleagues, passing each other so briefly down the hallway, and with a simple comment he sends me again questioning the status quo only to find the answers disheartening, but so necessary to ask, while more clearly revealing to me the truth of that red T-shirt I still proudly wear, with the phrase printed on my chest: "The working man is a sucka."

I Am a Working Man, But I *Ain't No Sucka*. (An Update)

As I revisit this essay, more than two years after writing it, I'm taken back by the prophetic quality of the piece. The fears, concerns, and vulnerabilities I was feeling as I wrote the initial draft seem eerily real as I read it over and realize that my fears and concerns have almost all come to fruition. Of course, I had to leave my position as an adjunct at Montclair

State University just as I predicted I would. I could no longer afford to stay on as a part-time employee with no job security and no benefits to boot. I refused to go back on the food stamp line. And so I've become another transient statistic of the university's adjunct majority that they don't even keep track of, just another ghost who passed by for a few semesters. I have since accepted a full-time position teaching online English courses at a for-profit university in Florida. Call me a practical Marxist, but the pressing necessities of life dictate that we seek and acquire financial stability, and with little promise of advancement as an adjunct, I've had to make the same tough decision countless others have made before me—and that many will continue to make after me. But the decision was a no-brainer.

Two years earlier I wrote, "The truth is, the situation is so precarious that I feel I'm just a car accident away from total ruin. It only takes one small accident or physical illness to prevent me from working, totally destroying my ability to provide for my family." The shocking twist is that the car accident and physical illness I had feared both actually happened. Only two months after I wrote the initial draft of this essay, I was afflicted by daily spells of vertigo. The affliction got so bad that I could barely stand and pace around the room lecturing to my classes without feeling as if the floor was sinking beneath me and I'd fall and collapse at any given moment. I even had to quit one of my part-time DJ jobs at a restaurant. Getting to school to teach everyday became an intense physical challenge. Of course, I never told my students about my severe dizzy spells, nor did I tell my supervisor for fear of being let go with no workman's comp as a safety net. I simply toughed it out day after day and pressed forward, working under conditions that any full-time, tenured faculty member would easily have taken medical leave for. But I was not afforded that luxury, even though I performed similar work as they did.

Later, on November 6, 2012 (election day), while still dealing with vertigo, I was driving to campus a half hour early to meet with one of my students when another driver blew through a stop sign and crashed into my driver's side door, causing my car to flip and roll over, landing back on three wheels—the fourth wheel broke off and flew onto someone's lawn. My first instinct was to look toward the back seat to make sure my seven-year-old son was okay. But then I realized I had already dropped him off at school and was grateful for that. In shock from the collision, my car mangled and filling with white smoke, I crawled out the broken passenger side window, still not fully aware of what just happened. I was taken to the hospital and released later that day. Two days after the accident, with a bruised back and neck and random vertigo spells, I was again walking across campus, lugging my heavy briefcase to class because—as you already know—I didn't have medical benefits and I simply could not afford to be out from work. It turns out the accident left me with a bulging disc and a herniated disc on my lower back and three herniations on my neck. Regardless, I had to endure the pain in order to feed my family and pay my bills. Shortly after, I got a call from the for-profit university offering me a full-time position. One month after that, I was on a plane flying toward financial stability, and two years later, I'm still employed here.

Doctoral Candidate X has now completed her degree, but the job market and the arrival of a child has led her to consider employment opportunities outside of the academy. It's not an easy decision. She has built solid relationships with senior faculty members, has been nominated for teaching excellence awards numerous times by her students, and has mentored many students academically, personally, and professionally. Unfortunately, the hustle of teaching at multiple campuses leaves little time for research and writing, which are the necessary components for building an academic career. One issue that has become much starker for Candidate X now that she has completed her degree is the gap between her economic reality and her status—two categories complicated by the fact that she faces multiple sets of expectations. First, Black women are not only expected to "pull their own weight" but also pull everyone else's. The question of whether one will or will not work outside the home is not one most Black women have traditionally been allowed to consider. In other words, Candidate X comes from a tradition that requires women to contribute beyond what would be considered equal to the economic stability of the family. So, although, her partner is a successful attorney at a prestigious law firm who can afford to support her and their child, earning significantly less is at odds with Candidate X's cultural upbringing. This is added to the second set of expectations that come with being a Black woman who is a product of elite private schools. Ivy League graduates of color feel a particular pressure to be visibly successful in part so they can be role models for their communities. Long-term contingent labor is not part of that narrative. All of this is compounded by the dynamics of a same-sex relationship in which both partners are from the same socioeconomic class and share the same cultural roots. Economic disparities in heterosexual couples are problematic within relationships but still fit into societal norms; in Candidate X's relationship, the economic disparity leads to status inequities that threaten the role she requires of herself but is also required of her. She explains, "If I were to do this all again, I might get a PhD in anthropology because I love this work, but to feel I really am part of my community I should have been a successful dentist or something."

Bensonsmith is currently teaching part time at Claremont Graduate University in the Applied Women's Studies program and admits to being pleasantly surprised by what it means to teach outside of the tenure model, particularly the Selective Liberal Art College (SLAC) tenure-track model that relies so heavily on student evaluations when assessing junior faculty. She explains that this in addition to a supportive director who gives her space to choose her subject matter. Teaching graduate students has made her feel "less encumbered," and her teaching evaluations have improved. The semester-to-semester work that is typical of most adjunct faculty certainly leaves her anxious, though she is quick to make clear that as a heterosexual married woman with support from her mother she knows her life has the kind of stability that allows her to enjoy the flexibility of adjunct work. She can spend more time with her children and participate in the civic life of her community. She writes:

I have taken the time as an adjunct to retool and focus my research agenda, which by necessity now includes collaboration. I say necessity because one of the primary drawbacks of temporary/adjunct status is the disconnect and isolation from the greater academic community on which we as scholars depend. This isolation expresses itself in many ways, but for me it's been the difficulty of presenting and sharing work at conferences/workshops where it's most deeply felt. For a scholar like myself, whose work is not within the mainstream of the discipline, conferences are a place where I get the most feedback and network with like-minded individuals. However, conferences are expensive—an out-of-pocket expense that is downright cost prohibitive for an adjunct who, unlike full-time faculty and grad students, does not qualify for reimbursement from their institutions. Once, your conference attendance drops off, you tend to "disappear" from the academic community, and invitations to speak and participate in workshops, round tables, and other vital activities also fade.

One of the best ways I've found to combat this is by collaborating with scholars from across disciplines. So I'm involved in two different research groups. One is a longtime collaboration with a scholar from Richard Stockton University—our projects focus on women's reproductive health and Black women's reproductive justice/rights. My second group is a transdisciplinary group of Religious Studies, positive psych, and Women's Studies scholars focusing on gender, culture, and empowerment (broadly *defined). Both collaborations have helped me remain current getting my work out and applying for grants. It works but again, it's painful at times, and I miss attending conferences and presenting. And this is not even speaking to the optics of it all, something that my colleagues and I (definitely me) are painfully aware.*

Having to work under these conditions is exactly why the system of adjunct hiring is broken. No one with an advanced degree and highly developed skill sets should have to endure this level of exploitation. The fragile reality afflicting the tens of thousands of adjuncts across the country is a real quality-of-life issue. It is an issue of "survive or die." At any moment, even the smallest tragedy could send an adjunct's life into a spiral of despair. Clearly, the system of exploitation is abusive and unjust.

This all seems particularly troubling because we expect the university, with all its books and knowledge, to operate on a higher moral platform than, say, a typical capitalist enterprise. But somehow, along the way, the university seems to have lost its basic humanity. The academy has lost its soul.

Although the for-profit system is not a perfect system, since we aren't granted tenure or long-term contracts, it is a much better alternative than the adjunct model. We have health insurance, workers' compensation, a dental plan, a 401k, and all the regular bells and whistles that come with a dignified career. The adjunct model offers none of this. Our opinions matter here. Our creativity and individual strengths are appreciated. In essence, we are treated with dignity and respect, and our working conditions reflect as much. If the adjunct model could move a little closer to this type of model for the thousands of adjuncts working at public universities nationwide, then I think it would go a long way toward fixing a very broken system of exploitation.

Notes

1. Patton, "The PhD Now Comes with Foodstamps."
2. Cottom, "The New Old Labor Crisis."
3. JBL Associates, "Reversing Course."
4. Ibid., 12.
5. Hart Research Associates. "Survey of Part-Time and Adjunct Higher Education Faculty."
6. Larsen, "The Underpaid Professor."
7. AQIP Team. "Adjunct Faculty Retention."

8. Hart Research Associates. "Survey of Part-Time and Adjunct Higher Education Faculty."

9. AQIP Team. "Adjunct Faculty Retention."

10. King, "Nonviolent Resistance," 451.

11. Larsen, "The Underpaid Professor," 9.

12. Montclair State University, "Annual Institutional Profile."

13. Hart Research Associates, "Survey of Part-Time and Adjunct Higher Education Faculty."

14. Maisto and Street, "Confronting Contingency."

15. Flaherty, "Adjunct Leaders Consider Strategies to Force Change."

16. Fried, "Opportunities for Efficiency and Innovation."

17. Vedder, "Why Does College Cost So Much?"

18. Edmundson, "On the Uses of a Liberal Education."

19. Lewin, "Private-College Presidents Getting Higher Salaries."

20. Schneider, "Big-Bucks College Presidents Don't Earn Their Pay."

21. Flaherty, "CUNY Adjuncts Ask Not to Be Called Professors."

22. Patton, "The PhD Now Comes With Food Stamps."

Activism(s)

Balancing the Passion for Activism with the Demands of Tenure*

One Professional's Story from Three Perspectives

April L. Few-Demo, Fred P. Piercy, and Andrew J. Stremmel
Virginia Polytechnic Institute and State University

This story will sound familiar to many assistant professors in the social sciences. Most of us chose this career because of our commitment to a profession that is relevant to people's lives and our desire to engage a transformative pedagogy that is grounded in social vision and moral praxis.[1] We want to take pride in work that makes a difference and improves the lives of children, women, and families through our efforts in education, family policy, and mental health services, to name a few. We did not leave our interest in social action at the doorstep when we entered academia. However, additional challenges emerge when our commitment to social justice meets the academy's definition of a highly productive faculty member.

What defines a highly productive faculty member, and how should productivity be measured? William Massy and Andrea Wilger provided several definitions of productivity.[2] One is the ratio of outputs (costs) to inputs (benefits). However, they found that faculty members from colleges and universities typically define productivity in terms of outputs. Their faculty respondents were influenced strongly by institutional rewards and provided broad and complex definitions that typically included two parts of the university mission: research and teaching. When asked "what mattered" most, respondents were more likely to identify refereed publications and research grants to the exclusion of teaching and service. The institution assumes that peer review for both publications and grants ensures high quality scholarship and impact.[3] Across institu-

*Few, April L., Fred P. Piercy, and Andrew Stremmel. "Balancing the Passion for Activism with the Demands of Tenure: One Professional's Story from Three Perspectives." NWSA Journal (now Feminist Formations) 19:3 (2007), 47–66. © 2007 by NWSA Journal. Reprinted with permission of Johns Hopkins University Press.

tional type, Gordon Winston found that this conceptualization can be attributed to hiring and promotion practices.[4]

Seldom does anyone examine the belief that the typical faculty member can achieve simultaneously high levels of productivity in both research and teaching.[5] Some scholars have examined the ratings of teaching effectiveness, one measure of quality but not of productivity,[6] whereas others have studied time allocation and rewards, not specific measures of productivity.[7] Massy and Wilger discuss faculty perceptions of teaching and research productivity, but they did not analyze the nature of this relationship in their national sample.[8] James Fairweather argues that less is known about the variation in expectations and norms for faculty working in distinct types of institutions or by discipline within an institution.[9] This finding speaks to a dearth in the literature about measures of various kinds of productivity. How do service and activism figure into productivity? Is there a place for them in academia?

In his 1990 book, *Scholarship Reconsidered: Priorities of the Professoriate*, Ernest L. Boyer critiqued the narrow range of what the professoriate calls scholarship and concludes that "the time has come to . . . give the term 'scholarship' a broader, more capacious meaning, one that brings legitimacy to the full scope of academic work."[10] Boyer called for the recognition of separate but overlapping forms of scholarship: discovery (pure research), integration (informed connections across disciplines), application (service that bridges the worlds inside and outside academia), and teaching. Perhaps because Boyer was the president of the Carnegie Foundation for the Advancement of Teaching from 1979 to 1995, or because his work was based on a national survey of faculty, his critique and suggestions became focal points for faculty discussions across the country. Some universities today base their tenure and promotion guidelines on Boyer's broad view of scholarship. Most, however, have maintained what Boyer termed "a more restricted view of scholarship."[11]

In this chapter, I share my story of balancing my commitment to diversity and social justice with the demands of tenure. I also asked Fred Piercy, head of the Department of Human Development, and Andrew Stremmel, departmental chair of the tenure and promotion committee, to reflect on this dilemma. It is our hope to stimulate conversation among our peers about challenging an institutional system where mainstream social constructions devalue activism and perpetuate a narrow view of scholarship.

Dr. April L. Few-Demo: My Story

This is a story about my efforts to meet the tenure demands of a research university without losing my passion for making a difference through outreach work related to diversity and feminism. First, let me summarize the context in which I find myself. I am one of twenty-four Black faculty (nine women, fifteen men) in a college of 396 faculty and one of thirty-nine tenure-track Black faculty in a university of 1,259 faculty. Only approximately 6 percent (i.e., 5.8%) of the student population is Black and even fewer Black students are found in my discipline of Family Studies. In fact, I usually have approximately three minority students in a class of sixty, or ten to fifteen in a class of 250. My service to the university has ranged from (1) serving as co-chair of the college's diversity committee; (2) co-organizing a Women's Studies faculty development workshop in which administrators, faculty, and students across campus discussed globalizing our curricula; (3) organizing a regional conference on domestic violence that included university and community presenters; and (4) serving as a mentor to several graduate and undergraduate minority students on campus. Moreover, as a newcomer to the area of southwest Virginia, I have presented seminars on domestic violence for social services and churches to facilitate my research on domestic violence in rural populations. Finally, I am active in the regular committee work that is expected of all new faculty members. On the national level, I was chair of a national committee of the American Association of Family and Consumer Sciences, secretary-treasurer of the Ethnic Minorities Section of the National Council on Family Relations, and a member of several other committees.

In my second-year review letter, the departmental tenure and promotion committee stated that they "would like to see [me] develop more collaborative relationships with senior faculty" and "to beware of getting too over-committed to tasks that will take [me] too far away from scholarship." Between my second and fourth review, I became co-chair of the college's diversity committee. My fourth-year review letter emphasized that I should focus more on publishing and restrain my service. After my fourth-year review, I had the opportunity to discuss my situation with two senior faculty members who are the coauthors of this paper. Dr. Fred Piercy is chair of the Department of Human Development and someone who understands the demands and expectations of a research university. Dr. Andrew Stremmel was chair of the tenure and promotion committee that conducted my fourth-year review. Both the department head and the former tenure and promotion chair value social action but also realize the imperative in the phrase "publish or perish." They want to encourage me to continue the activist pedagogy and service that nurtures my soul. At the same time, they want to see me survive and thrive within our department, which means writing a certain number of high-quality refereed journal articles. Because my challenge is one that many others face, we decided to use my story to illustrate several issues with which many new assistant professors grapple. Frederick Buechner, a theological scholar, suggests that "the story of any one of us is in some measure the story of us all."[12] Thus, my story provides space for Dr. Piercy's and Dr. Stremmel's stories to emerge in response to my construction of personally meaningful issues and perspectives.

I am glad that Dr. Piercy did not tell me to "just say no" to outreach activities, although I have heard this advice from others. Other minority professors have told me they could not help anyone else because they were their own diversity project. Just saying "no" is not as easy as it appears. Gloria Cuadraz gives but one example:

> But you tell me . . . how do you say no to a 21-year-old Chicana undergraduate, from another campus, in another state, who calls you, writes to you, and makes sure she meets you when you're in town to give the opening plenary talk for a conference, that you "don't have the time" to read her proposal for a senior thesis. . . . How do you say NO to her enthusiasm and to her desire to learn and be mentored? You don't. Because here is yet another consequence to saying no. That consequence is about the consequence to our spirit. If we deny ourselves these kinds of connections, ironically, we risk losing relationships that very often fuel and energize us. These are the individuals that oftentimes appreciate us and value us, when no one else, particularly institutionally, is doing so.[13]

Many minority and underrepresented students approach me after class to say I am the first Black professor they have ever had, that they are so happy I am here, and that because of me they have thought about going to graduate school for the first time or that they will be the first in their family to go to graduate school if I can help them. How do I, an assistant professor, tell such students that I do not have time to contribute to their professional growth? How do I say "no" to a Black community organization or church that asks for my time after I return home from campus? Why would I want to decline the chance to provide voice to the values I hold? The trick is, according to my department head, to write about these life-giving experiences—to make them part of my scholarly work—which is part of what this article is all about.

This is not a discussion about prioritizing service over research publications. I believe that I have been somewhat successful in balancing the demands to publish and in staying an active, committed professional. At the time of this writing, I have received two internal grants, published seven refereed journal articles and two book chapters, have four articles under review in top-tier journals, and have several other articles in progress. I have received awards from two sections of the National Council of Family Relations. The first was the Outstanding Student-Originated Contribution to Family Research and Theory Paper Award from the Family and Health Section. The second was the Jessie Bernard Outstanding Contribution to Feminist Scholarship Paper Award from the Feminism and Family Studies Section. I am a coauthor of the chapter on multicultural and critical race feminism in *Family Studies in the Sourcebook of Family Theory and Research*.[14] I am collaborating on research projects with several successful senior grant writers. I have instituted an international focus into our department's human sexuality class, the most popular class in the department. This class has anywhere from 150 to 250 students per semester and is a source of my highest teaching evaluations. Still, the most important means of opening the door to tenure appears to be refereed publications. Activism, whether teaching or service, is secondary. This is a discussion among colleagues about how one can maintain a professional self in academia without leaving one's activist self behind.

Activism and the University Mission

You look at the world differently when you leave graduate school and enter your first position as an assistant professor at a new university in a new community full of strangers. You carry with you certain expectations for yourself, your colleagues, and your students. I came to my position with the knowledge that I was one of the first Black professors in the Department of Human Development and that I may be the first ethnic teacher my students have ever experienced in their college career. During my first year at Virginia Tech, my own value system—and challenges to it—compelled me to engage in activist pedagogy and outreach as I also struggled to find time to write about my research.

Valuing the Scholarship of Activist Pedagogy

My first experience teaching at Virginia Tech was the Gender and Family Diversity course—it was a difficult, yet radicalizing experience for me. In a co-teaching context in which both professors were Black women scholars, white female students openly challenged our authority and our scholarship without fear of retribution. Some students also attempted a divide-and-conquer strategy to diminish our united instructional front. Having the presence of two assertive Black women professors in front of the classroom became a vortex of volatility for some students as we challenged how they negotiated the politics of location (i.e., race, ethnicity, class, gender, sexual orientation, nation) in their lives.[15] We were their first Black instructors (I was told this on several occasions), and although we were nurturing, we refused to play the role of "Mammies." I was surprised at the subtle and not so subtle ways we were punished. Perhaps I should not have been. Kendra Hamilton, assistant editor of *Black Issues in Higher Education*, observed, "White professors who teach challenging courses about race get patted on the back—even when we get pretty negative student evaluations. But people of color who teach about race are frequently punished in very, very serious ways: marginalized [and] . . . denied raises or promotions or tenure, largely on the basis of student evaluations."[16] Asian American English scholar, Bonnie TuSmith ruminated about how her physical presence created cognitive dissonance among her students in regard to their expectations of both professors and Asian Americans. TuSmith summarized the rote logic of her students' response to her presence: "Professors are white men. You are not a white man. Therefore, you are not a professor. English professors are white. You are Asian American. Therefore, you cannot be an English professor. Asian Americans are quiet, humble and submissive. You have strong convictions and you are not humble. Therefore, you are a failed Asian American."[17]

TuSmith wanted to find ways of doing her job without being punished for challenging her students to think outside of their comfort zone. In addition to fighting racist discourse in the classroom, she also had to negotiate internalized racism by Asian American students.

Our students found their power in evaluations and wrote negative comments that reflected their interpretations of our personality rather than our skill as experienced instructors. They also questioned our identity or "place" in the classroom and the scholarship we presented that featured works from ethnic family scholars. One white female student even wrote an assignment about the inferiority of Blacks to remind us that she felt Black women did not belong before a university classroom. Like TuSmith, we had to deal with similar cognitive dissonance in our students. Their evaluations reflected their notions of what defined a professor and a Black woman and the impossibilities of both existing in one person. In her evaluation, one student wrote that our very presence "made [her] angry every single class" and "everything being taught made [her] furious." I would later learn through another student that our angry student actively sought out co-conspirators to disrupt the classroom and undermine our authority. I never felt so disconnected from a class and so connected to my integrity and purpose. I also found some comfort by talking to a number of other junior and senior Black women scholars about this situation. I discovered that my teaching experience at a university where the majority of students are white was quite a common phenomenon to be endured and negotiated by Black professors.[18] One Black woman colleague shared with me that one of the reasons she left her previous post was that she felt unwelcomed by students and unsupported by her department. She felt her department refused to recognize the racism of its students. She stated that somehow sexism was easier for her colleagues to grasp.

Our collective "Blackness" and "woman-ness" challenged students' expectations of race, class, gender, education, and power and angered them when we expected more work and commitment than many were willing to give Black professors. That classroom experience fed a transformation in my vision of myself as a part of the department, the college, and the university. I also understand now that I am defined as a projection of what my students think I will be. Part of my role as an activist teacher is to modify those projections and help students understand the intersectionality of race, ethnicity, culture, class, and gender and that this knowledge tells them about themselves and the world, not just about me.

Standing alone before the class as a heterosexual middle-class Southern Black woman with a doctoral degree, I was the target of a diverse range of emotions. In teaching about intersectionality, I have observed how some students from privileged backgrounds become openly angry, hostile, confrontational, guilt-ridden, compassionate, supportive, or neutral or indifferent to my presentations on racism, sexism, classism, homophobia, and nationalism and how we all contribute to perpetuating socially hierarchical processes.[19] In those moments in the classroom when hearing and discussing the misuse of words such as "coloreds" or "orientals," I decided I was going to be neither derailed nor dismissed, and I would not succumb to feelings of hopelessness often fueled by explicit, subtle, or subversive student resistance.[20] I made a conscious effort to commit time to developing a liberatory, critical, and radical pedagogy. I wanted to tap into the multiple consciousnesses that we inhabit and through which we create opportunities for empowerment, and, according to Katie Cannon, emancipatory historiography.[21] Emancipatory historiography is a self-reflexive process wherein students can learn to challenge and deconstruct majority discourse, debunk myths, and (re)connect with different interpretations or accounts of individual or group history from the perspective of minority or oppressed groups. Engaging in this process helps students become more antiracist, antisexist, anticlassist, and antihomophobic by questioning the authority of hegemonic discourses. For a time, this kind of teaching became my primary scholarship—one valued by me but relatively invisible to the departmental tenure and promotion committee. I wanted to facilitate student processing of their own biases without allowing their fear to become the metanarrative of classroom experience. Teaching became a site of (r)evolution for me in terms of my commitment toward consciousness raising, social justice, and activist pedagogy. This, I thought to myself, is at the heart of what a committed scholar should be doing.

Doing critical pedagogy is doing activist pedagogy. Roger Simon described pedagogy as a political "practice within which one acts with the intent of provoking experience that will simultaneously organize and disorganize a variety of understandings of our natural and social world."[22] Teaching is indeed a political act. One of the primary concerns of practitioners of critical pedagogy is to expose social injustice and examine how to transform inequitable, undemocratic, or oppressive institutions and social relations in the classroom context. Henry Giroux defined critical pedagogy as "pedagogy [that] signals how questions of audience, voice, power, and evaluation actively work to construct particular relations between teachers and students, institutions and society, and classrooms and communities. . . . Pedagogy in the critical sense illuminates the relationship among knowledge, authority, and power."[23]

My approach to facilitating critical analyses of intersectionality in the classroom is grounded in the theoretical framework of Black feminism. Kathleen Weiler stated that to do pedagogy that is feminist in nature, "the authority of the feminist teacher as intellectual and theorist finds expression in the goal of making students themselves theorists of their own lives by interrogating and analyzing their own experience."[24] I am a teacher who is interested in creating spaces to deconstruct and analyze the consistencies and inconsistencies of our belief systems. Black feminism provides the liberatory underpinnings to orient the tone of my lectures, guide my selection of materials (e.g., articles, media, case studies), and serve as matchsticks for igniting emancipatory historiography and norm clarification. It also informs my ethic of care and collaboration in relation to my students. Black feminist Barbara Omolade states: "A Black feminist pedagogy is not merely concerned with the principles of instruction of Black women by Black women and about Black women; it also sets forth learning strategies informed by Black women's historical experience with race/gender/class bias and the consequences of marginality and isolation. Black feminist pedagogy aims to develop a mindset of intellectual inclusion and expansion that stands in contradiction to the Western intellectual tradition of exclusivity and chauvinism."[25]

Black feminist pedagogy is activism in that its goal is to eradicate stereotypes of marginalized and oppressed groups. Many multicultural and white feminists argue that a comprehensive understanding of social behavior is possible only when multicultural categories (i.e., race, ethnicity, gender, class, sexual orientation, nation, etc.) are highlighted as fundamental categories of analysis in both our pedagogy and research.[26] In a feminist classroom, I look positively for opportunities to interrogate hegemonic social stratifications and institutions. These are important teaching moments for the promotion of social change.

My investment in developing an activist, accessible pedagogy has been rewarding. I have seen my students experience multiple epiphanies throughout my courses as they finally connect, relate, and internalize how interlocking systems of oppression and privilege influence the decision-making behaviors of not only racial and ethnic families but also their own families and themselves. Teaching about individual and family diversity is more than an exercise in gathering articles and books on family diversity and presenting findings to a class. Teaching about diversity is about "working the hyphens," working the centers and margins of self and "other," and finding and sharing personal power in those social and psychic spaces where we feel most uncomfortable.[27] bell hooks described a feminist classroom as both "a place where there is a sense of struggle, where there is visible acknowledgment of the union of theory and practice" and "where we work together as teachers and students to overcome the estrangement and alienation that have become so much the norm in the contemporary university."[28]

In response to my fourth-year review letter and discussion with colleagues, I made a decision to divert more of my time to research and writing activities than to the scholarship of teaching. It was hard to do because teaching is my passion and central to my identity. It is my mission to mentor and socialize perspective-taking, culturally sensitive, and accountable citizens who will help create a better world. Most will work in areas that impact families and vulnerable populations (e.g., social work, education, health, therapeutic services, academia, and family policy). This semester was the first semester that I had to reduce those writing assignments that allowed undergraduate students to practice their analyses of and reflections on intersectionality.

These writing assignments provided students with the opportunity to apply Family Studies and feminist theoretical perspectives to personal experiences and interpretations of empirical articles, media, and narratives. In each paper, students practiced critical thinking by determining the main arguments or points of selected articles, substantiating or debunking arguments made by authors by using interdisciplinary research (e.g., Women's Studies, Africana Studies, Religious Studies), and identifying implications for future Family Studies research with attention to diversity and family policy. These papers required an inordinate amount of time on my part to provide extensive and thought-provoking feedback. Grading them was not a task that could be readily turned over to inexperienced graduate students with a limited background in critical theories. The writing exercises not only served to engage the students in critical thinking but also provided a space for students to connect with me as a mentor in their professional growth. Instead of planning for two or three papers, I had students write only one paper per semester. I did not want to reduce these assignments, but I was faced with the reality that I had to direct my time toward those goals that would increase my chances of getting tenure at a research-one university.

Activism in Service: "Second Shift" Scholarship

My teaching experiences have served as a catalyst for me to become more involved in diversity-related activities that seek to change the campus climate. Taken together, university service and outreach is the "second shift" for professors.[29] It is also important scholarship. Service is a genuine outlet for activism that defines our selfhood and altruism and supports life-giving connections. It is the glue that connects the university, community, and world. However, I also suspect that it is valued in most research universities about as much as the motherwork women perform to maintain the household and family well-being.[30] Activist service is considered by most tenure and promotion committees to be among those things that take us away from "real" scholarly pursuits.

In addition to allocating time for regular committee work and service within the university, Black professors have to attend to something else. In a conversation with another untenured Black colleague, I immediately recognized one specific challenge that Black professors at majority white universities and communities face. Both of us felt that fulfilling the university service mission did not stop on campus grounds for Black professors. There is the official service we do for the university and those organizations that further our research agenda and then there is our additional responsibility to our Black communities. My colleague stated that we have to be in the Black churches, Black community centers, and Black student organizations while trying to carve out time to make tenure. We don't say "no" to our community. This phenomenon is the second shift for geographically displaced, activist Black professors. Many Black professors feel isolated among colleagues, students, and their newfound community.[31] Thus, it is particularly important to stay connected to faculty members who care about diversity issues and to community members and students who share cultural characteristics and feelings of isolation. Bonita Butner, Hansel Burley, and Aretha Marbley emphasize the necessity for informal (and formal) social support as means of mental and physical well-being for Black faculty who are situated in majority white institutions.[32] They cite collaboration, collegiality, and community as the keys for professional success in academe. For me, these keys become a lifeline in the development of a "homeplace."[33] Pulling back from such service would magnify my feelings of isolation. Black Studies scholar Manning Marable refers to community service as a form of pedagogy and praxis.[34] It also can provide a focus for research.

It took nearly two years for me, an outsider on many counts, to gain a reliable reputation and the trust of rural community organizations where I wished to conduct my research on intimate violence—churches, social service agencies, and battered women's shelters.

Facing Tensions: My Final Reflections

Family Studies scholar Norma Burgess has written about the challenges that Black women face in the promotion and tenure process. Burgess identifies a lack of sponsorship and a restricted communication network as having negative impacts on productivity.[35] Because Black women scholars often work on the periphery of established networks, they are often hindered in their ability to access timely information and resources that lead to starting research programs, getting grants, publishing, consulting, and other activities that make their work visible to their peers and lead to tenure and promotion in the academy. Productivity and a sense of belonging increase when senior faculty members mentor junior colleagues to navigate through the "old boys' network" and to locate informal resources. Burgess also brings our attention to the fact that many Black women faculty members choose research projects that reflect Eurocentric notions of race, gender, and class and undermine minority or cultural theoretical perspectives.[36] And in doing so to survive professionally, they inevitably lose or subsume important parts of themselves.

I cannot help but resonate with some of Burgess's observations. Although I had mentors in the beginning, there were no projects to join immediately that would connect me to community and campus resources. The participants in my dissertation were Black women involved in abusive relationships. Before beginning my academic appointment, I had hopes of continuing to study Black women. However, this was difficult and required creative thinking for me to develop a research program. Advertising in local papers brought too few Black participants to begin a research program. Instead of studying abused Black women only, I had to broaden my focus to include studying rural white battered women in battered women's shelters with the hope of finding rural Black battered women. Now with a senior colleague, I am beginning a research project in state prisons to obtain a more diverse sample in a context that brings my activism to the forefront. Being an interdisciplinary scholar allows me to maintain an active engagement in

Women's Studies and Africana Studies, two disciplines that represent who I am personally.

I have poured much of my time into an activist pedagogy. My courses invite student resistance, but they also create opportunities for a critical examination of intersectionality and self-reflexivity. Although I realize that research is primarily what paves the road for tenure, I am aware that Burgess has echoed what senior colleagues have told me: poor teaching evaluations can be cited as reasons to deny junior faculty tenure and promotion.[37] Because I have focused on the teaching part of the university's mission, that first challenging semester remains an anomaly among my teaching evaluations. I have learned how to use student resistance to facilitate meaningful teaching moments. Consequently, my teaching evaluations are quite high. But I know that is not enough. In response to my tenure and promotion letters, I have curtailed service activities on campus and within my community. I am currently a co-chair of my college's diversity committee but will probably step down to become a member at the end of my term. I must rethink how much time I allot to servicing the needs of undergraduate and graduate advisees. Flexible advising hours have proven to be too costly. I will only serve on campus committees as a member, refusing most leadership opportunities. Thus, the reality I am beginning to experience is an institutionally supported sense of isolation. At the same time, I am looking harder for opportunities to serve and remain an activist scholar in my research and pedagogy. I like the fact that I am doing research with vulnerable populations (e.g., the transition processes of battered women and formerly incarcerated women) and hope this research will translate into transformative policies within agencies that serve those populations and their families. This is indeed social action. In serving as a mentor to graduate teaching apprentices, I have gained a course release that allows me to pass on my enthusiasm for integrating a social justice agenda into the classroom. It also allows me more time for research and writing. I am learning that a key to maintaining my activism is being creative and strategic about the kinds of service I commit myself to and writing about those opportunities.

In many ways, my coauthors have found ways to fit their activism into their careers successfully. What follows are the reflections of Andrew Stremmel, the chair of the departmental tenure and promotion committee, and Fred Piercy, the department head, about my efforts as a junior faculty to maintain my activism and still be successful within the system.

Reflections of Dr. Andrew Stremmel,
the Chair of the Tenure and Promotion Committee

In Dr. Few's fourth-year review, I, Dr. Andrew Stremmel, a middle-aged white associate professor, was the chair of the tenure and promotion committee and heard the committee echo the concerns of the department head, Dr. Fred Piercy. Some of us felt that Dr. Few was contributing significantly as a departmental and college citizen and making efforts to integrate her passion for teaching and service with her research scholarship. Others believed that, despite these efforts, Dr. Few was not publishing her work with a frequency expected in a comprehensive land-grant institution. All agreed that she needed to spend more time on writing and say "no" to anything that would not further this goal. I have mixed feelings about our letter to her. On the one hand, the committee was right, our colleague needed to be more engaged in the writing and dissemination of her ideas and findings. The harsh reality of university life is that we publish or perish. On the other hand, I struggled over the narrow academic specifications that our field seems to value and the single-minded view that everyone should look the same, be skilled in the same things, and engage in the same activities in order to be "successful" by university standards. Parker Palmer has noted that we spend so much of our lives abandoning our gifts or letting others disabuse us of them.[38] We are surrounded by the expectations of those who are not trying to discern our selfhood but fit us into certain categories or boxes. I do not think it has to be that way. As I reflect on Dr. Few's accomplishments and contributions over the past four years, our committee's discussion of their merits, and Dr. Few's story articulated so eloquently here, I am struck by several opposing ideas and values. They include values that I also embrace, ones that I find I must defend every day.

First, there is the elusive definition of success. On whose terms do we define this? If success is not on our own terms, if our lives do not reflect what we value, then can we be successful? Make no mistake: I am for rigor and setting high expectations; but I wonder if too often we approach our work and the evaluation of our colleagues asking the wrong question, "How successful is this person?" We might do better by asking, "How has this person been successful?"

Second, the idea of service and how we view it is a riddle. Anyone who has worked in a land-grant institution is well aware that service or "outreach" is one of three missions, albeit of lesser "value" than its counterparts of teaching and research. I believe this to be true even though time and again I have heard administrators refute this, particularly by emphasizing that teaching, research, and service go hand in hand. My colleague sees service as "a genuine outlet for activism that defines our selfhood and altruism and supports life-giving connections." Even the motto of our university is "Ut Prosim"—"That I may serve." Nevertheless, as the "soft" mission, excellence in service does not lead to tenure and promotion.

Third, Dr. Few strives to do not only what matters to her but also what nurtures her soul. Teaching, she notes, is a political act. She courageously teaches what she believes and who she is as a person; in doing so, she claims authentic selfhood and acts it out daily in her work as a professor. Her teaching is conducted with the hope that her actions and ideas will help to transform her students. If any one of us is going to take students with the seriousness they desire and deserve, then we will have little time to read and write and research. This, then, is the dilemma: How do we live with integrity, honoring the values and expectations of the university, while nurturing our passions, living with a sense of purpose, doing what energizes us and feeds our soul? We must pursue our academic duties and responsibilities with seriousness and commitment, but we cannot let our work seduce us into a disregard for doing what matters.

Reflections of Dr. Fred Piercy, Department Head

I love what both Dr. Few and Dr. Stremmel have written. We should all nurture our passions and do what feeds our souls. All of us need to feel good about what we do, and tenure does not guarantee that. At the same time, it does guarantee a job. The beauty of academics is that we have some say in what we study, teach, research, and write—what feeds our soul. Problems arise when new faculty take on activities that are invisible or are not valued in tenure and promotion evaluations.[39] And service demands on underrepresented faculty, as Dr. Few illustrates, can be considerable. For example, if Dr. Few had not agreed to be co-chair of our college's diversity committee, the chairs would both have been middle-aged white males (I am one of them). Her voice is important. Do we really want an underrepresented leader committed to social justice and diversity not using her talents toward these ends?

Leadership and service opportunities can help new (and particularly underrepresented) faculty feel engaged. They connect new faculty to the university and provide an opportunity to make a difference.[40] An outsider would probably see Dr. Few's service as too much, but I think it is also a big part of what helps her love her work. Should we tell her not to do what she loves? I hope not. Ideally, life shouldn't start after tenure. My wish is that we do what gives us joy but still do what we need to do to survive. It is possible for Dr. Few to connect her activities to activities that the academy respects—to do research on her teaching and to write papers on her service. This article is an example of this kind of "both–and" thinking.

I would be misleading my colleague if I said that numbers of publications were not important. The grapevine number of refereed publications for tenure here is about ten. I have served on twenty-four years of tenure and promotion committees and have voted against the tenure of assistant professors who didn't have the numbers. However, most did not do much of anything else either. Dr. Few's story raises different questions for me. She is good at everything she does, and her teaching and service are second to none. They are also good scholarship. But she is right—they are not as valued as publications or grants. That's the ballpark we play in. How much will this system accommodate to activist-minded assistant professors, and how much can or should scholars accommodate to the system?

The academic culture of research universities emphasizes grants and publications more and more. They are the coin of the realm, and not all of this is bad. Through publications researchers disseminate their work, which ideally influences policies and practices, and enhances their reputation and that of the university. Grant dollars make more sophisticated research possible and raise money to support graduate assistantships (and departments). So these standards are not without merit. In such a culture, how can we support energetic, activist, politically committed assistant professors? I like the idea of broadening our concept of scholarship, but that will not occur overnight. I also like supporting a culture where publications, grants, and good teaching and service inform and stimulate one another.

I can be most helpful to junior faculty by being clear about the expectations for tenure—including publications and grants—and suggest ways that they can do their work and meet these expectations without losing their souls or suffocating under someone else's expectations. I have always tried to make my own work play and to write and do research in the areas of my intellectual and personal passions. I want to help

Dr. Few and others figure out ways to connect their interests to what is valued at a research university. I would also like to have them find some joy in the process.

Collective Reflections: What and Who Shall Change?

Most new faculty spend a good deal of time trying to interpret tenure and promotion expectations from their faculty handbook, regardless of whether they work at a research-one university, private institution, or liberal arts teaching university. However, the handbook does not address the ways in which those expectations are interpreted at various levels (e.g., in departmental, college, and university tenure and promotion committees) and across different colleges (e.g., liberal arts, human resources, engineering). And, as we know, the social construction of "excellence" and "scholarship" can take many forms. We must challenge social constructions that devalue service and social action and institutions that perpetuate a narrow view of scholarship. In an e-mail correspondence with Dr. Few on October 15, 2004, Karen P. DePauw, dean of the graduate school, wrote:

> The existing culture of tenure and promotion should change.
> Yes, there are different types of institutions that define tenure and promotion differently and that do offer options for faculty, but this is not the only answer. The system currently in place makes the individual faculty member adapt or change, or leave the institution. Perhaps a more relevant question is . . . [how can] learning institutions . . . grow, adapt, change, and still maintain high standards? The traditional approach hasn't allowed for the richness of faculty contributions.
>
> What she and we, as authors of this manuscript are arguing is that institutional change should make room for the diversity in scholarly research, teaching, and service. One size should not fit all. While a lot of our comments relate to survival within a rigid system, we must also look for ways to shape the system in more inclusive and reasonable ways. The institution that evaluates us must move to a place where teaching and service accomplishments are acknowledged and rewarded as scholarship worth doing. We need, in other words, to move from victim blaming to institutional assessment and change. We all must be part of the solution.[41]

As we write this paper, for Dr. Few and others like her, tenure is not guaranteed. If she does not receive tenure, did she fail? Or did Drs. Piercy and Stremmel fail? Or did the system fail? Or perhaps we are giving the requirements of tenure too much power to control our lives. Although the focus of this paper is that of an assistant professor, it has implications for the university community at large. This article is a dialogue about working within the criteria that reflect the values of the institution. It is also a call to deconstruct which values should also matter. Clearly, we need professionals in the academy committed to the scholarship of teaching and social action. How do we keep them and celebrate their contributions and see them survive and thrive? These are critical open questions still to be answered.

As I, Dr. Few, think about what changes I have had to make in response to institutional demands or definitions of what is scholarly, I am reminded of bell hooks's warning of moving toward the center (i.e., mainstream of the profession or academe) and the possibility of losing self in that process: "Marginality [is] much more than a site of deprivation; in fact ... it is also the site of radical possibility, a space of resistance. It was this marginality that I was naming as a central location for the production of counter-hegemonic discourse that is not just found in words but in habits of being and the way one lives. As such, I was not speaking of marginality one wishes to lose—to give up or surrender as part of moving into the center—but rather of a site one stays in, clings to even, because it nourishes one's capacity to resist. It offers to one the possibility of radical perspective from which to see and create, to imagine alternatives, new worlds."[42]

Our Recommendations

Our recommendations are embedded in our reflections about Dr. Few's story and the challenges that all junior faculty, specifically ethnic junior faculty, face in the tenure and promotion process.

1. Do not give up who you are. Live your commitments, your passion.
2. Be strategic. Fit your commitment for service into your research and teaching.
3. Connect with your community and other informal sources of support.

Identify early who will be a genuine ally and mentor to you as you make the transition to a new community and profession. Do not wait for mentors to be assigned to you.

4. Do not fall for the too-pat suggestion to "just say no." Life is lived between "yes" and "no," and the margins do not have to be lonely or deadly, if you live well, with an eye for the rules of survival—both personal and institutional.

5. Radical as this may sound, "Do not diminish your intensity and passion for teaching." Teaching is about transforming society and oneself, and this means that teachers are obligated to encourage their students to reflect on, question, and reconstruct their own experiences. Further, teaching and research are not separate acts. Treated seriously, they are intellectual and ethical acts of inquiry, courage, and advocacy for change.

6. Being a little subversive is underrated. A life of moral commitment and social action is a life of meaningful subversion.

7. Rid yourself of nonessential demands on your time until your life reflects what you value. You can do this by setting fewer but more realistic goals and by trying to do a few things well. (We do not have to be excellent at everything!) Rather than "no," state, "I decided to commit my time and attention to—" Make your priorities transparent.

8. As you work both inside and outside the demands of the system, love what you do and do what you love. The best scholarship comes from passionate commitment.

9. Although it is wise to write about what elicits passion about your teaching, research, or service, be attentive that your writing reflects your professional identity or research program. If you claim an interdisciplinary identity, then consult mentors who can help you best articulate your multiple interests as a sound, coherent research or professional identity.

10. Live life now, not just after tenure.

Postscript

In June 2006, I earned tenure and promotion to the rank of associate professor at the Virginia Polytechnic Institute and State University. It has been a long journey waiting for the final vote of the board of visitors. Along the way, I have met a few assistant professors who found themselves in situations similar to the one I described in this paper. I have shared the recommendations my coauthors and I provide in this manuscript. In the end, I had to make some changes to meet the criteria to earn tenure and survive the system. I am, however, also encouraged that external reviewers and colleagues within my university community who were not privy to my experiences found value in my integration of scholarship and activism. Thus, the question remains: Who and what must change?

Notes

1. Allen, Floyd-Thomas, and Gilman, "Teaching to Transform."

2. Massy and Wilger, "Improving Productivity," 11.

3. Blackburn and Lawrence, *Faculty at Work*; Fairweather, *Faculty Work and Public Trust.*

4. Winston, "The Decline of Undergraduate Teaching," 8.

5. Fairweather, "The Mythologies of Faculty Productivity."

6. Feldman, "Research Productivity and Scholarly Accomplishment of College Teachers"; Hattie and Marsh, "The Relationship between Research and Teaching."

7. Fairweather, "Faculty Rewards Reconsidered"; Fairweather, *Faculty Work and Public Trust.*

8. Massy and Wilger, "Improving Productivity," 11.

9. Fairweather, "The Mythologies of Faculty Productivity."

10. Boyer, *Scholarship Reconsidered*, 16.

11. Ibid., 15.

12. Buechner, *The Sacred Journey*, 6.

13. Cuadraz, "Questions Worth Asking," 7–8.

14. Bengtson et al., *Sourcebook of Family Theory and Research.*

15. Williams, "The Angry Black Woman Scholar."

16. Hamilton, " 'Race in the College Classroom.' "

17. TuSmith, "Out on a Limb," 123.

18. Essien, "Visible and Invisible Barriers," 65–66; Smith, "The Tyrannies of the Untenured Professors of Color," 1106.

19. Allen, Floyd-Thomas, and Gillman, 319; Bohmer and Briggs, "Teaching Privileged Students about Gender, Race, and Class Oppression," 156.

20. Chan and Treacy, "Resistance in Multicultural Courses," 216–18; Hamilton, 32.

21. Cannon, "Emancipatory Historiography," 81.

22. Simon, *Teaching Against the Grain*, 56.

23. Giroux, *Disturbing Pleasures*, 30.

24. Weiler, "Freire and a Feminist Pedagogy of Difference," 462.

25. Omolade, "A Black Feminist Pedagogy," 32.

26. Bohmer and Briggs, 156; Collins, *Fighting Words*; Collins, *Black Feminist Thought*; Collins, "Learning from the Outsider Within"; hooks, *Talking Back*;

Rich, "Compulsory Heterosexuality"; TuSmith and Reddy, *Race in the College Classroom*.

27. Fine, "Working the Hyphens."
28. hooks, *Talking Back*, 51.
29. Hochschild, *The Second Shift*.
30. Collins, "Shifting the Center," 289.
31. Moses, "Black Women in Academe," 24.
32. Butner, Burley, and Marbley, "Coping with the Unexpected," 458–60.
33. hooks, *Yearning*, 42.
34. Marable, "Black Studies and the Black Intellectual Tradition."
35. Burgess, "Tenure and Promotion among African American Women," 229.
36. Ibid., 230.
37. Ibid., 232.
38. Palmer, *Let Your Life Speak*, 12.
39. Cuadraz, "Questions Worth Asking," 11.
40. Turner, "New Faces, New Knowledge," 35.
41. DePauw, E-mail correspondence.
42. hooks, *Yearning*, 149–50.

Cast Your Net Wide

Reflections on Activism and Community Engagement
When Black Lives Matter: Conversations with Ariana E.
Alexander, E. Frances White, and Jennifer D. Williams

Patricia A. Matthew
Montclair State University

The day before the first of six Baltimore officers charged with Freddie Gray's death was set to be tried, Morgan State University President David Wilson was interviewed by the *Chronicle of Higher Education* and asked to discuss the role of historically Black colleges and universities (HBCUs) in the aftermath of Gray's death. Wilson was asked what he had learned when the responses to Gray's death on April 12, 2015 caught city leaders unprepared, and his answer is interesting as protests about police violence have required administrators from colleges and universities to reconsider what matters to students of color, particularly Black students: "the discussions that we were having in the cabinet was around the power of listening, and the power of knowing that sometimes universities don't have the answers. You have to go into the neighborhoods and you have to have genuine conversations with the neighborhoods and ask the neighbors, if you will, what are the solutions? Because these are the individuals who are living these kinds of challenges every single day."[1]

It is the pressure of those everyday challenges that contributed to the protests that followed Gray's death. Wilson describes that day as one filled with phone calls from city officials that warned of unrest but could not prepare anyone for the mayhem that followed: looting, burning cars, school children let out of school into protests that turned violent, and the burning of CVS stores, most notably the CVS on the corner of Pennsylvania and West North avenues. Morgan students protested on campus in East Baltimore, blocking intersections on campus, before going to "ground zero" in West Baltimore, Wilson explained, to help escort children trying to get home and then assisting by the busload with the cleanup the following day. He touted Morgan's long history of social activism and told the *Chronicle* that the first student sit-in took place on the campus. He made the usual claims about valuing free speech and civil disobedience and then offered the boilerplate list of members of the community he was certain would participate in ongoing discussions and actions about the conditions that sparked the protests and the mayhem: "I do meet with our officials at the university, the executive director of public safety, our university police, the cabinet, the faculty, the students. We have ongoing conversations about our values at the university." His statement suggests that faculty members will engage with larger social justice issues, and it blurs the line between service (work that faculty take on to keep the university going) and activism (work that has the potential to upend the daily work of those same universities). Wilson says in his interview that the conversations on Morgan's campus are happening at other universities, and he is right. Students are moving beyond candlelight vigils to putting the lessons from the Black students' movement of the 1960s to use in the twenty-first century, and this moment is prompting faculty to think about their roles and the role of their research in what Gene Demby rightly calls the "New Civil Rights Movement."[2]

To some degree, all of the contributors to this volume are engaged in some form of what might be called "activism," though almost no one will apply the label to themselves or their work. They may call it "community service," "community building," or, as I prefer, "community engagement." Or they may resist labels by not calling it anything at all. All, however, are rooted in the understanding that their research and teaching need to have a material impact on the world outside of the work the academy recognizes. The challenge, then, is to think through the implications, through the risks and stakes. As Jafari Sinclair Allen notes, it's a different thing to sit on the board of a benevolent and politically neutral community group than it is to organize protests to challenge the things that make charitable groups necessary in the first place. "What," he asks, "does it mean to be a political citizen in the neoliberal university?" How does this work matter in academic careers when, as George Lipsitz observes: "Evaluation, recognition, and reward in academic life usually proceed through relentlessly individual and individualizing processes.... Prevailing professional practices encourage scholars to seek distinction for themselves as atomized individuals rather than as participants in a collective and collaborative conversation."[3] As the protests that reached a new level of intensity in Ferguson move from neighborhood blocks and street corners to university hallways and classrooms, and institutional leaders assemble task forces and committees in response to issues that will be around for a while, it's essential that administrators and faculty leaders remain mindful of what this labor costs faculty who engage in this work, particularly faculty of color. Talk of task forces and diversity initatives, meetings with students and administrative leaders are essential, but they come at a cost. It isn't easy for anyone to participate in these conversations, in this work. White faculty worry about missteps and misunderstanding and simply may not have much practice thinking about these issues in real time, even if their research focuses on the exact same questions that are physically manifested in protests. Faculty of color can face both the burden of representation and backlash from students, colleagues, and administrators.

As Jennifer Williams, an assistant professor at Morgan State, wonders, what is the difference between professors who join their students in protest and those who help them plan those protests? When does an appearance on MSNBC boost a university's profile, and when does it become a liability to a scholar's intellectual reputation? How can administrators whose job is to maintain the university's vision challenge it to reimagine itself? The questions about the connection between activism and higher education are not new, but they must be considered in new ways by every generation of academics. The spotlight on this moment is brighter, the pace of the conversation is quicker, and the sense of urgency is heightened as we bear witness almost daily to a crisis that many have been able to ignore or see as marginal to our research, especially those of us whose work does not bring us into direct contact with the harsh world in front of us. Stacey Patton captured this when, in the days after the Ferguson protests, she interviewed academics of color who, in addition to feeling brittle with anger and fear, also questioned the value of their work: "Broader questions intrude. . . . Does students' doctoral work matter? Does teaching matter? What about having a PhD? Should they continue to channel their passion and intellectual pursuits into higher learning or should they redirect that energy toward activism?" To these questions, I would add ones more tied to institutional concerns. How does the kind of service that is expected of faculty of color, especially working with students of color, change when these students are agitating for change and the notion of service to the institution slips into activism that seeks to upend its current practices?

These questions are partially answered by this promise in the "Austin School Manifesto," an evolving statement about the work of Black Studies scholars: "We believe that teaching and the production of insurgent knowledge is itself one form of 'resistance'; however, we struggle to push our work past discourse to praxis. We seek social transformation through both aspects of our work."[4] This question of "praxis" is one I asked three Black women academics to think about: Ariana Alexander[5], a doctoral candidate in history; Williams, at Morgan State University; and E. Frances White, professor of history and former vice provost for faculty development at New York University. None of these women would call what they do activism, and they vigorously oppose the label "activist." They each believe the term should be reserved for those whose livelihood relies on activist work, but they also know that their research is not just put in service to their individual fields of specialization or even to teaching but to their larger communities, even when they don't engage directly with movements getting the most attention right now. Alexander, as she prepares to defend her dissertation, captures the questions hovering over many of today's scholars and academics regardless of where they might be in their careers: "How can I see my intellectual work manifest itself in real ways?"

FOR HER DISSERTATION "Soles on the Sidewalk: The Bronx Slave Markets from the 1920s to the 1950s," Alexander uses personal correspondence, oral histories, legal records and surveys, and institutional reports to trace the lives of Black domestics in New York City to show that in the Northern struggle for Black freedom, "the treatment of black domestics in the context of modern slave markets reframes questions regarding migration, political activism, labor, urbanization, and local governance."[6] The starting point for her dissertation is the intersection of Westchester and Simpson streets in the Bronx—a spot she reads as a historical archive to show how various parts of the community from policy makers to journalists to church leaders responded to the presence of women forced to seek work in public spaces. "This archive on the sidewalk," she writes, "helps us imagine the personal narratives of the women waiting for work, the importance of community activism, and the execution of local power amidst a structured informal economy."[7]

Alexander has the kind of CV that could easily lead her to the tenure-track path: a postdoctoral fellowship or two followed by a few visiting assistant professorships and finally a tenure-track position. She is a Ford Fellow, has presented her research findings at the major conferences in her field, and has been a teaching assistant. She worked on the Bronx African American History Project to implement a digitizing system for oral history interviews, and she is a rigorous scholar who sees teaching as a way to transform students' perceptions about history. But she decided midway through her program that she didn't want to follow that specific path: "By my third year, I really loved teaching but really loved working with students more." Alexander's approach to her graduate education has been a mix of optimism and healthy skepticism. Instead of feeling closed off by the idea that the tenure track was not for her, she sought out ways to think of success beyond tenure at a research institution or a small liberal arts college. She wasn't "clamoring for the tenure track." In part, this was because she'd heard enough about it to know it wouldn't work for her and in part because she wants a career that puts her into regular direct contact with students. She does not think of work outside the tenure track as a consolation prize. Instead, she questions and actively interprets how her training can be of service. She is less interested in the idea of success that Lipsitz describes as rewarded in the academy (focused, individualized work) and more invested in how she contributes to activities that improve the material conditions of those in whatever community she finds herself in—at school, at church, and at the not-for-profits where she has worked. The question she faces is not how to survive the contingency gauntlet until she finds a tenure-track job but how her work will be meaningful.

The term "community" gets thrown around quite a bit, but for Alexander the idea of community shapes how she approaches her work: "You serve the community that you come from, you serve to help other people, you serve because we are all involved in a larger fight." In practical terms, this shapes how she imagines her career, working with students in an advisory capacity wherever she can find them. At NYU, this meant working in the Office of Pre-Professional and Advising; at Bryant and Stratton, a for-profit college in her home state of Ohio, it has meant working with at-risk students. It also shapes how she approaches work far away from the academy. Asked to organize a health fair for an organization, Alexander naturally reached beyond the normal corporate organizations usually found at such events, into the community organizations that focus on the underserved. I think this impulse is linked by two things: one is in how she approached her dissertation, and the other is in how that approach complements all of her work. Alexander's approach to her dissertation research reflects a thinker more interested in narrative than institutional boundaries. "I started thinking about narratives in nontraditional spaces and about underground archives," she explained to me. This, in turn, shapes how she works in the world: "My academic process in terms of thinking about how things influence each other influenced the choices I made about how to build a community for health." Her goal was to bring in organizations like Good Greens, a company whose goal is to make healthy food available to people regardless of their socio-economic status. This was essential to Alexander who wanted to move beyond simply including local businesses to organizations whose work extended into the community. Her goal was to show how underserved communities can have access to the kind of food (organic, locally sourced products) that can significantly impact their health, and she sees this as a political issue. The health fair served 300 people and is an example of how Alexander sees herself contributing to social justice work. As much as possible she chooses to work with young people and believes that, "the research, the approach, the tools that you get should be to serve people." As a result, when she's advising, teaching, or working with young people at local churches, she is working toward what she sees as the larger fight against economic inequity and the kind of absorption that she believes pulls young people away from building and maintaining meaningful communities.

The work that Alexander wants to do is not necessarily antithetical to a tenure-track career, but her experience in graduate school has shown her that one of the dangers of the academy is how it can separate people from their communities and the values that shape our work. She described it to me as "a fog" that makes it difficult to see the greater vision and impact of [our] work." Alexander was months away from finishing her dissertation when I talked to her about her work and where she thought it would take her. I asked her what advice she might have for graduate students still making their way through, and she advised them to remember this: "You're only working on a little brick . . . in combatting inequality." It's advice that is particularly useful for graduate students who, as Jeffrey McCune, an associate professor of Women, Gender, and Sexuality Studies and performing arts at Washington University in St. Louis, explains, have been pulled "out of their theoretical silos and into a space of activism, both in terms of getting physically involved and shifting how distant their work may be from the assault on black bodies in the every day."[8] In some ways Alexander has chosen what might be called the alternate academic (or "alt-ac") path, but this is only considered "alternate" in a model that sees a tenured position as the only way to define success. What is clear from how she goes about her work outside of the academy is what she's learned inside of it, particularly while completing a dissertation that focuses on the different ways women worked together to secure economic equity for domestic workers. In this process she has learned to see archives in non-traditional spaces and to understand how different narratives intersect in public spaces in powerful ways, for substantive change.

WHEN THE NOW INFAMOUS CVS in Baltimore was burned down in the wake of Freddie Gray's death, Williams went to the corner of Pennsylvania and West North avenues to join the protest and to see the aftermath of the fire. She explains that while she could have read about it in the *Baltimore Sun*, she believed seeing its remains would deepen her understanding of the events in the city where she lives and teaches. Williams is an assistant professor of American Literature and Women and Gender Studies at Morgan State University and a graduate of Howard University, founded the same year as Morgan. She brings to Morgan an approach to reading and critical analysis shaped by her experience as an undergraduate at Howard, where "activism was practically part of the curriculum." She entered Howard in 1989 soon after students protested and shut down the school for five days to protest Lee Atwater's appointment to the board of trustees, so that student body's tradition of protest and social justice is part of her intellectual and political DNA. Williams describes being at Howard as a kind of refuge from assumptions about inadequacy and the demanding white gaze, and she left Howard feeling prepared because she "had a sense of value that was not reliant on white approval." That mix of personal, intellectual, and political agency informs why and how she went to join that protest. Because of her Howard training she believes her role as an academic requires engagement with the city around her. That training also influences her pedagogy—both the kind of work that belongs in the classroom and her role as professor who also models for her students what critical engagement with communities looks like.

I've known Williams well for quite some time, but I'd never thought to talk to her about teaching at an HBCU until the student protests at the University of Missouri forced a change in the leadership and became a model for students of color at other schools. In addition to her scholarly work, she writes for *Ms. Magazine* (primarily on the blog but occasionally the print magazine) and has a blog that focuses on popular culture, gender, politics, race, and sexuality. What I noted was that attending vigils and community events and responses to the deaths of Black men and women were an integral, organic part of her days. She doesn't see them as extra but as part of how her life is structured. Part of this is a by-product of her Howard experience, and part of it is undoubtedly due in part to her research, which she describes as emphasizing "the interrelationships between gender, sexuality, race, and class . . . in relation to place and cultural memory." In her readings of twentieth-century literature she argues, "Black women's urban narratives complicate spatial divisions, such as those between home and the street or spaces of privacy and sociality." Williams attends events not simply to bear witness or express solidarity but because she sees in these twenty-first-century protests, in these streets where conflicts clash, the same patterns she reads and writes about. It's a perspective she brings to her teaching and not simply because she teaches at an HBCU.

An advanced assistant professor, Williams has taught at various institutions since finishing her doctorate in 2006, including Michigan State University and Goucher College. "I emphasize social justice more [at Morgan State], but my subject matter always lends itself to some kind of takeaway when it comes to the way that race, sexuality, and class function," she explained when I asked how teaching at an HBCU felt different than teaching at other schools, especially during this particular moment. I am curious and perhaps more skeptical than I should be about what happens in classrooms when issues about sexuality and gender—and especially race—enter the conversation. I worry too much about the line between teaching that leads to consciousness raising and proselytizing. I am suspicious of the ways theoretical jargon and rhetoric stand in the place of thoughtful instruction, so, although I should know better, I asked Jennifer about the difference. Her approach is not a gimmick for her to make classes topical or a way to make material "relatable" to students. It's also not the way she structures courses simply because she is teaching at an HBCU. She understands, and to some degree, shares my questions. "It's not as if I walk into class everyday saying, 'Be the change!'" she told me with a chuckle. "I wouldn't do that even if I could, but [students] are either part of the solution or part of the problem." Williams believes that part of her job is to help them see that part of getting a college education is understanding the difference between those two. It's also just sound pedagogy as she makes clear when she describes teaching canonical literature in its cultural context: "I don't have to make up ways to bring social consciousness to class. Students have to learn close reading, but if they're reading Anne Petry's *The Street*, they also have to know about what's happening in Harlem at the time." She's referring to the 1943 riot in Harlem, and the conditions (economic inequality and police brutality) are a lot like what's happening across this country now. Williams does not have to stretch to show her students Harlem in 1943 because for many of them it feels like Baltimore 2015. Her composition course focused on #BlackLivesMatter and used the current crisis for students, but the focus of the course was similar to most composition courses, and its aim was to teach students critical thinking, carefully writing, research, and so on. The texts she chose would work together without the label; in other words, they could have made sense on any syllabus and are consistent with the teaching I've heard her talk about for years. But, as Williams explains about teaching the course in the fall of 2015, "Shit was real."

The realness of fall 2015 was in response to how the April protests reverberated at Morgan State. President Wilson describes a day that began with anticipation that there would be unrest without fully understanding the intensity, scale, and scope of the protests: "As I recall, about two or three hours before the protests that the nation saw on television, I was on conference call with . . . Mayor Stephanie Rawlings-Blake. She had called a conference call to brief the university presidents on what the police were picking up, and how we should actually take that information to make sure that our campuses were prepared. But I think, then, what happened about three hours later or so was not what we thought would happen."[9] Wilson had to assure concerned parents that their students were safe, and those who called were not only parents whose children were already enrolled at Morgan but also those who planned to send their children to Morgan in the upcoming academic year. If, in the imagination of certain publics, HBCUs are training grounds for student activists, for the students who attend them and the parents who send them there, they are also and perhaps primarily institutions designed to provide an education for Black students in a space where they can feel freer than they might at a predominantly white institution. But as the media broadcasted protests, and schoolchildren headed home from school were caught in the violence, when West Baltimore was chaotic, parents were more concerned about safety than anything else: "It didn't take long," he explains, "for my office to get phone calls from parents and from students who had indicated a desire to come to Morgan. And they were wanting to know what's going on in Baltimore, and what is Morgan going to do to allay any concerns that we have about whether we should even come to your university?"

Wilson talks about the different responses of students and speaks respectfully of civil disobedience. He noted proudly that the first college sit-in in America took place at Morgan. And given that the second largest group of the 2015 class comes from Baltimore County, this work is also about participating in home communities. This is something Williams knows, but at an event in April she came to understand just how real the issues she raises in classes are to some students. In April 2015, Morgan State University sponsored an event with the African American Policy Forum; its cofounder, Kimberlé Crenshaw, moderated the event titled "Breaking Silence: A Town Hall Hearing on Women and Girls of Color in Baltimore." Crenshaw gave a generation of Black feminists language to describe what they knew was missing from the feminist movement and the discourse that surrounds it and offered a model for how to battle the hegemonic structures of white feminism. The African American Policy Forum, founded in 1996, used its resources and influence to address and highlight the plight of Black girls and women at a time when #BlackLivesMatter focused almost entirely on male victims of police violence and President Obama's initiative known as My Brother's Keeper was aimed at young Black boys. They produced the report *Black Girls Matter: Pushed Out, Overpoliced, and Underprotected*, which reveals alarming statistics about how Black girls are punished more often and more harshly than their white counterparts.

For Williams, the event was essential for her students and the community. As a member of the Women's and Gender Studies Department, as a feminist, and as a Black Studies professor, Williams does work about connecting the mission of the academy to the community and making sure that her students understand how these connections work: "Part of our work is teaching students, and teaching them to become informed citizens, and the Crenshaw event is an extension of what happens in the classroom." But she was also concerned about the limited efficacy of such an event. The women came to give testimony, and the community witnessed that, but Williams doesn't know what happened next, and it bothers her: "My worry in the end is that policy makers, lawyers, some political figures that could make substantive changes were there. They could listen to these women's testimonies, follow up, and make changes." But, she continues "because we haven't done a follow-up, did these women just come and lay out all of their trauma and then have to go back to all of their circumstances?" The forum was particularly instructive for Williams as she saw current and former Morgan students testify. It clarified for her, in the middle of this protest, the degree to which the crisis on the streets could well be in her own classroom. "It was interesting to see the bridge," she told me. "Generally, I love that. What I don't love is that we don't have the resources to give the students all they need." Her concerns are where Wilson's statements about dialogue and Morgan State's "values" clash with what faculty are expected to provide for students at all times but especially now. In some ways, Morgan is a hybrid—an institution that grants doctorates while understanding that the ethos of a liberal arts college is best for its students—and that requires a great deal of additional work for all of the faculty. Despite the place that activism and advocacy have in her work, Williams is first and foremost a scholar, and she feels the pull of being at a school that expects her to publish while also mentoring, advising, and supporting her students. Morgan touts small class sizes in much the same way that small liberal arts college do and demands publication at the same time.

Williams may not call herself an activist, but she is most passionate about the importance of it to the moral fiber of institutions when she talks about the role of community engagement. Throughout our conversation, Williams was candid but cautious—pushing back against any neat categories I've insisted on or assumptions about her relationship to her work, but when she talked about the stakes she was bold and unflinching: "Academia has to go to the street to do work that is socially meaningful. We need to think of research or 'the work' in a broader way. It's not just the work that's my book. I'm doing meaningful work when I work on my book, write for broader publics, and go into the community as a professor of Morgan State." And so, on the one hand, she understands the stakes for her work as an English professor; she knows that some of what she does won't "count" for tenure; and she is savvy enough to understand that the stakes are very different, depending not only on where a professor is in her academic career but also on the kind of activism she takes on. On the other hand, she won't be limited in where she takes her research: "Pennsylvania and West North avenues is an archive, and to bear witness to what happened there enriches my own knowledge. You can still smell the smoke there." She paused and then told me, "I mean, I suppose I could stay in the library all day." She paused again, and then explained why she doesn't: "I guess I'm a Black Studies professor."

TO SOMEONE LIKE E. FRANCES WHITE, who came up during the Black student movement, who defines herself as part of a Black radical feminist tradition, and who has had a successful career as a professor, dean, and vice provost, this current moment is as vibrant for her as the 1960s: "I think this is a great time to be in the academy and to be a faculty member. . . . I'm not saying there aren't difficulties. There are, but it reminds me of the Black student movement. I'm a product of that movement. It motivated my work." I visited with White in the months before she retired from NYU, and the last question I asked her was what advice she had for the next Frances White starting her career now. It was the kind of predictable question that always falls a little flat, and at first she didn't have an answer. As I was leaving her office, however, she called out "Cast your net wide. That's it: cast your net wide."

When I talked with her, I had scholars such as Alexander and Williams in mind, but I was also thinking of someone like Brittney Cooper, assistant professor of Women's and Gender Studies and Africana Studies at Rutgers and one of the cofounders of the Crunk Feminist Collective, a coterie of scholars, scholar-activists, artists, and writers who combine an interest in hip-hop culture with feminist principles for social justice and personal enlightenment. Cooper has her feet firmly planted in two worlds and is as likely to be lecturing on Black feminism, hip-hop, and pop culture as organizing in Ferguson while publishing in mainstream popular outlets and in traditional peer-reviewed journals. Her book *Race Women: Gender and the Making of a Black Public Intellectual Tradition* is forthcoming from University of Illinois Press, and she publishes in the leading journals of her field—*Signs*, *MELUS*, and *Meridians*—while publishing regularly in *Salon*, *The New York Times,* and *Cosmo.com* as well as appearing on MSNBC.

I was thinking of Stacey McCormick, who talked with me as she was leaving her adjunct position at Montclair and starting a tenure-track job as an assistant professor of English at Texas Christian University and was already scoping out both neighborhoods and the kind of community work she would do. Like Alexander, Jade Davis determined that a tenure-track post would not be as useful for her work as her current position as assistant director for Digital Learning Projects at LaGuardia Community College and Form Program Manager at the Humanities, Arts, Science and Technology Alliance and Collaboratory. Davis's doctorate is in Communication Studies (media, technology, and culture) from the University of North Carolina–Chapel Hill, and her cultural studies analysis is rooted in the work of Fanon, Barthes, McLuhan, and Hurston. I was thinking of Eve Dunbar, whose Gawker essay "Who Really Burns: Quitting a Dean's Job in the Age of Michael Brown" is one of the rare frank discussions of the intense pressures that come with making that administrative turn. And I was thinking about the doctoral candidate who shared on Facebook her concern that her activism will be an impediment on the job market. Each woman is building a career that requires her to maintain a balance between the push and pull of institutional expectations and her own commitments to social justice. Although men take on this work, too (Mark Anthony Neal and Marc Lamont Hill come to mind immediately), the labor and risks that Black women face are different, undervalued, or ignored all together.

When I asked White how community engagement (the term we agreed on when she, too, resisted my attempts to call her an activist) has fit into her academic career, I was surprised to hear her say it has a corner she's kept separate from her professional career. So often we are encouraged to list all we do, to account for all of our time, to justify what we do when we are not publishing or teaching, but White took a different approach: "I never counted the stuff I did outside. I thought it was something different. I was on the board of the Audre Lorde Project and the board of the Hetrick Martin Institute, but I never listed them." When I asked her why, she answered, "I didn't want my whole world to be one thing." She was also worried about the message it would send to her junior colleagues: "I wanted to make sure that I wasn't confusing younger faculty, that this was a thing that was going to get them tenure. This is your extra. You have a job and you have to do your job." She knows her approach doesn't work for everyone, but she stresses the importance of having corners in life that can be rooted in intellectual pursuits without being part of an official academic dossier to be counted and parsed during personnel processes. I think her approach reflects both a long career in the academy and the revolutionary nature of her research agenda as a historian. In this, she reminds me of Cheryl Wall and Houston Baker whose work in their teaching and scholarship was transformative because it existed in a cultural moment where mainstream academic conversations ignored the work of people of color.

Before White went into administrative work she'd been on the faculty in history departments at Fourah Bay College in Sierra Leone, Temple University, and Hampshire College and was writing about African women at a time when everyone was content to ignore them. She started her tenure-track career when the history department at Temple felt free to tell her, their new assistant professor, that they would not be listing her classes in the department's offerings. She had a joint appointment in history and Pan-African Studies, and while one department refused to include her courses in their major, the other struggled with a lack of resources and was uncertain about what to do with the Black radical feminist in their midst in the 1970s who would go on to write "Africa on Mind: Counter Discourse and African American Nationalism." White remembers that the chair of the department looked very happy to see her go. "Africa on my Mind," unsparing and thorough in its critique of sexism, is now practically canonical; in it she argues that Black nationalism is "an oppositional strategy that both counters racism and constructs conservative utopian images of African-American lives"[10] while cautioning against mythologizing Africa. It sounds like common sense to most of us now, but it pushed back against the accepted narratives that centered patriarchal goals.

White knew after her first department meeting that she was in the wrong school, and by the end of her second year she'd accepted a position at Hampshire College. She eschewed mainstream history, forgoing the American Historical Association's national conference after a few years, and, while she would not suggest this to new academics because the demands on tenure are stricter now, she believes this decision was good for her: "I am deeply inside me a historian; that's how I think of the world." She explains, however, the benefits of Hampshire: "I was able to live a kind of integrated life as someone who considered herself a Black radical and a Black feminist radical. It took me out of the mainstream in many ways, and that gave me the space to grow without certain kinds of tensions that I see now." She meant to stay at Hampshire for just a few years, but made a home there for seventeen years moving, it seems, almost seamlessly from being a member of the faculty to serving as a dean. Although I wanted to talk to White to get the prospective of a full professor, I was also interested in how she folded diversity into her career as an administrator. She joked about knowing that people saw her as going over to the "dark side," when she became a dean but I was curious to know how a self-described radical Black feminist whose research agenda emerged outside of mainstream historical culture made the change to leadership when institutions, I believe, are by design conservative.

On my way to meet White, who, in addition to being a woman of color, identifies as a lesbian, I kept thinking about what Joy James and

Edmund T. Gordon have to say about the limits of diversity as a way to reshape institutions: "The notion that mere appearance of progressives in institutionalized learning constitutes a disruption of the normative reproduction or the continuity of repression seems shortsighted. Just to have women, queers, and people of color in academe is insufficient, in and of itself, for social change.... The view that writing or teaching in a 'radical' vein, or building progressive units within the academy transforms educational institutions also seems myopic."[11] White was by any measure successful in both the work she required of all deans and provosts, but she was also successful in her efforts to develop the kind of program necessary to develop and maintain a diverse professoriate. At Hampshire College she served as dean of the School of Social Sciences working with forty faculty members and then dean of the faculty working with ninety faculty members. Diversity work wasn't something she originally planned, but, as she describes it, no one else was really doing it, and it was clearly necessary.

Whatever success she has had as an administrator (increasing enrollment, improving faculty diversity, raising twenty-five million dollars as part of a capital campaign at NYU, developing a postdoctoral program) she ascribes to her choice to work with a coalition across the campus communities she has joined. She described teaching at Hampshire College as "almost like having a second graduate experience" because of team teaching that expanded her understanding of sociology, anthropology, and European history. I think this kind of collaborative, interdisciplinary work shaped her sense of what is possible when faculty work across institutional structures and translated to her approach at NYU where she worked with the deans of fourteen colleges, all of which had slightly different needs, to build a postdoctoral program for underrepresented academics. I suspect that her team-teaching, which requires curricular collaboration and negotiation on a week-by-week, day-by-day basis, and her decision to work as a historian away from the mainstreams of her discipline resulted in more creative thinking about how to define and design successful programs. The NYU program was designed as a transition to a full-time career and not simply a placeholder for the institution. She explains that while she shaped and led it, she "didn't pull it off alone." The program was deliberately named the "Postdoctoral and Transition Program" to ensure that new PhDs could work in the arts and in traditional academic departments. It really was, White says, "a program to help people get somewhere." Now on the tenure track, Williams is one of those people with a book manuscript well underway in part because of that program.

White's discussion of the challenge she faced when trying to design diversity initatives speaks to the larger theme of this anthology. She explained that "[t]here was no opposition to it, but there was resistance nonetheless." It is this resistance without opposition that is so often a stumbling block to diversity at almost every level. It isn't necessary to argue against diversity initiatives but to simply argue for something else. White faced the argument that a resource-poor institution couldn't prioritize diversity, and as NYU tried to burnish its reputation, "There was this sense that in order to mak[ing] diversity a priority meant sacrificing the pursuit of big-name scholars." This attitude solidified and led to what White refers to as her "biggest defeat" when NYU's central School of the Faculty of Arts and Sciences refused to include any diversity initiatives as it increased its faculty. She describes the school's attitude as this: "We are trying to put all our resources into making NYU a premier institution, and we don't have time for that." It's clear that White still has strong feelings about the decision: "They had all this money to bring in new faculty, and diversity wasn't even mentioned. They didn't want anything to get in the way of bringing in named scholars." The idea that the college felt it needed to choose one over the other—diversity or named scholars, particularly when so many scholars of color are clamoring to live and work in New York—is a testament to how resistant institutions can be to the very notion of diversity. I think that what was particularly frustrating for White was that systems were in place and a coalition of deans and faculty supported the initiative but the leadership refused to make it a priority. For someone who regularly participates in panels on the subject and gives lectures and delivers keynotes nationally and internationally, it must have been particularly difficult to lose the battle. It also means that the school abandoned attempts to bring in junior faculty and mentor them as necessary.

White had the kind of advice for junior faculty that is common but not always heeded. I was particularly interested in her thoughts about writing in popular venues at a time when everyone seems obsessed with being or naming "public intellectuals." White is curious—"I wonder: How can they do that much writing and do the publishing that they have to do in those journals?"—but lands on a truth about rigorous tenure requirements that is inconvenient at a time when people want to chime in immediately about the current cultural and political crisis: "The standards are ridiculously high, but that's a reality." When I asked whether such writing was assessed during personnel processes and explained some silly theory I had about how deans think about time and how they calculated faculty work, she was mildly exasperated: "This is what I think people don't understand: it doesn't count!" When I pressed the point and asked about blogs and public writing, she was clear: "Mostly they don't know about it, don't care about it, and it doesn't register much." The coin of the realm at research institutions is still the single-authored book and publication in elite journals, and no amount of diversity will change that.

The leitmotif of our talk had been about working with other people, and even when White talks about how individual scholars can navigate the academy, she returned to this idea: "I've seen people go it alone, but that's not an easy path." She explained that she wouldn't advise people to pull away from their disciplines as much as she did and talked about how difficult, how scary it can be. Then, as I was leaving, with my hand literally on her office door, she crystalized what is underneath her approach in all areas of her work—as a scholar who thrived even when historians were inclined to ignore her work, as a teacher who embraced team teaching with colleagues in different disciplines, and as an administrator who understood that successful academic leaders need to work across their institutions to develop and maintain meaningful diversity—was the message, "Cast your net wide."

The idea of casting one's net wide gives young scholars permission to take the time they need to determine how the work they want to do fits in both with how they are trained and how they want to function in the academy at a time when the urgency of now makes it feel as if there is no time. Some of the work happening now is flashy and photogenic and hashtagged to death, but I think White would want young scholars to understand the value of work that comes as a result of the long view. She talks with great fondness about a former student who called her worried about not having time to do all that seems necessary right now. The worried student wrote that there just wasn't time. White said to me, "I guess I think that's wrong. I think we're better if we go for the long haul . . . the work is gonna be there."

For that work to happen, however, there needs to be a network of faculty who can offer an institutional counterpoint to the ideas in this statement from Morgan State president Wilson near the end of his interview: "Certainly, we encourage our students to be true to the great history of Morgan and to participate in civil disobedience but to always do so in a respectful manner." This is the point of view of a leader of an institution where the idea that Black lives matter is not only not new but also built into its foundation. The idea of being "respectful," of disrupting without being disruptive, is precisely why faculty need to be passionate but mindful, engaged but pragmatic. It also makes clear that the academy needs to cast its net wide, too. We look back now on the great scholar activists—Angela Davis, Audre Lorde, June Jordan, Cathy Cohen, and Amiri Baraka—but they had uneasy, tense relationships with the academy.[12] In some way, that tension must have been productive. As James and Gordon remind us, "Radical ideas can be easily commodified." But as Eve Dunbar extols, "'social justice' and 'social responsibility' are not tags in a course catalog or what happens after social unrest. They form the living and breathing bedrock for a compassionate and thriving community. They are utterly attainable goals—when leaders of powerful institutions actually listen."[13]

Notes

1. Eric Kelderman. "Morgan State Leads With Values in Wake of Protest," *Chronicle of Higher Education*, November 30, 2015 (video/online).

2. Gene Demby, "The Birth of a New Civil Rights Movement" *Politico Magazine*, December 31, 2014.

3. Lipsitz, "Breaking the Chains and Steering the Ship: How Activism Can Help Change Teaching and Scholarship."

4. E. T. Gordon, "The Austin School Manifesto: An Approach to the Black or African Diaspora" *Cultural Dynamics* 19(1) (March 2007): 93–97. From the author: "This manifesto is a collective living document. For this reason there is no definitive version. This version was presented by E. T. Gordon at Williams College in spring 2006 and revised in August 2006. It was based on the results of a collective writing effort initiated during the two-day Diaspora Symposium held at UT Austin in 2003, with a version produced by Jafari Allen from notes that he and Jemima Pierre took of discussions that took place over the course of two days during the Diaspora Symposium held in 2005. This was leavened with some of ETG's insights and those presented on the subject in commentary by Charles Hale as a discussant of papers presented by affiliates of UT's Diaspora Program on an AAA panel in 2004."

5. I asked my editors at UNC Press if I could have time to think about service and activism in this particularly turbulent time. They gave me that time, and I'm quite thankful for it. Ariana Alexander's early research on the subject has been essential to this version of the essay. The shape and direction of the conversations here reflect her thinking and are rooted in her ideas about scholarship as a kind of service to communities beyond the academy's walls. Jafari Sinclaire Allen

pointed me to key texts on the subject of activism in the academy and also read an early draft of this essay. I am eternally grateful for both.

6. Ariana Alexander, "Soles on the Sidewalk: The Bronx Slave Markets from the 1920s to the 1950s." Unpublished dissertation. New York University, New York.

7. Ibid.

8. Patton, "After Ferguson, Some Black Academics Wonder."

9. Kelderman, "Morgan State Leads with Values in Wake of Protest."

10. White, "Africa on My Mind," 75.

11. Gordon and James, "Afterword: Activist Scholars or Radical Scholars."

12. As Jelani Cobb reminds us in his reflection on Amiri Barka in the *New Yorker*, the former poet laureate of New Jersey was denied tenure by Rutgers at a time when scholars around the country were tenured based on articles and book chapters about his work.

13. Dunbar, "Who Really Burns."

Conclusion

Tweeting Diversity: Race and Tenure in the Age of Social Media

Patricia A. Matthew
Montclair State University

If Fred G. Wale were to repeat his project to integrate the faculty of predominately white institutions today, he might start with traditional mail exchanges or skip pen and paper and go straight to e-mail. Met as he was in the 1940s with silence by two-thirds of college leaders, he might start a blog to keep track of which university presidents responded, or, if he wanted to generate interest and pressure, he might start tweeting the responses and names of presidents and administrators who seemed to be ducking the issue. And if the scholars represented in this anthology were starting their careers today, their stories would evince many of the same obstacles and challenges they outline in their essays but would likely also include some reference to the resources that social media offer faculty of color and the risks that come with building academic careers at a time when the currency accrued to social media can also damage and destroy careers. In other words, this collection reflects pre-social media careers that evolved during a time when sharing information, stories, and strategies was more localized and difficult to communicate broadly and quickly.

Social media, particularly Twitter, is altering the experiences of academics of color by both connecting far-flung scholars who might never meet and by serving as a public, uncurated archive of the experiences of faculty of color. It makes it easier to draw attention to the problematic personnel processes in higher education and has the potential to make tenure processes more transparent. Prior to social media's ubiquity, faculty of color faced alone the transition from the relative comfort of graduate school to the social and professional isolation that can come with being one of the only people of color in a department, especially if they specialize in a field largely unfamiliar to their colleagues. Public discussions about the more personal experiences of academics were limited to the *Chronicle of Higher Education*'s "Miss Mentor" and personal essays by faculty A in field B teaching at mid-sized, northwestern university C—the latter of which sometimes featured faculty of color. Scholars working in new and emerging fields of scholarship had little or no way to connect with others in similar fields outside of annual conferences. The microaggressions and broad attacks that undermine personal confidence and institutional credibility went largely ignored or unanswered by those in positions of power. A contested tenure case might be discussed among the faculty and, if the professor was popular, protested by the students with pen-and-paper petitions circulated and then submitted to administrators who could put them in drawers and file cabinets and forget about them. It goes too far to claim that social media are transforming these transitions, trials, connections, and challenges,[1] but the ways in which social media are reshaping how academics of color move through their departments and institutions suggest that while institutional obstacles litter the path to success, social media can provide useful tools to directly combat or maneuver around those obstacles. So when faculty of color rightly fear that their experience with institutional racism is singular rather than part of a broader pattern, social media provide a space to find affirmation and solidarity. They can also serve as a barometer of the limits of academic freedom as we see rescinded job offers, locked Twitter accounts, and racist and sexist campaigns lobbied against the most vulnerable members of the academy— untenured faculty of color.

It's important to note that Twitter is as varied as its 500 million[2] users; among the Justin Bieber and *Scandal* fans, amid the political activists and groups they organize, in a corner of the Twittersphere a constellation of academics of color interact with one another every minute, hour, and day. This corner is populated by a mix of public intellectuals (Cornel West, Marc Lamont Hill, Michael Eric Dyson, Henry Louis Gates, and Melissa Perry Harris) prominent scholars (Sandy Darity, Brittney Cooper, Alondra Nelson, Anthea Butler, Tommie Shelby, Jelani Cobb, David Palumbo-Liu, Alan Liu), and numerous graduate students. They interact with journalists, political pundits, and news personalities. Their work moves between traditional academic discursive spaces and watercooler chat. They bring to bear critiques on popular culture rooted in traditional academic methodologies from history, anthropology, Ethnic Studies, and literary criticism. In addition to traditional academic peer-reviewed journals, they write for *Salon*, *Huffington Post*, and the online sites of the *Atlantic*, the *Nation*, and the *New Yorker*. It's also the space where advocacy groups (Crunk Feminist Collective, Blacks in Higher Education, Black PhD Network, Post Colonial Digital Humanities) announce news of particular interest to faculty of color. The space allows for casual exchanges that build informal connections that can evolve into substantive work relationships and collaborations. This is not a formally organized community but a collection of small groups of people who connect around a set of common interests linked through a sustained critique of race in higher education, popular culture, and national politics. It provides solidarity, intellectual exchanges, and it can make it easier for faculty of color to understand their work in a context that is not limited to traditional modes of scholarly discourse. It's not without its factions, squabbles, and schoolyard antics, but there is an ethos built around a common understanding of the power of solidarity in the face of institutions designed to exclude faculty of color.

While every academic understands that pursuing a tenure-track job means facing the possibility of moving to wherever a job in their field and specialization might be, it can be particularly daunting for academics of color if the only position in their field is in a town and city that is not diverse. And, while every newly minted PhD has to make the transition from graduate student to faculty member, the added layers of racialized tension and expectations make this transition more difficult for academics of color. Over the time it takes to finish the doctorate, graduate students of color are drawn to people who "get it" and shy away from those whose color blindness make them annoying or downright difficult. It's such a slow process as to be almost invisible. The gallows humor developed as a coping mechanism in response to racism in its myriad academic forms can hit a false note with new colleagues who may or may not share the same sensibilities or politics. The shorthand developed to talk about the realities of racism and cultural quirks doesn't always translate, and finding allies among white colleagues is a long process. Further, as the stories here have made clear, when moments of casual racism occur, it's not entirely clear to whom academics of color can turn for comfort, guidance, or just a bit of a rant.[3] Often it's difficult to even know whether or not one's experiences in an institution or department are isolated or part of a larger pattern, and white allies, for various reasons ranging from ignorance to discomfort to denial to fear, sometimes dismiss claims of racism without realizing how isolating it can feel for their colleagues. This institutional gaslighting can be paralyzing and chip away at the edges of faculty of color, eroding trust, respect for their colleagues and institution, and self-confidence. In 2013, the University of California–Los Angeles released the results of a survey of its faculty of color. While the majority of respondents were tenured, "they were still upset by the incidents of perceived bias, discrimination, or intolerance they had experienced at UCLA."[4] More important, nearly all of them said they felt that the offending parties were never forced to face consequences for their actions and explained that "UCLA's reaction to such complaints has consistently been to attempt to placate the injured faculty member without repercussions to the offending party."[5] If, as Marian Anderson explained decades ago, racism is like "a hair across your cheek. You can't see it, you can't find it with your fingers, but you keep brushing at it because the feel of it is irritating," then social media provides a magnifying glass to make visible those myriad hairs across the cheeks of faculty of color from around the country.

More than moral support comes from this kind of sharing. Social media have become a platform for promoting scholarship and building connections that can lead to meaningful collaborations. In 2013, Stanford University's Panel on Faculty Equity and Quality of Life released the results of a study that focused specifically on underrepresented minority (URM) faculty.[6] In the study, URM faculty reported they "often experience 'research isolation' when they lack colleagues whose research is similar enough to provide feedback or to collaborate with." More than 40 percent reported this intellectual isolation, even though they were not specifically asked to address this issue: "Faculty members felt that scholarship on race/ethnicity is marginalized in their campus units." While connections via Twitter cannot replace the professional relationships necessary for intellectually vibrant and cohesive academic departments, it can be a proving ground for working out ideas that can lead to innovative research.

A blog post read by a few people in the time before Facebook and Twitter can now be sent to thousands. Major figures in every field in the humanities can be found on Twitter, and the opportunity for dialogue and debate is great. In her post "From Tweet to Blog Post to Peer-Reviewed Article: How to be a Scholar Now," Jessie Daniels discusses how a tweet critiquing how the American Sociological Association overlooked race in panel after panel focused on online discourse at its 2010 conference evolved into a series of blog posts and, in 2013, an essay in

New Media and Society—a traditional, peer-reviewed journal. While this is not the only path to publication, it is certainly a more public one, and when race and diversity are the issue, scholarship benefits from arguments developed in a public sphere. As Daniels describes, "The suggestions for further citations came from people I know almost exclusively through our interactions via the blog or Twitter. That feedback from geographically remote, institutionally varied yet digitally close colleagues got me thinking about expanding that single blog post into a series of posts."[7] When Adeline Koh and Roopika Risam founded Postcolonial Digital Humanities, a "collaborative website" that "explores the theoretical and practical considerations of postcolonial digital humanities," they did so in part because of how publications in the emerging field of digital humanities seemed to develop different evaluative processes when work by scholars of color was under review. Koh and Risam have developed their website in full view of the digital humanities community, and the process has involved vigorous debate that requires everyone to think carefully about the varying projects digital humanities seek to undertake. Outside of the project of digital humanities, traditional scholars such as Georgetown History Professor Marcia Chatelain use social media in ways that provide a model for faculty and institutions alike. Chatelain was an untenured assistant professor when she developed the idea for #FergusonSyllabus. Attuned to the campus's activist energy in the wake of the George Zimmerman verdict, Chatelain explained that she didn't want to leave the death of Michael Brown and the country's response to it "undiscussed and untouched." Her original plan was not to make #FergusonSyllabus an institutional response, but as her own private contribution to a growing movement. She wrote in the *Atlantic*: "I have few talents in a crisis, but I do know I'm pretty good at teaching, and I knew Ferguson would be a challenge for teachers: When schools opened across the country, how were they going to talk about what happened?"[8] The end result was a crowd-sourced syllabus that was published on the *Atlantic*'s online site.

Perhaps more interesting than how the syllabus came about is how Chatelain successfully managed her institution's interest in her Twitter conversations around Ferguson. It offers a model of how faculty, particularly untenured faculty, can try to channel the energy of social media into their activist work while teaching their institutions how to value this labor. When one of Chatelain's senior colleagues sent a note to the department sharing news of her project, she knew he meant well but admits feeling a bit uneasy. Ultimately, she told me in phone conversation, she decided that she "fundamentally didn't care." She knew that, although she had started the hashtag as a private individual, the boundaries between persons and institutions are porous. She understood the risk and decided that it was one worth taking: "If I was not going to get tenure for something, I wanted it to be for this," she explains. "I had come into academia doing a lot of activism and wanted to do that for my students. If this was the going to be the thing that sunk me, I was going to be very proud of that."

Chatelain is what might be called a "late adopter" when it comes to social media. She didn't join until after she had her first academic post, mostly because her friends were on Facebook. Joining as an academic with institutional affiliation undoubtedly shaped how she saw her role in public. She didn't have to make the transition from graduate student on social media to faculty member using social media, and I suspect this is why it has worked so well for her. Once she knew her colleagues were aware of #FergusonSyllabus, she met with the president's office to discuss her project and was pleasantly surprised to find that her efforts were in line with how both her president and her provost planned to respond to Ferguson. Chatelain spoke with real institutional pride about this response, clearly understanding how leadership at the highest levels, particularly around current events, can galvanize colleges and universities: "[this] fundamentally changed the school year for everyone," and students and faculty were "energized by the possibility that their activism would be supported."

Despite the overwhelming success of #FergusonSyllabus at every level—as a substantive contribution to the Ferguson movement and as a catalyst for organizing at her institution—Chatelain was unsure about how to discuss it in her tenure file: "Even though I was getting positive feedback, the anxiety about being taken seriously pushed me to downplay it." It wasn't until her senior colleagues noticed that a discussion of #FergusonSyllabus was missing from her tenure file that she decided to include it; even then, she was unclear about how to discuss it and where. Was this teaching, research, or service, or some kind of mix that doesn't fit into neat institutional boxes? Her reticence and eventual decision to discuss the work speak to what kind of support is required of departments and institutions whose faculty participate in social media. It isn't enough to post guidelines for language and require faculty to make clear they are only posting for themselves; more than simply governing how faculty work in social media, universities need to figure out how to support and reward this work at its best.

The #FergusonSyllabus is an example of social media, particularly Twitter, at its most productive. It's at its best and perhaps most bracing when the kinds of flagrantly racist comments that often go unanswered in the ivory tower are made public; the response can be swift and fierce and become an opportunity for solidarity and, more important, a platform to explain and explore through blog posts, op-eds, and Storyfied tweets how singular incidents reflect systemic problems. Twitter is the most influential social platform for facilitating and sometimes fomenting this discussion. Take, for example, the case of Tressie McMillan Cottom vs. the *Chronicle of Higher Education*. In 2012, McMillan Cottom was a doctoral candidate in Emory University's sociology program. According to her blog, she studies education, inequality, and organizations: "[My] research has surveyed for-profit students and the organizational mechanisms of the for-profit college sector."[9] McMillan Cottom was like any number of graduate students—sharp, resourceful, driven, and passionate. She is bolder than some and certainly more charismatic than most, with an uncanny ability to crystalize problems that others miss entirely—first with sharp rhetoric and then with even sharper organizational critiques. She is quick on her keyboard and a provocative tweeter who quickly dispatches those she disagrees with using an arsenal that includes everything from Durkheim to critical race theory to snappy retorts ("Girl, bye," she once tweeted to a white woman who tried to challenge her criticism of mainstream feminism). Even with her admirable skill on social media, however, what makes her unique is how she has put social media to use to amplify her voice to make bold critiques of educational systems and the tools used to measure their effectiveness. Despite being a new doctoral candidate, McMillan Cottom was already distinguishing herself and drawing the attention of online media organizations and had to balance requests for columns, public speaking, and interviews with the work of finishing her dissertation. Social media has had a profound impact on her academic career: "Social media was a lifeline for me when, as a first year graduate student, I found myself without an adviser or a clue. I have built professional relationships in virtual spaces that have been invaluable for my career and personal well-being. Many of my closest mentors and advocates started as Twitter follows or blog commenters. I have also used public discourse to engage powerful actors in media and academe, sometimes to contribute and other times to agitate. That I have done this as a graduate student strikes some as brave and others as foolish."[10]

She has been a steady presence on social media for years, but her profile increased sharply when she wrote a blog post in response to a particularly nasty attack on African American Studies. On April 30, 2012, a blogger on the *Chronicle of Higher Education*'s "Brainstorm" page wrote the following after reading an article in the publication highlighting the work of three doctoral students: "If ever there were a case for eliminating the discipline, the sidebar explaining some of the dissertations being offered by the best and the brightest of Black-studies graduate students has made it. What a collection of left-wing victimization claptrap. The best that can be said of these topics is that they're so irrelevant no one will ever look at them."[11]

Blogger Naomi Schaefer Riley went on to mock the dissertations of three graduate students—Keeanga-Yamahtta Taylor, La Tasha B. Levy, and Ruth Hays—dismissing their work in the broad, hyperbolic rhetoric that guarantees blog hits. Riley offered nothing new in her critique: she simply used reductive rhetoric to rehearse the broadest claims from the culture wars of the 1980s. Her harsh critique of doctoral candidates echoed criticisms and debates that shape pedagogical, curricular, and personnel debates at even the most progressive institutions. The anger and disdain she sparked was also not particularly new. African Americans who specialize in Ethnic Studies are often rightfully angered by empty critiques and broad dismissals of their research and teachers. What was different, however, was how social media amplified the responses to Schaefer Riley's screed and the speed with which the *Chronicle of Higher Education* responded to the backlash. She was fired seven days after her initial post. Before that, however, she doubled down:

> Unless the *Chronicle* features you in a piece, being a graduate student is just like being "invisible" (Ralph Ellison, please call your office.) A word to the wise: If you're trying to convince the wider world that Black people in America are oppressed, I'd skip using the experience of Black graduate students as an example.
>
> Finally, since this is a blog about academia and not journalism, I'll forgive the commenters for not understanding that it is not my job to read entire dissertations before I write a 500-word piece about them. I read some academic publications (as they relate to other research I do), but there are not enough hours in the day or

money in the world to get me to read a dissertation on historical Black midwifery. In fact, I'd venture to say that fewer than twenty people in the whole world will read it. And the same holds true for the others that are mentioned in the piece.[12]

Liz McMillen, the editor-in-chief of the *Chronicle*, wrote an editorial note replying to the "outrage" and "disappointment" of the "several thousand" commentators who responded to the post. Rather than taking on the content of Schaefer Riley's critique, she explained that the post "did not conform to the journalistic standards and civil tone that you expect from us" and that Schaefer Riley had been terminated.

It's impossible to point to a single comment, blog post, or tweet that pushed Schaefer Riley off the pages of the most influential news publication in higher education, but McMillan Cottom's response to the attack, a post on her blog and the petition she started, must have been a contributing factor. Not content to rant in an e-mail or kvetch over coffee, she used social media to publically criticize the *Chronicle of Higher Education* and marshaled an impressive collection of allies to hold them to account. In her blog post "The Inferiority of Blackness as a Subject" she got to the heart of Schaefer Riley's attack:[13] "Schaefer Riley went after, arguably, the most powerless group of people in all of academe: doctoral students who lack the political cover of tenure, institutional support, or extensive professional networks. She attacked junior scholars who have done nothing but tried to fulfill the requirements of their degree program and who had the audacity to be recognized for doing so in academia's largest publication. Their crime is not being fucking invisible."

She went on to bring into sharp focus what it means to be an African American graduate student:

> Maybe it has been awhile since you have been a graduate student. Maybe you have never been a Black graduate student. Let me tell you a little about my experience of that.
>
> You are almost always perceived as crazy and different for doing something few in your family or peer groups would ever consider doing. Even if you are among the best and brightest in college you are somewhat of an oddity in graduate school. You are either the voice of all Black people or the voice of no one. You can be, in any combination and at any given moment: an affirmative action case, an overachiever, lazy, aggressive, scary, and your University's poster child for diversity.

Two things make this episode particularly interesting—the speed of the firing and the fact that at the helm was a graduate student with relatively little institutional power. The speed is a result of the qualities that separate Twitter from other social media platforms. Prior to the ubiquity of social media, Schaefer Riley's rant would have been met with a few stern letters to the editor—some supportive, some critical. A collective statement written by a department or professional group decrying her unprofessionalism and mischaracterization of an academic discipline might have been submitted.[14] But to the same degree that social media rewards outrageous, aggressive rhetoric, it can also be relentless if enough of its practitioners are offended by such rhetoric.

Twitter rewards crisp, pithy, often snarky critiques of culture and also allows individuals to quickly mobilize like-minded peers to pressure academic administrations by calling out problematic statements. When Schaefer Riley attacked Black Studies, McMillan Cottom's blog post and petition were disseminated by her Twitter followers and people they follow. In a presentation at the Association of Black Sociologists' 2013 conference, she recounts how quickly her post spread: "I went to Wal-Mart and I was still hopping mad. On the return trip home I pull over and write a blog post refuting Schaefer Riley's argument and calling on the *Chronicle* to exercise editorial ethics by removing it and censuring Schaefer Riley. It's Atlanta so a 10-mile ride took me about an hour. By the time I got home, a link to my blog post had been retweeted over 300 times and my sleepy blog which averaged, prior to that, maybe 100 readers a week had been read by almost 10,000 unique visitors in three countries."[15]

THE SPEED AND SCOPE OF McMillan Cottom's campaign is not just about the technology of Twitter but about how people interact on it. As Joel Penney and Caroline Dadas explain in their essay "(Re)Tweeting in the Service of Protest," "The specific architecture of Twitter has been noted by scholars for its particular emphasis on rapid textual exchange among a multitude of actors and publics."[16] They continue, "In particular, the way in which Twitter has allowed users from disparate locations to continuously tweet and retweet information about the movement outside of the strictures of mainstream media recalls Warner's definition of a counterpublic: 'it enables a horizon of opinion and exchange; its exchanges remain distinct from authority and can have a critical relation to power.'"[17] McMillan Cottom explains it thusly: "[Twitter's] fundamental strength is its ability to separate the wheat from the chaff, or put another way, to cull the signal from the noise. This is an invaluable benefit, particularly to social movements."

Carrie Brown, Elizabeth Hendrickson, and Jerry Litten discuss how the possibility of Twitter can increase the diversity in the media in their presentation to the International Symposium for Online Journalism. Their working thesis is that since people of color use social media to stay abreast of events in their communities and use Twitter more than white people,[18] news outlets would be wise to see this as an opportunity to develop a new audience. The Pew Research Center finds that people of color use Twitter at twice the rate of whites and that Twitter users are economically diverse.[19] They point out that while Facebook users are interested in connecting with friends and family, Twitter users are more likely to reach out to those outside of their social circles, and while people of color and white people use social media in similar ways, people of color seem to be using the medium more conversationally than other racial and ethnic groups. The same opportunities that Brown et al. claim will make media more diverse are already being capitalized on by faculty of color on Twitter. It can be good for academics of color and, by extension, their home institutions if they can feel more connected. Ideas can be challenged (sometimes unproductively) and worked out. Friendships can form, and alliances can be built. A first-year graduate student might find herself in a conversation with Sandy Darity, chair of Africana Studies at Duke, or David Palumbo-Liu, professor of Comparative Literature at Stanford.

While Twitter offers new opportunities for faculty of color, McMillan Cottom qualifies her praise of social media as platform for substantive change, arguing that "mobilizing a message is not the same as mobilizing people. It can be a necessary condition but not a sufficient one for social movements as we generally define them in academic terms." And as Sava Sahell Singh points out, "The flip side of building networked communities of scholars is that we run the risk of creating echo chambers on Twitter, using them only to propagate the things we deem important."[20] Penney and Dadas explain that Twitter "privileges circulation *almost* to the exclusion of other concerns."[21] And the same space that can pull people together can damage the reputations of scholars at all stages of their careers. In her *Inside Higher Ed* piece, McMillan Cottom explains the risk of engaging with the world through public scholarship: "I have argued that social media and online spaces provide a means for women and minority scholars to build networks as protective factors against institutional forces that marginalize them. But I offer that argument with a caveat: doing so is not without risk. The inequalities women and minorities face in traditional academic models only exacerbate the potential risks of contributing to public scholarship. That is potentially devastating to those who would benefit most from the kind of visibility, credibility, and network building that public scholarship can provide."[22]

SHE KNOWS WHAT SHE IS talking about. Her posts, articles, and columns regularly incite virulent racist and sexist attacks, the best of the worst of which she sometimes shares on Twitter. In an essay for *ADA: A Journal for Gender and New Media*, she explains, "Really angry commenters want to have me fired, sanctioned by the university, and my brains violently excised from my body."[23] She has a remarkable ability to pivot away from such responses and continues to write in a constellation of forums—peer-reviewed journals in her chosen field, online news magazines, her blog, and education papers. But the anger and violent threats that McMillan Cottom deflects with seeming ease is pernicious, and the first two wishes her detractors have—to see her fired and to see her institutionally sanctioned—have become a regular part of the arsenal used more and more by people of all stripes to punish faculty of color for what they say on social media. These incidents always spark questions about academic freedom, and when the targets are scholars such as Anthea Butler, Saida Grundy, and Zandria Robinson, academic freedom gets tangled up in racist and sexist attacks. For each of these women, social media engagement moved beyond single tweets or private threats. They were each targeted by groups of people determined not only to threaten them but also to damage their careers. They failed: Butler is a tenured associate professor with sterling credentials and a bulletproof CV; Grundy was supported by her union and her search committee, and both of her scheduled classes for her first semester were fully enrolled; and Robinson's attackers were focusing on the University of Memphis when she had already moved on to the arguably more prestigious Rhodes College.[24]

While the coordinated attack on Anthea Butler was the most extreme and the attempts to discredit Zandria Robinson[25] confirm that people are actively seeking targets for conservative rage, Saida Grundy's experience of being "dragged" on social media is a call for all tenured faculty to help emerging scholars of color develop strategies for navigating social media. A few months before Grundy's tenure-track contract at Boston University went into effect, several of her tweets were used to prove that she hated white people in general and white male students in particular. A few days after an Oklahoma frat was videotaped singing a racist chant, she asked, "Why is white america [*sic*] so reluctant to identify white college males as a problem population?" According to Boston University's faculty website, Grundy is a "feminist sociology of race and ethnicity," so while her tweets were intemperate, they were no doubt rooted in that research. But the "reverse-racism" crowd used this tweet and a few others to whip up and focus the anger of people who would rather talk about anything than white supremacy and racism. At first, it seemed to be working. Boston University president Robert A. Brown, whose office was critiqued for shutting down the university's African Presidential Archives and Research Center,[26] issued a statement that claimed to defend Grundy's academic freedom and then tried to have it both ways: "Boston University does not condone racism or bigotry in any form, and we are committed to maintaining an educational environment that is free from bias, fully inclusive, and open to wide-ranging discussions."[27] For her part, Grundy released a response conceding that her tweets were problematic and then explained, "As an experienced educator, I take seriously my responsibility to create an inclusive learning environment for all of my students. . . . I am unequivocally committed to ensuring that my classroom is a space where all students are welcomed."

In the midst of the chatter, tweets, blog posts, and articles, Grundy's department stood silent. Her faculty union was unequivocal in its support and, among other things said, "We are disheartened that President Robert Brown does not highlight the cultural value of such intellectual labor in his letter to the community."[28] But I was most interested in her departments' responses; she has a joint appointment in Sociology and African American Studies. Those departments seemed best positioned to defend the truths underneath those tweets. My sense is that they probably worked with the union on the statement, but this seemed like a missed opportunity. In an interview with Boston Public Radio (WBUR), Nancy Ammermann, a member of Grundy's search committee, explained what everyone already knows: "Twitter's hard, and many of us who are in the academy are trying to exercise some voice in social media and Twitter, but we all know that it's very difficult to make a nuanced argument in 140 characters." She continued, "And we know that the words we use can often be taken the wrong way when they're out in such a very public kind of forum."[29] She's right, of course, but it's important to move beyond naming the risks.

As Kerry Ann Rockquemore says at the beginning of an advice column about social media, if telling "millennial scholars not to engage in social media is like telling fish not to swim,"[30] what do senior faculty of color owe to emerging scholars of color whose careers are developing either in the glare of social media or in its shadow? They are all advised to have blogs and websites (some of which bring to mind the Ilyana Fix My Life aesthetics that suggests that some scholars are promoting a brand instead of their research) and to promote their work. Sharing work and ideas on social media must feel like it increases the impact of their scholarship, especially at a time when the country is wrestling, quite violently, with racism, sexism, and transphobic attitudes, and so the need for institutions to develop plans and strategies to support the role of social media in faculty careers is more urgent than ever. To be clear, the threats to academics are not new. As Chatelain noted, "Academics have always been targets, and people have always wanted to come for us. Now they have better mechanisms. We are still in the culture wars, but there are now more warriors." Academics of color need their own mechanisms and strategies.

Chatelain, who is a role model by almost any measure, admits, "There were moments that I had on Twitter that were not my best." She cautions, "Everyone doesn't exist the same way on Twitter. We are not all the same on this digital space just because we all have access." My own social media choices are pretty deliberate, especially on Twitter. I am always conscious about how my critiques of racism and white supremacy might make my students feel, so I was offended by Grundy's tweets—not their rightness or wrongness (her question is entirely legitimate) but how they might make students feel. But I suspect I'm more conservative than I'm willing to allow and that this conservative streak has helped me succeed in an academy that tends to like their Black folks assimilated. And so I ask myself regularly what I can do to make social media and the academy a safer place for those who are more strident than I might like. I can talk about strategies and mechanisms all day, but I keep returning to the fact that there is no real advice to offer because, like any other part of the profession, these choices are deeply personal, especially when it comes to how one uses social media for community and outreach at the same time. One person's prudent is another person's respectability politics. And the real problem, of course, is that the rage of white supremacy can't be mentored around. If we council, wring our hands, advise, and warn, we run the risk of silencing voices that we need the most—the future Anthea Butlers, Zandria Robinsons, Saida Grundys, and the future Tressie McMillan Cottom—a woman whose Twitter profile once offered both a warning and a promise: "I fail at shutting up."

McMillan Cottom popped up on my Twitter timeline when her response to the *Chronicle* post was repeatedly retweeted by the relatively few people I follow. Long before I met her, I decided to write about her battle with the *Chronicle*. The nature of Schaefer Riley's screed and the fact that she was successfully challenged by a young African American doctoral student suggested to me that Twitter was more than just a way to promote projects. Despite how impressive the blog post was and the response it generated, I was skeptical of McMillan Cottom and couldn't tell if her response was luck or a sign of an individual who had tapped into Twitter in the same way as Occupy Wall Street organizers had earlier. I initially followed her on Twitter and then almost immediately unfollowed her, thinking she was a one-blog-post wonder. There are countless blogs that I have come to think of as "oppression diaries"— blogs with posts that recount the very real troubles marginalized academics face but without sustained institutional critiques that move their posts beyond the realm of public journaling. These blogs rely too much on jargon (to the point they are sometimes unreadable), and while I appreciate their place and understand their importance, I don't find them particularly interesting. McMillan Cottom's posts kept popping up in my timeline, however, and I kept finding them compelling. So when I received an invitation to teach for an online for-profit college, I immediately thought to ask her about it. When she posted on her timeline that she needed help copy editing an essay, I recommended my research assistant Liam, who I paid to format the anthology for review. Over the course of a year via Twitter and e-mail, we have had an ongoing discussion about a range of topics: race in higher education, mainstream feminism's problem with women of color, the work of being an academic, hair, pop culture, and intraracial politics. She is a prolific writer with multiple blog posts up every week. Read them regularly and it's clear that her personal narratives are a springboard for a larger critique of how systems work to keep class and race (and gender) structures in place. She doesn't, in other words, write about herself simply as a way to vent; rather, she manages to successfully situate her experiences within larger social systems, making her arguments accessible to a wide audience without reducing complex ideas into mere anecdotes. Our relationship has evolved organically, and I have gone from seeing her primarily as an example of how social media can ameliorate the slings and arrows of racism in the academy to being a fan of her work. I now think of her as a friend.

We met over lunch when she was in Manhattan to give two papers at the Association of Black Sociologists. In person she is as quick, witty, and fierce as she is on Twitter. She is also constantly writing. Several times during our conversation she opened her moleskin to jot down a note, idea, or phrase one of us had used. While she is extremely popular with an enviable profile, feet planted in both the world of public intellectual discourse and as a scholar, I was curious to know what place she would find if she chose to stay on the traditional academic path and ended up in a tenure-track position. While I was curious, she was worried. She knew the realities of the job market, and she knew through a combination of gut instinct, sharp observational skills, and common sense that she would have cultural and institutional obstacles to overcome. She understood that the charisma and boldness that make her media friendly would play out differently in an academic department.

In her presentation, she talked about the blog post that led me to her work. The presentation was not simply a discussion of the blog post and the change it helped spark but was also about why she critiqued the *Chronicle of Higher Education*:

> *Chronicle of Higher Education* did not intend to harm the reputation and careers of junior Black scholar (for the rest of their careers this story will show up when their names are googled).
> It intended to generate profit for its organization. That the two coincide is a lesson for why organizational level analysis matters. Organizational practices make intent relatively meaningless.
> If citizenship paperwork is printed in English only that is likely not because some white man somewhere hates immigrants. It's a bureaucratic decision, however, that can have the same net effect: minimizing access to marginalized groups. Racist intent, or this perversion of race as an individual failing as Omi and Winant and Bonilla Silva would argue, obscures the reality of our bureaucratic

iron cage wherein organizational processes can formally rational-
ize inequality, obscuring their saliency via ostensibly neutral
bureaucratic acts without all the messiness of intending to be
racist or sexist. . . .

Even though her post critiquing the *Chronicle* was read in twenty-seven
countries by 80,000 people, she is reluctant to overstate the power of
Twitter. In an e-mail message she argues: "Social media is likely con-
strained in similar ways to traditional social movements. I think it can
only work once, you know? I mean the same methods and tools can be
applied to new situations but they have to constantly be reevaluated, re-
imagined, and reconfigured because organizations are very, very savvy
about absorbing dissent."

She is probably right, but steeped as I am in old-school scholarship, a
tenured university professor who navigated her entire career without the
benefit of social media, it's been tempting to see the future in Tressie's
successful deployment of social media and to imagine her prospects. She
was more skeptical than I am about her future. When we met for lunch,
she wanted to know why specifically I thought she would be successful.
Whereas I had lofty ideas, she thought about things like income, health
insurance, and a retirement plan. She also, I learned as we've continued to talk, spends a great deal of time thinking about the difference
between the traditional research models with publication in top-tier academic journals and with storied university presses and newer models
that might seem to have more impact but that might not always have the
same staying power as the research agenda she is launching. She is not
interested in clicks and traffic to her website but about intervening in
her field in ways that are both broad and deep.

Her concerns are echoed by Houston Baker, Jr., who sees the value
of social media but reminds us that scholarly engagement requires the
kind of time and space for reflection that is anathema to the pace of
social media. Baker is no intellectual Luddite, but he has resisted the al-
lure of academic "fame" that others seem to seek, a model that measures
success by the number of op-eds and television appearances a scholar
makes. He eschews "hot take" academia that seems to value clicks over
substance, and he is concerned—rightfully so, I think—that the work
suffers when it's shaped by the pace and demands of social media.
Baker draws a sharp distinction between the necessary, often invisible
work of deeply rooted scholarship and quick takes that tend to rely on

provocative numbers and rhetoric. Chatelain agrees and points to another challenge, explaining that it can be all too risky for young scholars to confuse the currency of social media ("speaking truth to power") with what the academy requires of scholars (ideas that are the result of careful research and reflection). After the success of #FergusonSyllabus, Chatelain found herself in a strange competition—one between her social media reputation and her success as a scholar. Her book *South Side Girls: Growing Up in the Great Migration* (Duke UP 2015) is very different than the #FergusonSyllabus, but the latter often brings her more attention than the former. As a result, she has to structure speaking invitations to make sure that the focus is not just on activism but on the research and writing she does away from social media.

My sense in August 2013 was that McMillan Cottom was poised to move beyond the occasional Huffington Post reference and column in *Inside Higher Education* and that she might be one of those great "public intellectuals" that people seem obsessed with naming. But before we could talk fully about my ideas (or anything), she had to leave. She was attending a task force meeting about Twitter and sociology. We were a bit late getting back from lunch, so all the seats at the main table were taken. This was before she left Atlanta for a year to participate as a graduate fellow at the Center for Poverty Research at UC Davis and accepted a position as a columnist for *Slate*. It was before her post "The Logic of Stupid Poor People" was cross-posted to "Talking Points Memo" and Andrew Sullivan's "The Daily Dish." It was before Michael Moore thanked her personally and Junot Díaz cited her. And it was before she showed up as part of a Room for Debate for the *New York Times*. Since then, she's been a fellow at Berkman Center for Internet and Society at Harvard. I watched as she put a book manuscript under contract on hold so she could put it through an additional peer-review process to make sure that her structural critique was as powerful as her seductive prose. She's also a new assistant professor at Virginia Commonwealth University. But in August 2013, the table was full, and she wasn't sure if she would end up with a tenure-track position; if she did, what would that mean for her career? As I left her, a solicitous white man brought in a chair for her, and I saw her sitting at the back of the room, taking it all in, tweeting her critique of the American Sociologist Association's discussion of social media to academics around the globe.

Notes

1. For more on tenure denials and social media see Dunn, "Lost Your Tenure Case?"

2. Smith, "How Many People Use 800+ of the Top Social Networks."

3. I originally discussed this transition on the *Written/Unwritten* blog in the post "Lesson from the Collections I: The Missing Cohort."

4. Ceasar, "Study Faults UCLA's Handling of Faculty's Racial Bias Complaints." Another faculty member, who is Latino and works in health sciences, described an incident in 2008 when a "senior faculty member" in the same department loudly called him a racial epithet in front of students. The professor said he went to the assistant dean of his department but was advised against going further because it "would cause more trouble," the report said. The faculty member said he feels threatened by his colleague, who is still at UCLA. A fully tenured white professor said he has spoken out against inappropriate conduct. He said, however, that he was retaliated against by his department chair, who refused to recommend him for a merit pay increase. The professor later retired from UCLA.

5. Ibid.

6. Stanford University, "Quality of Life Survey Follow-Up Study."

7. Daniels, "From Tweet to Blog Post to Peer-Reviewed Article."

8. Chatelain, "How to Teach Kids."

9. McMillan Cottom blogs at tressiemc.com.

10. McMillan Cottom, "Risk and Ethics in Public Scholarship."

11. Riley, "The Most Persuasive Case for Eliminating Black Studies?"

12. Riley, "Black Studies, Part 2: A Response to Critics."

13. McMillan Cottom, "The Inferiority of Blackness as a Subject."

14. The graduate students responded with their own post. See Taylor, Levy, and Hays, "Grad Students Respond to Riley Post on African-American Studies."

15. McMillan Cottom, "Using Social Media to Rage Against the Machine."

16. Penney and Dadas, "(Re)Tweeting in the Service of Protest."

17. Ibid.

18. Riley, "Black Studies, Part 2: A Response to Critics."

19. The Pew Research Center finds that people of color use Twitter at twice the rate of whites and that Twitter users are economically diverse: "Ten percent of users with middle-class household incomes between $54,000 and $74,999 use Twitter, the same proportion as those with less than $30,000 household incomes . . . urban residents are twice as likely to use Twitter as their rural counterparts" (7).

20. Singh, "Tweeting to the Choir."

21. Penney and Dadas, "(Re)Tweeting in the Service of Protest."

22. McMillan Cottom, "Risk and Ethics in Public Scholarship."

23. McMillan Cottom, "Who Do You Think You Are?"

24. Krantz, "Controversy Trails New Professor to BU"; Robinson, "Zeezus Does the Firing 'Round Hurr."

25. See Butler, "Conservatives Bashed Me for Speaking Out about the Zimmerman Verdict," and Charles McGuiness, "Anthea Butler Gets Attacked."

26. Svrluga, "Boston University Debates Discrimination."

27. Brown, "Letter from President Brown."

28. DeLuca, "What We Know About Saida Grundy."

29. Thys, "Incoming BU Professor Criticized for Tweets on Race."

30. Rockquemore, "Let's Talk About Twitter."

Campus Lockdown and the *"Talking Tenure"* Newsletter

From fall 2007 to March 2008, graduate and undergraduate students at the University of Michigan at Ann Arbor organized a conference around a spate of tenure denials of women of color scholars and hosted a broader dialogue about the legibility of women-of-color–based scholarship and the conditions of knowledge production in the imperial university. "Campus Lockdown: Women of Color Negotiating the Academic Industrial Complex" was a one-day conference that addressed the following issues: the relationship of campus climate and resources to the retention of students and faculty of color; the politics of tenure, disciplinary formations, and multiculturalism; the relationship between social justice, Ethnic Studies, and the "academic–industrial complex"; and the role of pedagogy and publicly engaged scholarship in the academic–industrial complex. The conference included plenary sessions with women of color scholars, all of whom waived honoraria to participate in this important moment of protest and solidarity, which included plays, art installations, workshops, newsletters, and petitions.

The Tenure Research Group, a subset of the larger group of graduate students working on the tenure issue, emerged to produce research on the state of women of color faculty at Michigan and throughout higher education. With input from faculty and a staff member from the Center for the Education of Women, we researched the history of women of color faculty at Michigan and began working on a publication that would highlight the growing tenure dilemma for women of color faculty in higher education. The result was the *"Talking Tenure"* newsletter, which was a truly collaborative effort between students and faculty. The Michigan Civil Rights Initiative, also known as Proposal 2, was a 2006 piece of legislation authored by Ward Connerly to ban state "preferential treatment" programs and policies, which, we argue, adversely impacts the retention of students and faculty of color at the University of Michigan. In 2007, only 3 percent of full professors at the University of Michigan were women of color, and between 2006 and 2007, the university was unable to retain twelve of 200 women of color faculty.

The conference organizers were alarmed at the potential loss of critical faculty in Ethnic Studies, Women's Studies, American Culture, History, and other departments across campus. Receiving national and international media coverage, the conference generated overwhelming interest. On March 14, 2008, more than 700 people affiliated with more than forty universities from twenty states were convened at the university. For those who were not able to attend the conference, we maintained a website for a year afterward that included all resource materials generated from the conference and the campaign. It was our vision as organizers that this dialogue would continue beyond the momentum and energy embodied in the conference, and we envision this newsletter and other resources as a continuation of this work.

Kirisitina Sailiata, Matthew Stiffler, and Lee Ann Wang provided the description for Campus Lockdown. They would like to acknowledge the larger collective, dozens of unnamed organizers, whose fierce and loving labor made this event possible.

The authors of *Talking Tenure* are Maria Coter, Paul Faber, Roxana Galusca, Anneeth Kaur Hundle, Rachel Quinn, Kirisitina Sailiata, Jamie Small, Andrea Smith, Matthew Stiffler, and Lee Ann Wang.

Talking Tenure

"Being isolated in any situation is never fun, but in academia it is so hard because there is so much to do that if you are doing it all alone, not only are you not getting synergy and not getting help and assistance, but you are also not going to be successful."   Woman of Color Faculty Member in the Social Sciences, University of Michigan

The statement above highlights the marginalization of women of color faculty at the University of Michigan. Institutionalized inequities within the University create an environment where marginalization transcends mere social discomfort to ultimately prevent both scholarly growth and personal wellbeing. In the five-year period between 2001 and 2006, women of color faculty have been leaving the University of Michigan at an average of 5 women per year. These numbers are significant considering the fact that women of color currently comprise less than 7% of the total faculty membership. As we look further up the academic hierarchy, these numbers become even more troubling with women of color at the rank of full professor accounting for a mere 1.6% of this group. Quantitative data on the recruitment and retention rates for women of color faculty at the University of Michigan alert us to and help us identify the problem. However, in order to understand how and why the rates are what they are, we need access to the particularities of women of color's lived experiences. In the fall of 2007 I began a qualitative study which included interviews with 28 women of color

faculty across all University colleges and departments. The purpose of this study was to act as a step in the direction of seeking to understand, through the experiences and insight of women of color faculty members themselves, what the University community can do to improve their rates of recruitment and retention.

Within each faculty member's story and across stories, a deeper complexity is revealed that helps illuminate elusive concepts such as climate, marginalization, exclusiveness and collegiality. In addition, the narratives explicate the challenges in fulfilling the expectations in joint appointments and the University's expressed commitments to interdisciplinarity that unfavorably impact the academic success of women of color attempting to juggle research, teaching and service requirements across two or more departments. These women's personal revelations are vitally important given the often subtle and insidious nature of discrimination, and the difficulty in defining how it actually operates and impacts individual and collective lives. Peering through the lens of these women's narratives, we have no choice

but to acknowledge and validate the impact and consequences of deeply embedded structural inequalities. The words of the women of color provide clues as to where constructive intervention can take place and, additionally, help predict the strategies that may be most effective.

Bringing the perspectives of women of color faculty to the forefront validates and honors their critical analysis as a blueprint for tackling institutional change. It is, however, the perspectives of women of color that are often made invisible and delegitimzied through claims that their stories are just that stories – personal, clouded by emotion, and disconnected from larger social realities. This study and potentially revolutionary spaces such as the Lockdown Conference challenge this notion while reclaiming the strategy of bearing witness to and asserting the authority of underrepresented voices.

Aimee Cox received her Ph.D. from the University of Michigan. She will start a tenure-track position at Rutgers University this fall.

3% of full professors at the University of Michigan are women of color in 2007.

12 Decrease in number of women of color faculty between 2006 and 2007.

4 Number of Native women who are tenured or in tenure-track positions at the University of Michigan.

1,483 Number of white men who are tenured or in tenure-track positions at the University of Michigan.

Office of Budget and Planning, University of Michigan, Ann Arbor

MYTHS OF INTERDISCIPLINARITY

"We will expand the effort to bring our interdisciplinary culture to the classroom and to our research enterprise. Disciplines help us both to see and not to see; interdisciplinary teams help us to see more widely."

—University President Mary Sue Coleman in 2004

"No other university offers faculty and students our scope and scale of fields of study, and the opportunities to push their ideas in new directions. Great universities like Michigan must transcend disciplines to be truly effective in addressing societal needs. Over the next five years, we will fund 100 tenure-track faculty positions, to expand interdisciplinary work and to increase faculty connections with undergraduates."

—University President Mary Sue Coleman in 2007

MYTH: Interdisciplinarity means combining the methods and approaches of several disciplines.
REALITY: Interdisciplinarity is keeping the main approach and method of your home discipline and borrowing a few scattered reference points from another discipline. Hence the question: "Where is your methodology?"

MYTH: The University of Michigan encourages and nurtures interdisciplinary work.
REALITY: Departments do not have the structures necessary to support this work, nor are they interested in creating them. In effect, faculty, mostly of color and mostly junior, who do interdisciplinary work face obstacles and must continuously justify their scholarship in front of their departments.

BEARING WITNESS...

"They brought in all of these wonderful young scholars, black, Asian, you know ... but mostly African Americans and then it was almost like there was virtually no interest in hearing what they had to say about the direction of the department and absolutely no interest in engaging their work. It was like, okay, you make us look good, we appear diverse now be quiet. And then, as there was all of this incredulity when these assistant professors started to leave and go to other universities. I had to leave too there was too much hypocrisy and no commitment to the scholarship and work we were doing."

Woman of Color Former Faculty Member
University of Michigan, Ann Arbor

REALITY: In addition to overt forms of discrimination that may receive media coverage, women of color faculty face subtle forms of marginalization on a daily basis. An African-American participant in Aimee Meredith Cox's interview study on the challenges that women of color face in academia describes the stereotypes that she encounters from her colleagues: "If they're on the borderline, liking you might make a difference. The man I told you [interviewer] about, the one who asked if I was going to name my daughter 'Shaniqua,' he's on the tenure committee. So, you can't go off. You'd be crazy to go off. You just smile and say no and you move on because you don't want to be the angry black woman. It could mean not getting tenure...even if you've been offended."

MYTH: Departments in the Humanities seek to nurture scholarship across disciplines.
REALITY: The burden of interdisciplinarity falls squarely on the shoulders of the individual, usually a junior faculty of color, also most of the time jointly-appointed, who is expected to "make it work across the strict departmental guidelines and boundaries." These scholars are supposed to produce "amazing, creative things that aren't really even supported through structures, resources, or respect" (a faculty member with three appointments across departments).

REALITY: At a prestigious research university like the University of Michigan, teaching skills play a relatively minor role in tenure decisions. The university evaluates assistant professors primarily on their research record. Furthermore, women of color faculty often mentor large numbers of undergraduate and graduate students who seek them out for their intellectual prowess and their shared understanding of marginality in the academic industrial complex. Thus, in addition to their pedagogical labor in the classroom, women of color faculty assume extra responsibilities for mentoring students outside the classroom.

WELCOME FROM THE WOMEN OF COLOR IN THE ACADEMY PROJECT

Despite a discourse of institutional support for women of color faculty at the University of Michigan, the numbers of tenured and tenure-track faculty have increased at a snails pace over the past two decades. **Since 1985 to the present, women of color at the full professor rank has increased from less than one percent to approximately 3% of the total faculty at this institution.** Women of color faculty have increased at a greater percentage among the ranks of assistant and associate faculty members, however, across all ethnic minority groups, women of color still comprise only 12% and 10% respectively. While women in general remain underrepresented among faculty, the situation for women of color in particular remains dire and has not shown meaningful improvement over time. Further, **a consistent pattern of tenure and 3rd year review denials points to systematic barriers for women of color, both in terms of valuation of their unique and often increased teaching and service contributions, as well as their innovative and often culturally-specific programs of research.** Unfortunately, these issues have great urgency in this post-Proposition 2 era whereby the support for affirmative action policies in the state of Michigan has been outlawed.

Issues related to the recruitment, retention and promotion of women of color gave rise to the development of the Women of Color in the Academy Project (WOCAP) in June 1994. After a series of discussions with women of color from various schools and colleges, the Center for the Education of Women and the Women's Studies Program jointly submitted to the Office of Academic and Multicultural Affairs a proposal for a series of activities to be undertaken over the course of three years on behalf of women of color faculty and students at the Ann Arbor campus of the University of Michigan. The project has been ongoing since that time and has been jointly funded by the Office of Academic and Multicultural Affairs and the Office of the Vice President for Research.

Current goals of WOCAP include:
- Highlighting the contributions that women of color make to the university community and to society at large, both academically and culturally;
- Building a network of women of color faculty that serves as a support system for their research undertakings, academic career development, and enhanced career satisfaction, thus supporting their retention;
- Advocating on behalf of women of color faculty and graduate students by working collectively for progressive institutional change with the goal of creating healthy and equitable environments in which to engage in scholarly activity; and
- Serving as a model for future recruitment and retention programs for women of color faculty at the national and international level.

It is with these goals in mind that WOCAP enthusiastically supports (as a co-sponsor) the Campus Lockdown conference organized by conscientious and committed graduate students and supporters.

We welcome you to the University of Michigan and look forward to working together to address the structural constraints faced by women of color in academia.

FACULTY OF COLOR IN THE ACADEMIC INDUSTRIAL COMPLEX

Excerpt from talk delivered at the 2008 SCOR Conference: "Decision Time: Lifting Smokescreens Dropping Knowledge"

Professor Maria E. Cotera

Out of the six women of color who underwent the tenure process this year, only two made it through their departmental votes unscathed. Four of these women were jointly appointed and had to negotiate both the extra labor and the extra level of political maneuvering that such joint appointments signify. While all the cases will be reviewed at the level of the college, and may well be approved, we cannot ignore the message that their difficulties at the departmental level suggest. Now, tenured faculty in departments may have any number of reasons for voting negatively on a given candidate's case, ranging from personal antipathy, yes, it happens, to political disagreements with the candidate's work, to serious concerns about the scholarship, but I'm not about to parse the reasons behind these decisions. What I am more interested in is the mechanics of that "peculiar institution" called tenure, and more specifically about the ways in which it regulates, even produces good citizens of the neoliberal institution through its processes. The most obvious way in which this happens is that faculty who don't tow the line, don't get tenure. In this instance, tenure is a punitive process meant to punish faculty who disobey the rules of the neoliberal institution, and to excise them as bad citizens of our scholarly community.

As part of our recent struggles against the tenure decisions in the Department of Women's Studies, junior faculty, lecturers, and graduate students came together to support the women of color who received negative recommendations. In the process of crafting a response strategy, which involved a letter writing campaign to the deans, we met with senior faculty allies who offered advice on how we might phrase our letter: what elements of the specific cases we might want to highlight, how we might want to structure our argument in favor of the candidates and so forth. What became immediately clear in this process was the extent to which our rhetoric had to be shaped by the logic of the very institution that had denied the validity of the scholarship we were defending. For example, despite the fact that the Women's Studies Department claims to value work that integrates activism and scholarship, and regardless of the fact that one of the candidates was recruited and hired as a scholar/activist, we were told that we shouldn't highlight the national recognition that this scholar had received for her activism, because it might actually hurt her case with the college. We also wanted to talk about the relevance of public scholarship to the historical development of Women's Studies, and how most of the central canonical texts of feminist theory that we teach in our core curriculum were produced with activist audiences in mind, not academic audiences. We hoped to use this logic to contextualize the candidate's non-academic writing as not only relevant, but central to the production of knowledge in Women's Studies. Again, we were told that this line of reasoning could actually undermine the candidate's case. As a result, our letter focused, as did the tenure review, exclusively on the candidate's academic scholarship and teaching, limiting both the force and the scope of our intervention.

What I am trying to convey in this depressing recitation of the barriers we faced in trying to rewrite the dominant script of the institution, is not that resistance is futile, but that the power of the academic industrial complex lies in its ability to construct the very terms upon which we stake our resistance. In order for our intervention to be legible to the people who would ultimately determine the fate of these candidates, it had to be made on their terms and within the narrow domain of the logic of the neoliberal institution which values individualism, private property, hierarchy, and profit above all else. What was most striking to me during this process was the way in which it translated our dissent into the idioms of the institution. Which is to say that tenure is much more than a hazing ritual, or perhaps it is the ultimate hazing ritual, designed to place us in submission, make us suffer through the illogic of dominance, accepting it eventually as the only logic, so that we may emerge, chastened and newly reborn, as compliant academic subjects.

So if our very gestures of dissent can be transformed into a pedagogical project that teaches us to submit to the logic of the norm, then, is there any way we can remain in the institution as resisting subjects? I'm not sure, but to my mind this question is connected to the larger question of who our knowledge production serves, a question that must always stand at the center of our work as scholars of color.

Maria Cotera is an Assistant Professor of American Culture and Women's Studies at the University of Michigan, Ann Arbor.

JOINT APPOINTMENTS AND WOMEN OF COLOR

The continued rise in the number of joint appointments over the last two decades has negatively impacted junior faculty in general and especially women of color. Within the college of LSA, women of color disproportionately hold jointly appointed tenure-track positions.[1] On the surface, a joint appointment looks as if it would allow women of color faculty the opportunity to conduct cutting edge scholarship that crosses traditional disciplinary boundaries and institutional restrictions. In actuality, as the numerous reports from faculty working groups, the Provost, the Senate Advisory Committee, and research organizations like Advance have decreed over the last decade, joint appointments are precarious for junior faculty and especially women of color because of their unwieldy nature.[2] As Maria Cotera has written, herself a jointly-appointed scholar, women of color "[have] to negotiate both the extra labor and the extra level of political maneuvering that such joint appointments signify." Prof. Cotera calls attention to the fact that women of color scholarship is already difficult for the university system to process because it has the tendency to be collaborative, interdisciplinary, and "public," which contradict the values of the "neo-liberal university": "individualism, private property, hierarchy, and profit above all else."[3]

In February 2007, a committee of faculty was charged with writing a report about issues of faculty recruitment and retention in conjunction with the university's diversity initiative. The committee's recommendations call for more support of "interdisciplinary/diversity faculty with joint appointments through flexibility around tenure," increased "research support for work that may not be as easily funded through standard channels," a recognition of team scholarship efforts and recognition of emergent or community-based scholarship.[4] These changes to university procedure and the tenure structure would certainly benefit women of color scholarship. But this type of rhetoric has been pervasive for years with no real move towards structural change, evident in the recent tenure cases.

Although the institution recognizes the precarious position that junior faculty and especially women of color are in vis a vis joint appointments, small departments and academic units, particularly in

the under-funded humanities, continue to rely on joint appointments because of their fiscal viability, proving again that the university is at heart a corporation. Sadly, even though the University of Michigan has recognized for more than a decade that women of color faculty were at risk in the tenure process, there has been a failure to make any changes to the outdated tenure procedure, which is established on a century-old idea of "acceptable" scholarship. A chilling example of this comes from a 1998 Provost's office report on "interdisciplinarity." The report stresses that "women and minorities" who may be "more vulnerable in the evaluation processes of the University may feel an understandable reluctance to engage in interdisciplinary activity." The report continues, "It would be a tragedy if two of the University's highest values, diversity and interdisciplinarity, proved (or were felt to be) mutually incompatible in this way."[5] The tragedy is evident. [Footnotes on Back Page]

Matthew Stiffler is a Ph.D. Candidate in the Program in American Culture at the University of Michigan, Ann Arbor.

From *The Michigan Daily* website on March 6, 2008. "I had a class with Andrea Smith in my senior year, and she was absolutely very passionate about what she taught, the discussions we had in that class were great, really brought to light some angles that I have never considered before. And she is a leader in Native American rights and Women rights, she's also a brilliant writer. I'm a guy, but I found the class very inspirational and memorable. How do you get tenure here, if Andy [Smith] can't get it?"

BEARING WITNESS...

As a doctoral student in the Department of Anthropology, I found the recent series of negative tenure recommendations profoundly disheartening. For those of us engaged in progressive work, doctoral education is critical--not only for our individual research projects, but as a practice and process of negotiating and understanding the positionality from which we engage with those projects in the first place. To this end, women of color scholars like myself require role models with experience. We need women of color faculty for the knowledge and tools they provide to us, the critical contributions they make to our academic communities, and for the possibilities for collective work that emerge from their situated knowledge. Women of color at the faculty level in other departments have been essential for the progress of my own intellectual development, and I have looked to them for the mentorship and professional development that I need. I come from a discipline that is historically notorious for scholars who write "about" race by either reinforcing parochial and essential racial categories or deconstructing race so that its significance no longer matters. The decreasing number of tenured women of color faculty means that the entire university community loses out on the innovative contributions of these outstanding scholars.

Aneeth Kuar Hundle is a graduate student in Anthropology at the University of Michigan, Ann Arbor

BACK PAGE

Compiled by Jamie Small

Myth #1

"The university denies tenure to women of color faculty because they are shitty teachers."

Fact: At a prestigious research university like the University of Michigan, teaching skills play a relatively minor role in tenure decisions. The university evaluates assistant professors primarily on their research record. Furthermore, women of color faculty often mentor large numbers of undergraduate and graduate students who seek them out for their intellectual prowess and their shared understanding of marginality in the academic industrial complex. Thus, in addition to their pedagogical labor in the classroom, women of color faculty assume extra responsibilities for mentoring students outside the classroom.

Myth #2

"Feminist activism has no place in the academic environment – it muddies objective scholarly work with anger, and it is an inappropriate use of public funds."

Fact: All academic work is inherently political: the development of research questions, methods, analysis, and conclusions are all informed by power dynamics in the social world. Attempts at objectivity are just that – *attempts*. Therefore, it is more intellectually rigorous to recognize one's location within webs of power. This is precisely what feminist activists endorse. So while feminist activists may be angry about past and current injustices, this anger does not spoil their scholarly diligence. Rather, this anger sharpens their analytical edge, and it

locates the university as a crucial site for social justice. If the University of Michigan wants to be an intellectual leader in the twenty-first century, it must seriously recognize the challenges of feminist activists.

Myth #3

"Departmental and College tenure review committees base their decisions on systematic and transparent criteria."

Fact: It is unclear which criteria are used to evaluate tenure cases. Tenure decisions are made behind closed doors; records are not released; and the standards seemingly vary across different cases. This lack of transparency renders it difficult, if not impossible, for junior faculty to prepare their tenure files as thoroughly as possible. Furthermore, this policy of obscurity enables departments and the college to hide behind individualizing rhetoric when explaining negative tenure decisions. That is, they assert that each case must be decided on its own merits, but they refuse to recognize the alarming patterns of discrimination that this policy of "meritocracy" enables.

Myth #4

"Women of color are the only faculty group that faces discrimination at the University of Michigan."

Fact: In 2005, former Law professor Peter Hammer filed a lawsuit against UM in which he alleges that the university denied him tenure because he is openly gay. Lansing Circuit Court Judge James Giddings recently decided that the case would go to a jury trial. The university's defense of their tenure decision sounds remarkably similar to recent tenure decisions against women of color. *The Michigan Daily* quoted university attorney Richard Seryak on March 7, 2008. Seryak claimed, "The Law School provided more special accommodation for this candidate than for anyone else in the history of the Law School and at the end of the day, this decision was based on his scholarship." own merits, but they refuse to recognize the alarming patterns of discrimination that this policy of "meritocracy" enables.

Contributors and Partners

Roxana Galusca
Rachel Afi Quinn
Jamie Small
Matthew Stiffler
Paul Farber
Aneeth Kuar Hundle
Maria Cotera
Aimee Cox
Members of the Women of Color
   in the Academy Project
Members of the "Tenure Research
   Committee"
Organizers of the Campus
   Lockdown conference

Myth #5

Women of color already account for a disproportionately large percentage of faculty at the University of Michigan.

Fact: Although the University of Michigan promotes itself as committed to diversity, its recruitment and retention of women and people of color remains less than stellar. In 2006, women of color accounted for just 7.1% of faculty at the entire university. In addition, it is unclear how effectively UM retains these groups because individual tenure cases are not released publicly. Anecdotal evidence suggests that women of color faculty leave – either by choice or because of negative tenure outcomes – UM at disproportionately high rates.

1. In 1998, 34% of the faculty in LSA had some sort of joint appointment, which was the highest percentage of any school or college at the University (http://www.provost.umich.edu/reports/slfstudy/pdf/facappend5.pdf). Just a brief glance at the websites for some of the larger LSA departments and academic units that employ the highest percentages of women of color, including American Culture, CAAS, and Women's studies, will show that a large percentage of these faculty members are jointly appointed.
2. See for example the Senate Advisory Committee for a Multicultural University's 2003 report, http://www.umich.edu/~sacua/cmu/cmu-april-2003-report.htm.
3. Maria Cotera. 2008. "Faculty of Color in the Academic Industrial Complex." Unpublished paper delivered at the Students of Color of Rackham (SCOR) Conference at the University of Michigan. Feb. 15.
4. Report of the Faculty and Staff Recruitment and Retention Subcommittee. 2007. Diversity Blueprint Task Force, University of Michigan, Ann Arbor. http://www.diversity.umich.edu/about/bp-faculty-staff-report.pdf.
5. Subcommittee on Interdisciplinarity. 1999. "Issues at the Intersection: Report and Reccomendations." Office of the Provost, University of Michigan, Ann Arbor. http://www.provost.umich.edu/reports/issues_intersection/interdisciplinarity.html

Appendix B

University of Southern California Analysis of Data on Tenure

While it is relatively easy to find data about the demographics of the professoriate (the National Center for Education Statistics publishes them regularly), it is difficult to find data about tenure rates. Most institutions don't make such information public, regardless of whether or not they keep track of it.[1] And even tracking tenure rates can't capture retention rates. This is one of the reasons why it was such a surprise when the *Chronicle of Higher Education* published political scientist Jane Junn's analysis of the University of Southern California's tenure rates.[2] To be clear, the findings themselves were newsworthy—startling to some, confirmation for others—but the mere presence of the study is significant as a way to help us think about the impact that inequitable tenure processes have on diversity.

Although the *Chronicle of Higher Education*'s focus on Junn's analysis connected it to her colleague Mai'a K. Davis Cross's 2012 tenure denial, this memo shows the analysis is actually in response to a series of tenure denials, including Jane Iwamura's in 2010. Iwamura and Davis Cross were in different departments, but their cases have some similarities, at least on the surface. Supporters of both women point to sterling publishing records and university awards for teaching and mentorship. They also note that Iwamura and Davis Cross were denied tenure at the administrative level. In Davis Cross's case, although she received a unanimous vote at the college level, when her file reached the provost's level Dean Howard Gillman was directed to cold call experts in her field, despite the fact that she'd followed the university's external review process. Every institution has its own external review process, but Gillman's claim that calling field experts not listed in a candidate's file fell within normal practices was countered by a faculty grievance committee that found that his conduct "lacked appropriate protocols." The problem with Gilman is not simply that he ignored the assessments in Davis Cross's file but that he undermined a complex process that suggests a lack of trust in the candidate, her department, and those who agreed to evaluate her file. His decision to overturn these recommendations (from colleagues and specialists in Davis Cross's field) not only speaks to the issue of faculty governance but also undermines the notion of external review, which is supposed to function more neutrally than university assessment.[3]

In the study, Junn focused on 106 Social Sciences and tenure cases put forward between 1998 and 2012. This memo to Philip Ethington, president of the USC Faculty Council, shows her findings and how she reached them. They were challenged by USC for being too subjective, and in a particularly dismissive statement to the *Daily Trojan*, Provost Martin Levine dismissed the question entirely:

"Every few years, someone raises the question of possible discrimination in tenure statistics. Each and every time, analysis of a multi-year period shows there are no statistically significant differences between the tenure success at USC of female and male faculty, or minority and non-minority faculty."[4]

LAURA PULIDO, USC Professor of American and Ethnic Studies, notes that there are very few data to support Levine's claim and that the institution is not holding itself to the same standards it requires of its faculty. Junn explained that her analysis was based on published information in the course catalogs about the actual faculty members because USC does not share data. Hiding behind the notion of "privacy," it seems USC denies requests to provide data to support its assertions about their tenure rates. As Pulido points out, "If faculty were to conduct a study without showing their data, it would be considered unscientific and would be rejected." In response to a series of irregularities, faculty dismissal, and an overall lack of transparency, Pulido founded the Committee for Tenure Justice at USC—as a sustained effort to address a messy, problematic tenure system that seems to disproportionately affect faculty of color. Davis Cross is now an assistant professor of political science and international affairs at Northeastern University.

Notes

1. See "Faculty Tenure Flow Rates"; "Tenure Outcomes by Race/Ethnicity and Gender"; Dooris and Guidos, "Tenure Achievement Rates at Research Universities."
2. June, "Tenure Decisions at Southern Cal Strongly Favor White Men."
3. Serhan, "Special Feature: Prof Loses Tenure Bid After Appeal."
4. Ibid.

TO: Philip Ethington, President of the USC Dornsife Faculty Council
FROM: Jane Junn, Professor of Political Science, USC Dornsife
DATE: 19 October 2012
RE: Analysis of data on tenure at USC Dornsife

A series of denials of tenure to minority junior faculty in the Social Sciences and Humanities in the College at the University of Southern California raised questions about whether there is a pattern and practice of discrimination in the promotion process. A recent denial prompted this analysis within the context of a grievance filed by the faculty member. This analysis presents five findings from an aggregate analysis of 106 individual cases of junior faculty in the Social Sciences and Humanities between 1998 and 2012.

Study Methodology

The University of Southern California does not make records of its tenure decisions public. In the absence of publicly-available information, systematic data on the composition of tenure-track and tenured faculty in USC College (now known as USC Dornsife) can be collected from the annual course catalogs. A database of assistant professors who were evaluated under the tenure and promotion process at USC College between 1998 and 2012 was built using the annual course catalogs. Individual faculty members listed as untenured Assistant Professors were tracked over time until they either moved to the rank of Associate Professor, or disappeared from the course catalog. Junior faculty who moved from Assistant Professor to Associate Professor can be observed with full certainty. The disposition of cases not moving from Assistant to Associate Professor at USC was determined by direct correspondence with the faculty member, report of the individual's status by tenured members of the faculty member's department, or information from other knowledgeable individuals.

Untenured Assistant Professors who left USC before experiencing the tenure process were excluded from the analysis. These cases were excluded from the analysis because these faculty were not – based on the knowledge obtained from the sources cited above – evaluated under the tenure and promotion process at USC. Instead, only those cases where there was a high degree of certainty that the candidate had entered and experienced the tenure and promotion process at USC were included. Thus the cases included in the analysis represent the universe of cases rather than a sample, and any observed differences in outcome variables between groups is a meaningful difference. The analysis presents the variation in having been awarded tenure at USC versus not being awarded tenure. The category of not being awarded tenure includes the status of having been formally denied tenure as well as not having a decision rendered on tenure despite the presence and evaluation of a dossier.

Data were collected for a total of 106 Assistant Professors at USC College between 1998 and 2012. Roughly half (N=54) were in the social sciences, and the other half (N=52) were in humanities departments. Faculty may have had dual appointments with other College departments or with other units at USC such as the School of Cinematic Arts. In the case of appointments with other units, faculty were coded with the USC College department. For joint appointments within the College, faculty were coded on the basis of the recollection of informants regarding the department that took the lead on the tenure case. Social science departments included in the analysis are Anthropology, Economics, International Relations, Linguistics, Political Science, Psychology, and Sociology. Humanities departments included in the analysis are American Studies and Ethnicity, Art History, Classics, East Asian Languages and Culture, English, History, Philosophy, Religion, and Slavic Languages.

During the fourteen-year period included in this study, 67.9% of the Assistant Professors appearing in the course catalogs were observed to advance to the rank of Associate Professor at USC. Of the 106 faculty included in the database, 53.8% were male and 46.2% were female. Whites made up 60.4% of the faculty included in the database, 9.4% were African American, 23.6% were Asian American, and 6.6% were Latino/Hispanic. The largest demographic grouping by gender and race was white male junior faculty who made up 34.9% of all Assistant Professors who went through the tenure process between 1998 and 2012. The second largest group was white female junior faculty (25.5%). The remaining 39.6% were junior faculty of color (the sum of 18.9% male minority faculty and 20.7% female minority faculty).

Five findings are described below, and analysis of patterns of being awarded tenure by categories such as gender and race is accompanied by tests of statistical significance (i.e., Chi-Square). As noted above, any observed differences in the average rate of being awarded tenure is a substantively important difference because the data represent the universe of cases rather than a sample of Assistant Professors who experienced the tenure process at USC between 1998 and 2012.

1. Ninety-two percent of white male faculty were awarded tenure at USC. Over the fourteen-year period under study, 37 white male Assistant Professors (representing approximately 35% of all faculty at this rank in the social sciences and humanities) were evaluated for tenure. On the basis of information gleaned from multiple sources, only 3 white males of the 37 total were not awarded tenure at USC in the social sciences and humanities. The rate of tenure for white male junior faculty is 91.9%. Of the 3 white males who were denied tenure, 1 was awarded tenure after reconsideration and remains on the faculty in a social science department. Another white male who was denied tenure remains at USC as a "professor of the practice" in another social science department. The lone white male who was denied tenure in the humanities is no longer at USC. There is a similar pattern of high success of being awarded tenure for white male junior faculty in the social sciences (88.2%) and humanities (95%).

2. Fifty-five percent of female and minority faculty were awarded tenure at USC. In stark contrast to the 91.9% success rate among white male junior faculty, all other faculty in the social sciences and humanities observed during this period had a much more modest rate of success of 55.1%. This group includes white women, minority women, and minority men (Asian Americans, Latinos, and Blacks). The difference between the tenure success rate for white males of 91.9% compared to that of women and minority faculty of 55.1% is statistically significant at the .000 level. Figure 1 provides a visual representation of the comparison between white male junior faculty and women and minority junior faculty at USC College.

Figure 1: Comparison of Tenure Awarded: White Males v. Women and Minority Faculty

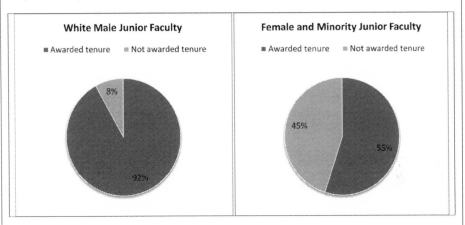

The relationship between being white and male and being awarded tenure at a substantially higher rate at USC College is consistent across the social sciences and humanities. In the social sciences, 88.2% of white male faculty were awarded tenure compared with 51.4% of female and minority junior faculty (statistically significant at .009). In the humanities, 95% of white male faculty were awarded tenure compared with 59.4% of female and minority junior faculty (statistically significant at .005).

3. White junior faculty are awarded tenure at a higher rate than minority junior faculty. Consistent with the high degree of success of being awarded tenure among white male junior faculty, comparison of the success rates between white junior faculty at USC College and minority junior faculty shows a wide disparity. Eighty-one percent of white junior faculty (including both men and women) between 1998 and 2012 were awarded tenure, while 47.6% of minority junior faculty (including both men and women) were promoted to Associate Professor with tenure. This relationship between race and being awarded tenure at USC is statistically significant at .000. Figure 2 presents a visual representation of the comparison.

Figure 2: Comparison of Tenure Awarded: White v. Minority Junior Faculty

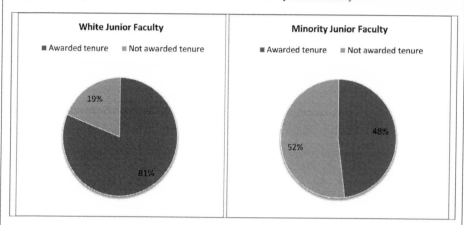

Patterns of significantly higher rates of tenure awarded to white junior faculty compared with minority junior faculty at USC College are consistent across the social sciences and humanities. In the social sciences, 79.3% of white junior faculty were awarded tenure while 44% of minority junior faculty were awarded tenure (statistically significant at .007). In the humanities, 82.9% of white junior faculty were awarded tenure while 52.9% of minority junior faculty were awarded tenure (statistically significant at .023). There were small differences between groups of minority faculty, with 50% of African American junior faculty being awarded tenure, 48% of Asian American junior faculty, and 42.9% of Latino/Hispanic junior faculty successful in the USC tenure process.

4. Asian American female faculty are awarded tenure at a lower rate than white female faculty. While the data are clear about the near-universal rate of USC awarding tenure to white male junior faculty (91.2%), white female faculty were awarded tenure at a lower rate of 66.7%. The success rate for Asian American female faculty, however, was even lower at 40% being awarded tenure by USC. Overall, the relationship between race/ethnicity and gender of faculty and being awarded tenure is significant at .003.

<u>5. Data on comparative tenure rates between minority and white faculty in Social Sciences and Humanities at USC College show a different pattern from information published by USC.</u>

The University of Southern California's Manual of the University Committee on Appointments, Promotions and Tenure specifies the following information in its 2011 publication.

UCAPT Manual (January 2011), page 1:

"1.a-2. How does UCAPT embody USC's commitment to equal opportunity?
UCAPT's recommendations are made individually on a merit basis. Analysis of the data between 2005 and 2009 shows no statistically significant difference between minority and non-minority candidates in success rate for promotion to tenure. (The success rate for minority candidates happens to be five percentage points higher.) During the same period, over a quarter of UCAPT's members were themselves minority."

These figures are inconsistent with results of tenure cases in the Social Sciences and Humanities at USC College observed during this time period. Between 2005 and 2009, there were 42 cases, of which 26 were white scholars and 16 were minorities. White junior faculty were awarded tenure at a rate of 88.5%, while 56.3% of minority junior faculty were awarded tenure. The relationship between race and being awarded tenure during this time is statistically significant at .017.

Appendix C
Making Labor Visible

In the spring of 2007, the director of the Minority Student Affairs office at Barnard College invited me to a brown-bag lunch usually attended by students and administrators to introduce myself and talk about Africana Studies and the paucity of faculty of color from my perspective as a newly arrived professor. I had been hired earlier that academic year to run the faltering Africana Studies program in the wake of student protests over the departure of two high-profile black tenured faculty. Their resignation left the college with only three black professors, none of whom had tenure.

Barnard College is unique in that it is the only small liberal arts college that does not control the outcome of its own tenure process. After the college agrees to award a candidate tenure, a separate committee at Columbia University reviews the case, a process that often puts the values of teaching and service in the small liberal arts context in conflict with the demands of a research-one university. The tenure process for assistant professors takes from sixteen to eighteen months.

I wanted to educate the protesting students and responding administrators by making explicit to the community exactly what we are asking for when we demand the hiring of faculty of color to build diversity in the curriculum. I also needed to make clear how Barnard's past exclusionary practices—whether or not intentional—hindered the search for black faculty. In my drive to make visible to the administration the many barriers to tenure at Barnard and the burden on me as the sole tenured black on the faculty, I had already reached out to feminist faculty at other institutions for research on "invisible labor" and received many useful suggestions. My challenge was to distill the research for a casual audience, so I gave the group this chart along with a page from the introduction to *Spirit, Space & Survival: African American Women in (White) Academe*, which discusses some of Barnard's earlier dismissals of antiracist and black staff. The irony of my spending time researching invisible labor and creating the chart, which would at most appear in an ignored item on my year-end personnel report, was not lost on me.

My specific focus for the chart was on black faculty who work in Africana Studies at Barnard College; however, many of the issues and demands apply to many faculty of color and any faculty who works in interdisciplinary programs. It also only deals with professional demands. It does not address the labor of home and family that we are encouraged to make invisible in professional arenas: unequal burden of childrearing and housework and the larger demands of family borne by working class, first-generation, and minoritized faculty.

Despite the daunting challenges the college structure poses and the unique burdens presented to its faculty and thanks to the collaborative efforts of feminist faculty, at the time of this writing the Africana program is now a department with four tenured black women with half-time appointments. The college now has eleven tenured and tenure-track faculty who identify as Black or African American. We hope to maintain some momentum, but institutional memory, tenacious in maintaining certain structures of privilege, is short when it comes to the perspectives of people on the margins: with each change in a central administrative position, we start over with some part of the process of change.

Kim F. Hall

Expectations for successful tenure applicants at Barnard

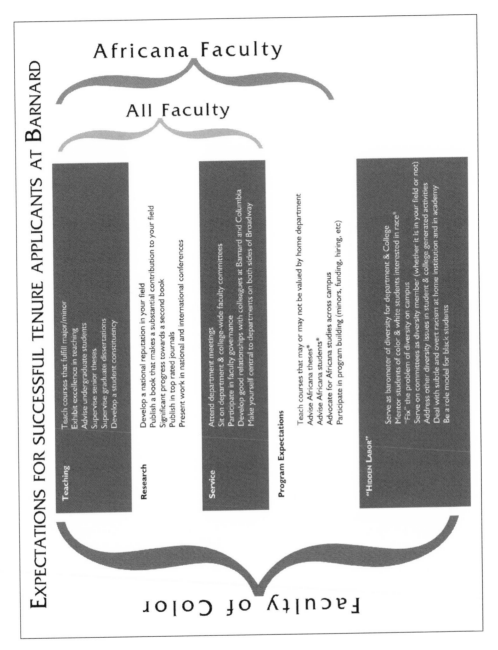

Africana Faculty

All Faculty

Teaching
Teach courses that fulfill major/minor
Exhibit excellence in teaching
Advise undergraduate students
Supervise senior theses
Supervise graduate dissertations
Develop a student constituency

Research
Develop a national reputation in your field
Publish a book that makes a substantial contribution to your field
Significant progress towards a second book
Publish in top rated journals
Present work in national and international conferences

Service
Attend department meetings
Sit on department & college-wide faculty committees
Participate in faculty governance
Develop good relationships with colleagues at Barnard and Columbia
Make yourself central to departments on both sides of Broadway

Program Expectations
Teach courses that may or may not be valued by home department
Advise Africana theses*
Advise Africana students*
Advocate for Africana studies across campus
Participate in program building (minors, funding, hiring, etc)

"Hidden Labor"
Serve as barometer of diversity for department & College
Mentor students of color & white students interested in race
"Fix" the problem of diversity on campus
Serve on committees as diversity member (whether it is in your field or not)
Address other diversity issues in student & college generated activities
Deal with subtle and overt racism at home institution and in academy
Be a role model for black students

Faculty of Color

Bibliography

Academic Personnel Manual. University of California–Davis. (28 November, 2010), http://manuals.ucdavis.edu/apm/220.htm#IVD.

Adalberto, Aguirre Jr. "Women and Minority Faculty in the Academic Workplace: Recruitment, Retention, and Academic Culture." *ASHE-ERIC Higher Education Report* 27(6) (2000), 1–110.

Ahmed, Sara. *On Being Included: Racism and Diversity in Institutional Life*. Durham, NC: Duke University Press, 2012.

Alexander, Ariana. "Soles on the Sidewalk: The Bronx Slave Markets from the 1920s to the 1950s." Unpublished dissertation.

Alger, Jonathan. "When Color-Blind is Color Bland: Ensuring Faculty Diversity in Higher Education." In *Racial and Ethnic Diversity in Higher Education*, edited by Caroline Turner et al., 137–50. Boston: Pearson Publishing, 2002.

Allen, Katherine R., Stacey M. Floyd-Thomas, and Laura Gillman. "Teaching to Transform: From Volatility to Solidarity in an Interdisciplinary Family Studies Classroom." *Family Relations* 50 (2001): 317–25.

Allen, W. R., E. G. Epps, E. A. Guillory, S. A. Suh, and M. Bonous-Hammarth. "The Black Academic: Faculty Status among African Americans in U.S. Higher Education." *Journal of Negro Education*, 69(1/2) (2000): 112–27.

American Association of University Professors (AAUP). "Faculty Governance at Historically Black Colleges and Universities: Tables on Shared Governance." (n.d.), http://www.aaup.org/AAUP/pubsres/academe/2005/MJ/Feat/minotab.htm.

———. "The Historically Black Colleges and Universities: A Future in the Balance." (n.d.), http://www.aaup.org/NR/rdonlyres/DB4D0473-E966-4464-BBCE-A322CA68D456/0/HBCUs.pdf.

———. "How to Diversify the Faculty." (n.d.), http://www.aaup.org/AAUP/protect/legal/topics/howto-diversify.htm.

———. "National AAUP Committees: Historically Black Institutions and Scholars of Color." (n.d.), http://www.aaup.org/AAUP/comm/default.htm#hbicomm.

———. "Resources on Minority Serving Institutions." (n.d.), http://www.aaup.org/AAUP/issues/MSIs/MSIresources.htm.

———. "Shared Governance, Junior Faculty, and HBCUs." (n.d.), http://www.aaup.org/AAUP/pubsres/academe/2006/ND/Feat/GuyS.htm.

———. "Statement on Government of Colleges and Universities." (n.d.), http://www.aaup.org/AAUP/pubsres/policydocs/contents/governancestatement.htm.

American Council on Education/American Association of University Professors (ACE/AAUP). "Does Diversity Make a Difference? Three Research Studies on Diversity in College Classrooms, 2000." (2000), http://www.aaup.org/NR

/rdonlyres/F1A2B22A-EAE2-4D31-9F68-6F235129917E/0/2000_diversity
_report.pdf.

Anderson, James. D. "Race, Meritocracy, and the American Academy during the Immediate Post-World War II Era." In *Racial and Ethnic Diversity in Higher Education*, edited by Caroline Sotello Viernes Turner, 6. Boston: Pearson Custom Publishing, 2002.

Anonymous. "Not Just a Diversity Number." (13 June, 2012), https://www .insidehighered.com/advice/2012/06/13/essay-how-colleges-treat-diversity-hires.

AQIP Team. "Adjunct Faculty Retention." Colorado Mountain College, Fall 2008. 07 June 2012.

Austin, J. L. *How To Do Things with Words*. Oxford, UK: Clarendon Press, 1962.

Baez, Benjamin. *Affirmative Action, Hate Speech, and Tenure: Narratives About Race and Law in the Academy*. Oxford, UK: Routledge Falmer 2002.

Baez, Benjamin. "Race-Related Service and Faculty of Color: Conceptualizing Critical Agency in Academe." *Higher Education* 39(3) (2000): 363–91.

Baker, Houston A. *Betrayal: How Black Intellectuals Have Abandoned the Ideals of the Civil Rights Era*. New York: Columbia University Press, 2010.

———. *The Trouble with Post-Blackness*. New York: Columbia University Press, 2015.

Banh, Ivana. "Professor Denied Tenure Despite Decade of Service." (n.d.), http:// bamboooffshoot.com/2010/09/18/professor-denied-tenure-despite-decade-of -service/.

Bell, Derrick. *Faces at the Bottom of the Well: The Permanence of Racism*. Epigraph. New York: Basic Books, 1992.

Belles, A. Gilbert. "The College Faculty, the Negro Scholar, and the Julius Rosenwald Fund." *The Journal of Negro History* 54(4) (October 1969): 383–92.

Bengtson, Vern L., Alan C. Acock, Katherine R. Allen, Peggye Dilworth-Anderson, and David M. Klein, eds. *Sourcebook of Family Theory and Research*. Thousand Oaks, CA: Sage, 2005.

Bernstein, Mary. "Celebration and Suppression: The Strategic Uses of Identity by the Lesbian and Gay Movement." *American Journal of Sociology* 103(3) (1997): 531–65.

Bhabha, Homi K. *The Location of Culture*. New York/Oxford, UK: Routledge, 1994.

Blackburn, Robert T., and Janet H. Lawrence. *Faculty at Work: Motivation, Expectation, Satisfaction*. Baltimore: Johns Hopkins University Press, 1995.

Bohmer, Susanne, and Joyce L. Briggs. "Teaching Privileged Students about Gender, Race, and Class Oppression." *Teaching Sociology* 19 (1991): 154–63.

Bonilla-Silva, Eduardo. *Racism without Racists: Color-Blind Racism and the Persistence of Racial Inequality in the United States*. New York: Rowman & Littlefield, 2003.

Bow, Leslie. *"Partly Colored": Asian Americans and Racial Anomaly in the Segregated South*. New York: New York University Press, 2010.

Boyer, Ernest L. *Scholarship Reconsidered: Priorities of the Professoriate*. San Francisco: Jossey-Bass, 1990.

Bramen, Carrie Tirado. "Minority Hiring in the Age of Downsizing." In *Power, Race, and Gender in Academe: Strangers in the Ivory Tower?* edited by Shirley Geok-Lin and Maria Herrera-Sobek, 112–31. New York: MLA Press, 2000.

Brodkin, Karen. *How Jews Became White Folks and What That Says About Race in America.* New Brunswick, NJ: Rutgers University Press, 1999.

Brooks, David. "The Limits of Policy." *The New York Times.* (4 May 2010), A 31.

Brown, Robert A. "Letter from President Brown." Boston University Office of the President. (12 May 2015), http://www.bu.edu/president/letters-writings /letters/2015/5-12/.

Brown, Wendy. "The Impossibility of Women's Studies." *Differences: A Journal of Feminist Cultural Studies* 9(3) (1997): 83.

Buechner, Frederick. *The Sacred Journey.* San Francisco: Harper, 1982.

Burgess, Norma J. "Tenure and Promotion among African American Women in the Academy." In *Black Women in the Academy: Promises and Perils,* edited by Lois Benjamin, 227–34. Gainesville: University Press of Florida, 1997.

Butler, Anthea. "Conservatives Bashed Me for Speaking Out about the Zimmerman Verdict." *The Guardian.* (29 May 2013), http://www.theguardian .com/commentisfree/2013/jul/29/george-zimmerman-conservative-backlash.

———. "Burning Acts: Injurious Speech." *Roundtable* 3(1) (1996).

———. "Giving an Account of Oneself." *Diacritics* 31(4) (2001): 22.

Butner, Bonita K., Hansel Burley, and Aretha F. Marbley. "Coping with the Unexpected: Black Faculty at Predominantly White Institutions." *Journal of Black Studies* 30 (2000): 453–62.

Cannon, Katie. "Emancipatory Historiography." In *Dictionary of Feminist Theologies,* edited by Letty M. Russell and J. Shannon Clarkson, 81. Louisville, KY: Westminster John Knox Press, 1996.

Ceasar, Stephen. "Study Faults UCLA's Handling of Faculty's Racial Bias Complaints." *Los Angeles Times.* (18 October 2013), http://www.latimes.com /local/la-me-ucla-discrimination-20131019,0,2297269.story#axzz2ideMQzlt.

Chabram, Angie. "The role of Chicana/o Literature in Teaching Spanish to Native Speakers." In *Language and Culture in Learning,* edited by Barbara Merino, Henry Trueba, and Fabian Samaniego, (124). London: Falmer, 1993.

———. "The Spanish Colon-ialista Narrative." In *Mapping Multiculturalism,* edited by Avery Gordon and Christopher Newfield, (215–37). Minneapolis: University of Minnesota Press, 1996.

Chan, Connie S., and Mary J. Treacy. "Resistance in Multicultural Courses: Student, Faculty, and Classroom Dynamics." *American Behavioral Scientist* 40 (1996): 212–22.

Chatelain, Marcia. "How to Teach Kids about What's Happening in Ferguson." *The Atlantic.* (25 August 2014), http://www.theatlantic.com/education/archive /2014/08/how-to-teach-kids-about-whats-happening-in-ferguson/379049/.

Chin, Frank, and Jeffrey Paul Chan. "Racist Love." In *Seeing Through Shuck,* edited by Richard Kostelanetz, 65–79. New York: Ballantine, 1972.

Cixous, Hélène. *Portrait of Jacques Derrida as a Young Jewish Saint.* New York: Columbia University Press, 2004.

Clay, Andreana. "Intergenerational Yearnings and Other 'Acts of Perversion': Or, Where Would I Be without Lesbian Drumming?" *Journal of Lesbian Studies* (Special Issue), 19(3) (2015): 384–99.

Coates, Ta-Nehisi. "A Religion of Colorblind Policy." *The Atlantic.* (30 May 2013), http://www.theatlantic.com/national/archive/2013/05/a-religion-of -colorblind-policy/276379/.

Cohen, Andrew. "Speak, Clarence, Speak!" *The Atlantic.* (14 January 2013), http:/ /www.theatlantic.com/national/archive/2013/01/speak-clarence-speak/267169 /.

Cohen, Patricia. "In Tough Times, The Humanities Must Justify their Worth." *New York Times.* (25 February 2009), C1.

Collins, Patricia Hill. *Black Feminist Thought: Knowledge, Consciousness, and the Politics of Empowerment.* London: Routledge, 1991.

———. *Fighting Words: Black Women and the Search for Justice.* Minneapolis: University of Minnesota Press, 1998.

———. "Learning from the Outsider Within: The Sociological Significance of Black Feminist Thought." *Social Forces* 33 (1986): 514–32.

———. "Shifting the Center: Race, Class and Feminist Theorizing about Motherhood." In *Shifting the Center: Understanding Contemporary Families,* edited by Susan J. Ferguson, 287–305. Mountain View, CA: Mayfield, 2001.

Cornelius, Llewellyn J., et al. "The ABCs of Tenure: What All African-American Faculty Should Know." *Western Journal of Black Studies* 21(3) (1997): 150–55.

Cox, Aimee. "Women of Color Faculty at the University of Michigan: Recruitment, Retention, and Campus Climate." Center for the Education of Women. (April 2008), http://www.cew.umich.edu/sites/default/files/ AimeeCoxWOCFull2_1.pdf.

Crenshaw, Kimberlé. "Demarginalizing the Intersection of Race and Sex: A Black Feminist Critique of Antidiscrimination Doctrine, Feminist Theory, and Antiracist Politics." In *The Politics of Law: A Progressive Critique,* edited by David Kairys, 57. New York: Pantheon Press, 1990.

———. "Mapping the Margins: Intersectionality, Identity Politics, and Violence Against Women of Color." *Stanford Law Review* 43(6) (1991): 1241–99.

Cuadraz, Gloria H. "Questions Worth Asking: Observations from an Assistant Professor." Keeping Our Faculties: Addressing Recruitment and Retention of Faculty of Color in Higher Education. Conference symposium proceedings, Minneapolis 1998, 1–12.

Daniels, Jessie. "From Tweet to Blog Post to Peer-Reviewed Article: How to Be a Scholar Now." The London School of Economics and Political Science. (25 September 2013), http://blogs.lse.ac.uk/impactofsocialsciences/2013/09/25 /how-to-be-a-scholar-daniels/.

"David Harold Blackwell: National Visionary." National Visionary Leadership Project. (2002–13), http://www.visionaryproject.org/blackwelldavid/.

D'Emilio, John. "The Campus Environment for Gay and Lesbian Life." *Academe* 76(1) (January/February 1990), 16–19.

DePauw, Karen. 2004. E-mail correspondence to April L. Few-Demo, 15 October.

Derrida, Jacques. "Force of Law: The 'Mystical Foundation of Authority.'" In *Deconstruction and the Possibility of Justice*, edited by Drucilla Cornell et al., (3–67). New York: Routledge, 1992.

——. *Otobiographies: The Teaching of Nietzsche and the Politics of the Proper Name*, translated by Peggy Kamuf. New York: Schocken Books, 1985.

Dhillon, Kiran. "The Most Popular Law Schools of Supreme Court Justices." *Time*. (8 May 2014), http://time.com/91646/the-most-popular-law-schools-of -supreme-court-justices/.

Dooris, Michael J., and Marianne Guidos. "Tenure Achievement Rates at Research Universities." (May 2006), https://www.soe.vt.edu/highered/files /Perspectives_PolicyNews/08-06/TenureAchievementRates.pdf.

Dozier, Raine. *The Experiences of LGBT Faculty at Western Washington University: A Report Submitted to the LGBT Advisory Council*. Bellingham, WA: Western Washington University (2012), http://www.wwu.edu/president/docs /Experiences%20of%20LGBT%20Faculty%20at%20WWU.pdf.

du Cille, Ann. "The Occult of True Black Womanhood: Critical Demeanor and Black Feminist Studies." *Signs* 19(3) (Spring 1994): 591–629.

Dukes, Richard L., and Gay Victoria. "The Effects of Gender, Status, and Effective Teaching on the Evaluation of College Instruction." *Teaching Sociology* 17 (1989): 447–57.

Dunbar, Eve. "Who Really Burns: Quitting a Dean's Job in the Age of Michael Brown." *Jezebel*. (2 December 2014), https://jezebel.com/who-really-burns -quitting-a-deans-job-in-the-age-of-mi-1665631269.

Dunn, Sydni. "Lost Your Tenure Case? Get Ready for the Online Petition." *Vitae*. (2 May 2014), https://chroniclevitae.com/news/474-lost-your-tenure -case-get-ready-for-the-online-petition.

Edmundson, Mark. "On the Uses of a Liberal Education: As Lite Entertainment for Bored College Students." *From Inquiry to Academic Writing*, edited by Stuart Greene and April Lidinsky, 322–37. Boston: Bedford/St. Martin, 2012.

Essien, Victor. "Visible and Invisible Barriers to the Incorporation of Faculty of Color in Predominantly White Law Schools." *Journal of Black Studies* 34 (2003): 63–71.

Evans, Patricia. "Books." (n.d.), http://www.patriciaevans.com/books.html. 29 November 2010.

——. *Verbal Abuse Survivors Speak Out*. Avon, MA: Adams Media, 2003.

Evans, Stephanie. *Black Women in the Ivory Tower: 1850–1954*. Gainesville: University Press of Florida, 2007.

"Faculty Tenure Flow Rates." Pennsylvania State University. (n.d.), http://www .opia.psu.edu/sites/default/files/spring10-tenureflow.pdf.

Fairweather, James S. "Faculty Rewards Reconsidered: The Nature of Tradeoffs." *Change* 25 (1993): 44–47.

——. *Faculty Work and Public Trust: Restoring the Value of Teaching and Public Service in American Academic Life*. Boston: Allyn & Bacon, 1996.

———. "The Mythologies of Faculty Productivity: Implications for Institutional Policy and Decision Making." *Journal of Higher Education* 73 (2002): 26–49.

Feldman, Kenneth A. "Research Productivity and Scholarly Accomplishment of College Teachers as Related to Their Instructional Effectiveness: A Review and Exploration." *Research in Higher Education* 26 (1987): 227–98.

Fiedler, Leslie. *An End to Innocence: Essays on Culture and Politics*. Boston: Beacon Press, 1955.

Fine, Michelle. "Working the Hyphens: Reinventing Self and Other in Qualitative Research." In *Handbook of Qualitative Research*, edited by Norman K. Denzin and Yvonna S. Lincoln, 70–82. Thousand Oaks, CA: Sage, 1994.

Finkelstein, Martin J. "Diversification in the Academic Workforce: The Case of the U.S. and Implications for Europe." *European Review* 18 (2010): S142.

Flaherty, Colleen. "Adjunct Leaders Consider Strategies to Force Change." *Inside Higher Ed.* (9 January 2013), https://www.insidehighered.com/news/2013/01/09/adjunct-leaders-consider-strategies-force-change.

———. "CUNY Adjuncts Ask Not to Be Called Professors in Course Syllabus to Highlight Working Conditions." *Inside Higher Ed.* (6 February 2013), https://www.insidehighered.com/news/2013/02/06/cuny-adjuncts-ask-not-be-called-professors-course-syllabuses-highlight-working.

Freud, Sigmund. *A General Selection from the Works of Sigmund Freud*, edited by John Rickman. New York: Doubleday, 1957.

Fried, Vance H. "Opportunities for Efficiency and Innovation: a Primer on How to Cut College Costs." *American Enterprise Institute*. (24 June 2011), http://www.aei.org/publication/opportunities-for-efficiency-and-innovation-a-primer-on-how-to-cut-college-costs/.

Fries, Christopher J., and R. James McNinch. "Signed Versus Unsigned Student Evaluations of Teaching: A Comparison." *Teaching Sociology* 31 (2003): 333–44.

Fuss, Diana. *Identification Papers*. New York: Routledge, 1995.

Gamson, Joshua, and Dawne Moone. "The Sociology of Sexualities: Queer and Beyond." *Annual Review of Sociology* 30 (2004): 47–64.

García-Echeverría, Olga A. "Lengualistic Algo: Spoken-Broken Word." In *Telling Tongues*, edited by Louis G. Mendoza and Toni Nelson Herrera, 22–25. National City, CA: Calaca, 2007.

Giroux, Henry A. *Disturbing Pleasures: Learning Popular Culture*. New York: Routledge, 1994.

Gold, Allan R. "Black Students End Occupation of Office at Harvard Law School." *The New York Times*. (12 May 1988), http://www.nytimes.com/1988/05/12/us/black-students-end-occupation-of-office-at-harvard-law-school.html.

González, Norma, Luis C. Moll, and Cathy Amanti. *Funds of Knowledge: Theorizing Practices in Households, Communities, and Classrooms*. Mahwah, NJ: Erlbaum Associates, 2005.

Gordon, Edmund T, and Joy James. "Afterword: Activist Scholars or Radical Scholars." In *Engaged Contradictions: Theory, Politics, and Methods of Activist Scholarship*, edited by Charles Hale. Berkley: University of California Press, 2008.

Griffin, Farah Jasmine. *Inclusive Scholarship: Developing Black Studies in the United States. A 25 Anniversary Retrospective of Ford Foundation Grant Making, 1982–2007.* New York: Ford Foundation, 2007.

Griffin, Kimberly A., and Richard J. Reddick. "Surveillance and Sacrifice: Gender Differences in the Mentoring Patterns of Black Professors at Predominantly White Research Universities." *American Educational Research Journal* 20(10) (2011): 1–26.

Grimes, William. "David Blackwell, Scholar of Probability, Dies at 91." *The New York Times.* (17 July 2010), http://www.nytimes.com/2010/07/17/education /17blackwell.htmlhttp://www.visionaryproject.org/blackwelldavid/.

Guzman Mendoza, Celeste. "Native Tongue." In *Telling Tongues,* edited by Louis G. Mendoza and Toni Nelson Herrera, 93–97. National City, CA: Calaca, 2007.

Haag, Pamela. "Is Collegiality Code for Hating Ethnic, Racial, and Female Faculty at Tenure Time?" *Education Digest: Essential Readings Condensed for Quick Review* 71(1) (2005): 57–62.

Hale, Charles R., ed. *Engaging Contradictions: Theory, Politics, and Methods of Activist Scholarship.* Berkeley: University of California Press, 2008.

Hall, Stuart. *Race, the Floating Signifier.* Documentary transcript. Northampton, MA: Media Education Foundation, 1997.

Hamilton, Kendra. "'Race in the College Classroom': Minority Faculty Often Face Student Resistance When Teaching about Race." *Black Issues in Higher Education* 19 (2002): 32–37.

Handman, Max Sylvius. "Economic Reasons for the Coming of the Mexican Immigrant." *American Journal of Sociology* 35(4) (1930): 601–11.

Harris, Trudier. *Summer Snow: Reflections from a Black Daughter of the South.* Boston: Beacon, 2003.

Hart Research Associates. "Survey of Part-Time and Adjunct Higher Education Faculty." *American Academic* February 2010. AFT Higher Education.

Hattie, John, and Herbert W. Marsh. "The Relationship between Research and Teaching: A Meta-Analysis." *Review of Educational Research* 66 (1996): 507–42.

Hendrix, Katherine G. "Student Perceptions of the Influence of Race on Professor Credibility." *Journal of Black Studies* 28 (1998): 738–64.

Hernández-Linares, Leticia. "Spanglish Superhighway: A Road Map of Bicultural Signs of Life" (2000–03). In *Telling Tongues,* edited by Louis G. Mendoza and Toni Nelson Herrera, 84–92. National City, CA: Calaca, 2007.

"Hidden Hurt: Domestic Abuse Information." (28 November 2010), http:// www.hiddenhurt.co.uk/.

Hochschild, Arlie Russell. *The Second Shift.* New York: Avon Books, 1989.

hooks, bell. *Talking Back: Thinking Feminist—Thinking Black.* Boston: South End Press, 1989.

———.*Yearning: Race, Gender, and Cultural Politics.* Boston: South End Press, 1990.

Hughes, Langston. "I, Too, Sing America." In *The Collected Poems of Langston Hughes,* edited by and Arnold Rampersand, 46. New York: Vintage, 1995.

Hull, Gloria T., Patricia Bell Scott, and Barbara Smith, eds. *All the Women Are White, All the Blacks are Men, But Some of Us Are Brave—Black Women's Studies.* New York: The Feminist Press, 1982.

Indiana University–Bloomington. "Tenure Guide." (n.d.), http://www.iub.edu/~shs/docs/tenureguide.pdf.

Jaimes, M. Annette. "American Racism: The Impact on American-Indian Identity and Survival." In *Race*, edited by Steven Gregory and Roger Sanjek, 41–61. New Brunswick, NJ: Rutgers University Press, 1994.

Jaschik, Scott. "Hiring Themselves." Insidehighered.com. (13 November 2013), http://www.insidehighered.com/news/2013/11/13/study-finds-law-schools-perpetuate-elite-legal-education-values-faculty-hiring.

JBL Associates, Inc. "Reversing Course: The Troubled State of Academic Staffing and a Path Forward." Report for the American Federation of Teachers. (7 June 2012), http://www.aft.org/sites/default/files/reversingcourse1008.pdf.

Johnson, E. Patrick. *Black Queer Studies: A Critical Anthology.* Duke, NC: Duke University Press, 2005.

———. "In the Merry Old Land of OZ: Rac(e)ing and Quee(r)ing the Academy." In *The Queer Community: Continuing the Struggle for Social Justice*, edited by R. Johnson III, 85–103. San Diego: Birkland, 2009.

Johnson, Mat. *Pym.* New York: Random House, 2011.

June, Audrey Williams. "Tenure Decisions at Southern Cal Strongly Favor White Men, Data in Rejected Candidate's Complaint Suggests." *Chronicle of Higher Education* (13 November 2012).

Katznelson, Ira. *When Affirmative Action Was White: An Untold History of Racial Inequality in Twentieth-Century America.* New York: W. W. Norton & Co., 2005.

Kelderman, Eric. "Morgan State Leads with Values in Wake of Protest." *The Chronicle of Higher Education.* (30 November 2015), video/online.

King Jr., Martin Luther. "Nonviolent Resistance." In *The Little Brown Reader*, edited by Marcia Stubbs and Sylvan Barnett, 451–54. New York: Longman, 2011.

Krantz, Laura. "Controversy Trails New Professor to BU: Educator's Comments on White Males Stir Debate on Race, Academic Freedom." *Boston Globe.* (27 June 2015), https://www.bostonglobe.com/metro/2015/06/27/grundy/6DsS3QckMwa4Y4mXpsBPOM/story.html.

Larsen, Jean. "The Underpaid Professor: Visiting Professors Contributions Are Underappreciated." *Claremont Portside.* (May 2012): IX.5, 6–7.

Laszloffy, Tracey, and Kerry Ann Rockquemore. *The Black Academic's Guide to Winning Tenure—Without Losing Your Soul.* Boulder, CO: Lynne Rienner, 2008.

Laymon, Kiese. "Recipe #150: How to Lay Claim to Dignity." https://www.kieselaymon.com/p=1697.

Leap, Terry. L. "Tenure Discrimination, and African-American Faculty." *Journal of Blacks in Higher Education* 7 (Spring 1995): 103–5.

Levitt, Aimee. "Wash. U. Finally Gives an African-American Woman Tenure." *River Front Times.* (22 September 2010), http://blogs.riverfronttimes.com/dailyrft/2010/09/wash_u_finally_gives_an_african-american_woman_tenure.php.

Lewin, Tamar. "Private-College Presidents Getting Higher Salaries." *New York Times*. (4 December 2011), http://www.nytimes.com/2011/12/05/education/increase-in-pay-for-presidents-at-private-colleges.html.

Lewis, Amanda E., Mark Chesler, and Tyrone A. Forman. "The Impact of 'Colorblind' Ideologies on Students of Color: Intergroup Relations at a Predominantly White University." *Journal of Negro Education*. 69(1/2) (Winter–Spring 2000): 74–91.

———. "Knocking at Freedom's Door: Race, Equity, and Affirmative Action in U.S. Higher Education" *Journal of Negro Education* (Winter–Spring, 2000): 112–27.

Lim, Shirley Geok-Lin, Maria Herrera-Sobek, and Genaro M. Padilla, eds. *Power, Race, and Gender in Academe: Strangers in the Tower?* New York: Modern Language Association of America, 1999.

Lipsitz, Greg. "Breaking the Chains and Steering the Ship: How Activism Can Help Change Teaching and Scholarship." In *Engaged Contradictions: Theory, Politics, and Methods of Activist Scholarship*, edited by Charles Hale. Berkley: University of California Press, 2008.

Liptak, Adam. "Justice Clarence Thomas Breaks His Silence." *New York Times*. (14 January 2013), http://www.nytimes.com/2013/01/15/us/clarence-thomas-breaks-silence-in-supreme-court.html?_r=0.

———. "Justice Thomas's Dissent Hints of Supreme Court's Intentions on Same-Sex Marriage." *New York Times*. (9 February 2015), http://www.nytimes.com/2015/02/10/us/justice-thomass-dissent-hints-of-supreme-courts-intentions-on-same-sex-marriage.html.

López, Manuel Paul, ed. "Mi Cantito." In *Death of a Mexican and Other Poems*. Chico, CA: Bear Star Press, 2006.

Mabokela, Reitumetse, and Anna L. Green, *Sisters of the Academy: Emergent Black Women Scholars in Higher Education*. Sterling, VA: Stylus Publishing, 2001.

MacLean, William Patrick. "Participation in a Professional Association's Annual National Conference: A Phenomenological Inquiry into the Perceptions of Underrepresented Educational Leadership Faculty." Ph.D. diss., Washington State University, 2010.

Maisto, Maria, and Steve Street. "Confronting Contingency: Faculty Equity and the Goals of Academic Democracy." *Liberal Education* 97(1) (2001), 6–13.

Manning, Johnathan. "Sulphur Slaying Case Before U.S. Supreme Court." *American Press*. February 4, 2013.

Marable, Manning. "Black Studies and the Black Intellectual Tradition." *Race and Reason* 4 (1997–98): 97–98.

Marcal, Kate. "Tenured Professor Overcomes Obstacles of Race and Gender." *Student Life*. (22 September 2010), http://www.studlife.com/scene/2010/09/22/tenured-professor-overcomes-obstacles-of-race-and-gender/.

Martin, Biddy. "Success and Its Failures." *Differences: A Journal of Feminist Cultural Studies* 9(3) (1997): 104.

Massy, William, and Andrea Wilger. "Improving Productivity: What Faculty Think about It—and Its Effect on Quality." *Change* 27(1995): 10–21.

Matthew, Patricia. "Lesson from the Collections I: The Missing Cohort." *Written/Unwritten*. (19 May 2011), http://writtenunwritten.wordpress.com /2011/05/19/lesson-i-the-missing-cohort/.

———. "Review of *Mentoring Faculty of Color*." *Western Journal of Black Studies* 38(4) (Winter 2014): 283–84.

McGough, Michael. "Justice Clarence Thomas' Silence is 'Disgraceful'? Not Really." *Los Angeles Times*. (21 February 2014), http://www.latimes.com /opinion/opinion-la/la-ol-clarence-thomas-supreme-court-silence-20140221 -story.html.

McGuiness, Charles "Anthea Butler Gets Attacked by Malkin's Twitch-Mob." *The Social Seer*. (13 September 2012), http://www.socialseer.com/2012/09/13 /anthea-butler-gets-attacked-by-malkins-twitch-mob/.

McIntosh, Peggy. "White Privilege: Unpacking the Invisible Knapsack." Excerpt from Working Paper 189, "White Privilege and Male Privilege: A Personal Account of Coming To See Correspondences through Work in Women's Studies" (1988), Wellesley College Center for Research on Women. Wellesley, MA: Author, 1988.

McMillan Cottom, Tressie. "The Inferiority of Blackness as a Subject." (2 May 2012), http://tressiemc.com/2012/05/02/the-inferiority-of-blackness-as-a -subject/.

———."The New Old Labor Crisis." *Slate*. (24 January 2014), http://www.slate .com/articles/life/counter_narrative/2014/01/adjunct_crisis_in_higher_ed_an _all_too_familiar_story_for_black_faculty.html.

———. "Risk and Ethics in Public Scholarship." (9 December 2012), http://www .insidehighered.com/blog/8948.

———. "Using Social Media to Rage Against the Machine: *Chronicle of Higher Education*, Naomi Schaefer Riley, and Black Studies." Unpublished conference paper.

———. " 'Who Do You Think You Are?' When Marginality Meets Academic Microcelebrity." *ADA: A Journal of Gender, New Media and Technology*. (18 June 2015), http://adanewmedia.org/2015/04/issue7-mcmillancottom/.

Mencke, Bernadette Kristine Buchanan. "Education, Racism, and the Military; A Critical Race Theory Analysis of the G. I. Bill and its Implications for African-Americans." Unpublished diss., 2010.

Merino, Barbara, Henry Trueba, and Fabian Samaniego, eds. *Language and Culture in Learning*. London: Falmer Press, 1993.

Mireles, Oscar, "Lost and Found Languages." In *Telling Tongues*, edited by Louis G. Mendoza and Toni Nelson Herrera. National City, CA: Calaca, 2007.

Monsiváis, Carlos. "Prologue." In *La otra cara de Mexico: El pueblo Chicano*, edited by David R. Maciel. Mexico City: El Caballito, 1982.

Montclair State University. "Annual Institutional Profile of Montclair State University, Fall 2010." (15 October 2010), http://www.montclair .edu/oit/institutionalresearch/AssessmentDocs/Excellence /MSUInstitutionalProfile2010.pdf.

Moraga, Cherríe L. *Loving in the War Years*. 2nd ed. Boston: Beacon, 2000 [1983].

Moses, Yolanda T. "Black Women in Academe: Issues and Strategies." In *Black Women in the Academy: Promises and Perils*, edited by Lois Benjamin, 23–37. Gainesville: University Press of Florida, 1997.

Natt, Lorena. "U.S. Probes Alleged UCD Hispanic Bias." *Sacramento Bee*, 14 March 1990.

"No Blacks in the Pipeline: The Standard Explanation for Low Percentage of Black Faculty Continues to Be Much of a Red Herring." *Journal of Blacks in Higher Education* 33 (2001): 77–78.

Obergefell v. Hodges, U.S. 556 U.S. 28 (2015).

Omolade, Barbara. "A Black Feminist Pedagogy." *Women's Studies Quarterly* 15 (1987): 32–39.

Ong, Paul, Edna Bonacich, and Lucie Cheng, eds. *The New Asian Immigration in Los Angeles and Global Restructuring*. Philadelphia, PA: Temple University Press, 1994.

Ortega, Mariana. "Being Lovingly, Knowingly Ignorant: White Feminism and Women of Color." *Hypatia* 21(3) (Summer 2006): 56–74.

Palmer, Parker J. *Let Your Life Speak: Listening for the Voice of Vocation*. San Francisco: Jossey-Bass, 2000.

Patton, Stacey. "After Ferguson, Some Black Academics Wonder: Does Pursuing a PhD Matter?" *Chronicle Vitae*. (12 September 2014), http://chroniclevitae .com/news/703-after-ferguson-some-black-academics-wonder-does-pursuing -a-ph-d-matter.

———. "How a White Historian Nurtures Diverse PhDs." *Chronicle of Higher Education*. (15 May 2015), http://chronicle.com/article/How-a-White-Historian -Nurtures/230153/.

———. "The PhD Now Comes with Foodstamps." *Chronicle of Higher Education*. (6 May 2012), http://chronicle.com/article/From-Graduate-School-to/131795/.

Penney, Joel, and Caroline Dadas. "(Re) Tweeting in the Service of Protest: Digital Composition and Circulation in the Occupy Wall Street Movement." *New Media & Society*. (23 January 2013), http://www.academia.edu/4094532/ _Re_Tweeting_in_the_Service_of_Activism_Digital_Composition_and _Circulation_in_the_Occupy_Wall_Street_Movement.

Porter, Philip W. "Book review of *Who Am I? An Autobiography of Emotion, Mind and Spirit*." *Ethics, Place, and Environment* 3(3) (2000): 331–40.

Pratt, Mary Louise. "Arts of the Contact Zone." In *Ways of Reading* (5th ed.), edited by David Bartholomae and Anthony Petroksky. New York: Bedford/ St. Martin's, 1999.

Princeton University Reports. "Program in African American Studies." (18 September 2006), http://www.princeton.edu/reports/african-20060918/# comp0000481800aed0000000042a0048.

Rich, Adrienne. "Compulsory Heterosexuality and Lesbian Existence." *Signs* 5 (1980): 631–60.

Riley, Naomi Schaefer. "Black Studies, Part 2: A Response to Critics." *Chronicle of Higher Education*. (2 May 2012), http://chronicle.com/blogs/brainstorm /black-studies-part-2-a-response-to-critics/46401.

———. "The Most Persuasive Case for Eliminating Black Studies?" *Chronicle of Higher Education*. (1 May 2012), http://chronicle.com/blogs/brainstorm /the-most-persuasive-case-for-eliminating-black-studies-just-read-the -dissertations/46346.

Robinson, Zandria. "Zeezus Does the Firing 'Round Hurr." *New South Negress*. (n.d.), http://newsouthnegress.com/zeezusyear/.

Rockquemore, Kerry Ann. "Let's Talk About Twitter." (20 May 2015), https://www .insidehighered.com/advice/2015/05/20/essay-issues-facing-young-academics -social-media.

Rubin, D. L. "Help! My Professor (or Doctor or Boss) Doesn't Talk English." In *Readings in Cultural Contexts*, edited by Judith N. Martin, Thomas K. Nakayama, and Lisa A. Flores, 127–40. Mountain View, CA: Mayfield, 2001.

Russ, Travis L., Cheri J. Simonds, and Stephen K. Hunt. "Coming Out in the Classroom . . . An Occupational Hazard? The Influence of Sexual Orientation on Teacher Credibility and Perceived Student Learning." *Communication Education* 51(3) (2002): 311–24.

Sánchez, Rosaura. "Language Variation in the Spanish of the Southwest." In *Language and Culture in Learning*, edited by Barbara Merino, Henry Trueba, and Fabian Samaniego. London: Falmer, 1994.

Schneider, Mark. "Big-Bucks College Presidents Don't Earn Their Pay." American Enterprise Institute. (22 December 2010), https://www.aei.org /publication/big-bucks-college-presidents-dont-earn-their-pay/.

Scott, Joan Wallach, ed. *Women's Studies on the Edge*. Durham, NC: Duke University Press, 2008.

Serhan, Yasmeen. "Special Feature: Prof Loses Tenure Bid after Appeal." *The Daily Trojan*. (2 May 2013), http://dailytrojan.com/2013/05/02/prof-loses -tenure-bid-after-appeal/.

Sherwin, Elizabeth. "Change Advised in the Spanish Curriculum." *Davis Enterprise*, March 1990, 1.

Simon, Roger I. *Teaching Against the Grain: Texts for a Pedagogy of Possibility*. New York: Bergen and Garvey, 1992.

Singh, Sahell Sava. "Tweeting to the Choir: Online Performance and Academic Identity." Selected Papers of Internet Research [online], March 2013.

Smith, Craig. "How Many People Use 1000+ of the Top Social Media, Apps and Digital Services." (n.d.), http://expandedramblings.com/index.php/resource -how-many-people-use-the-top-social-media/3/.

Smith, Pamela. "The Tyrannies of the Untenured Professors of Color." *University of California Davis Law Review* 33 (2000): 1105–33.

Smolowe, Jill. "Anita Hill's Legacy." *Time*. (19 October 1992), http://content .time.com/time/magazine/article/0,9171,976770,00.html.

Soto, Gary. "Spanish." In *Red Hot Salsa*, edited by Lorie Marie Carlson, 2–7. New York: Henry Holt & Co., 2005.

Spivak, Gayatri Chakravorty. "Can the Subaltern Speak?" In *Colonial Discourse/ Post-Colonial Theory: A Reader*, edited by Patrick Williams and Laura Chrisman, (66–111). New York: Columbia University Press, 1994.

Stanford University. *Quality of Life Survey Follow-Up Study of Underrepresented Minority Faculty at Stanford University.* Stanford University's Panel on Faculty Equity, and Quality of Life. (May 2013), https://facultydevelopment.stanford .edu/sites/default/files/documents/URM-Report1-exe-sum_0.pdf.

Stanley, Christine A. "Coloring the Academic Landscape: Faculty of Color Breaking the Silence in Predominately White Colleges and Universities." *American Educational Research Journal* 43(4) (Winter 2006): 701–36.

Straumsheim, Carl. "Interdisciplinary and Out of a Job." *Inside Higher Ed.* (8 March 2013), https://www.insidehighered.com/news/2013/03/08/liberal -arts-instructors-rally-around-interdisciplinary-studies-after-tenure-denials.

Svrluga, Susan. "Boston University Debates Discrimination on Campus." *Washington Post.* (15 May 2015), http://www.washingtonpost.com/news/grade -point/wp/2015/05/15/boston-university-debates-discrimination-on-campus/.

Taylor, Keeanga-Yamahtta, La Tasha B. Levy, and Ruth Hays. "Grad Students Respond to Riley Post on African-American Studies." *Chronicle of Higher Education.* (May 2012), http://chronicle.com/blogs/brainstorm/grad-students -respond-to-riley-post-on-african-american-studies/46421.

Taylor, Verta, and Nicole Raeburn. "Identity Politics as High-Risk Activism: Career Consequences for Lesbian, Gay, and Bisexual Sociologists." *Social Problems* 42(2) (1995): 252–73.

"Tenure Outcomes by Race/Ethnicity and Gender from 2014–2014 in CAS." University of South Florida.

Thys, Fred. "Incoming BU Professor Criticized for Tweets on Race; Students Rally to Support." WBUR. (13 May 2015), http://www.wbur.org/2015/05/13/ saida-grundy-bu-professor-tweets.

Toobin, Jeffrey. "Clarence Thomas Speaks, Finally." *New Yorker.* (14 January 2013), http://www.newyorker.com/news/news-desk/clarence-thomas-speaks-finally.

Tuan, Yi-Fu. *Who Am I? An Autobiography of Emotion, Mind, and Spirit.* Madison, WI: University of Wisconsin Press, 1999.

Turner, Caroline. "New Faces, New Knowledge." *Academe* 86 (2000): 34–38.

TuSmith, Bonnie, and Maureen T. Reddy. "Out on a Limb: Race and the Evaluation of Frontline Teaching." In *Race in the College Classroom: Pedagogy and Politics,* edited by Bonnie TuSmith and Maureen Reddy, 112–25. New Brunswick, NJ: Rutgers University Press, 2002.

———. *Race in the College Classroom: Pedagogy and Politics.* New Brunswick, NJ: Rutgers University Press, 2002.

U.S. Department of Education, Winter 2009–10, Human Resources component, Fall Staff section. National Center for Education Statistics compiled by University of Washington, MLIS candidate, Camille S. Davidson.

University of Missouri–Kansas City. "Selected Recommendations for Supporting Women and Minority Faculty.*" (n.d.), http://www.umkc.edu /provost/chairs/toolkit/supporting-women-and-minority-faculty.pdf.

University of South Carolina Upstate. "Common Data Set." (n.d.), http://www .uscupstate.edu/uploadedFiles/About_upstate/Planning_and_Organizational _Development/Institutional_Research/CommDataSet2009_2010.rtf.

Valenzuela, Angela. *Subtractive Schooling U.S.–Mexican Youth and the Politics of Caring*. Albany: NY, SUNY University Press, 1999.

Vedder, Richard. "Why Does College Cost So Much?" *American Enterprise Institute*. (23 August 2005), https://www.aei.org/publication/why-does-college-cost-so-much/.

Vizzini, Ned. "High Anxiety." *New York Times Book Review*. (13 May 2007), http://www.nytimes.com/2007/05/13/books/review/Vizzini-t.html.

Walesby, Anthony. "Facts and Myths of Affirmative Action." *Higher Ed Jobs*. (16 December 2010), https://www.higheredjobs.com/articles/articledisplay.cfm?ID=246.

Wall, Cheryl. "Foreword: Faculty as Change Agents—Reflections on My Academic Life." In *Doing Diversity in Higher Education: Faculty Leaders Share Challenges and Strategies*, edited by Winifred R. Brown-Glaude, ix–xvi. New Brunswick, NJ: Rutgers University Press, 2008.

———. "What Does It Mean to Be a Black Woman Who Reads for a Living?" Presentation at Rutgers University. (23 June 2009), http://www.youtube.com/watch?v=YdFHT3CICKA.

Weiler, Kathleen. "Freire and a Feminist Pedagogy of Difference." *Harvard Educational Review* 61 (1991): 449–74.

White, Deborah Gray. *Telling Histories: Black Women Historians in the Ivory Tower*. Chapel Hill: University of North Carolina Press, 2008.

Williams, Charmaine. "The Angry Black Woman Scholar." *NWSA Journal* 13 (2001): 87–97.

Williams, Patricia J. *Seeing a Color-Blind Future: The Paradox of Race*. New York: Farrar, Straus & Giroux, 1997.

Winston, Gordon K. "The Decline of Undergraduate Teaching: Moral Failure or Market Pressure?" *Change* 26 (1994): 8–15.

Acknowledgments

To the authors, coauthors, and interview subjects whose work made this anthology possible, I offer my gratitude and respect. Thank you for trusting me with your stories and for your patience and fortitude.

My thanks go to the English department at Montclair State University for its support throughout this project, especially colleagues who recommended contributors, read early drafts of chapters, and offered publishing advice and moral support: Janet Cutler and Jim Nash, Fawzia Afzal- Khan, Rashida Batte-Bowden, Lee Behlman, Phyllis Brooks, Kim Harrison, Laura Jones, Johnny Lorenz, Alex Lykidis, Stacey McCormick, Marietta Morrisey, Larry Schwartz, Art Simon, and La Shana Walters. A sabbatical approved by Provost Willard Gingerich gave me time to complete the research for this project. The English Council approved my application for research assistance, making it possible for me to work with the indefatigable Liamog Drislane. I am especially grateful to the late Paul Arthur, the brilliant film scholar and fierce conversationalist who made me promise to use my academic freedom to always do the work I thought mattered most.

We have been lucky to find a home with the University of North Carolina Press and its impressive, knowledgeable staff. Alison Shay and Joe Parsons have made a process that might have been daunting and alienating intellectually satisfying and a true pleasure. I am also thankful for the efforts of Jay Mazzocchi, Ian Oakes, (Michelle Witkowski at Westchester Publishing Services), and Dino Battista. I especially appreciate Joe's guidance and patience.

I am grateful to the friends and family who have supported me in myriad ways over the years it has taken me to finish this anthology: Dominique Riviere Gonsalves, Ariana Alexander, Jafari Sinclair Allen, Tennille Allen, Althea Anderson, George Bailey, Grady Ballenger, Charlotte Baker Pierce, Angie Chabram, Karen Cardozo, Jennifer Clark, Brian Cliff, Ta-Nehisi Coates and The Horde, Jade Davis, Eve Dunbar, Bonnie Joy Gunzenhauser, Kim Hall, F. Jefferson Hendricks, Claudia Matthew Hobbs, Nichele Hoskins, Norma Johnson, Nadia Jones, Kiese Laymon, Dwayne Mack, Debra Marek, Carmen Matthew, Neil Matthew, Syneira Matthew, Michelle Moravec, Susan Newton, Kelly Nims, Vimala Pashputi, Cynthia Raatle, Fred Raatle and her online communities, Aviva Schuman, Margaret Schwartz, Danny Simmons, Siri Suh, Nate Therien, Joan T. Walrond, Steve Weddle, everyone at Nero Doro, Jennifer Williams, and Tressie McMillan Cottom.

Mr. Bill and Ma'Onie have made all things possible and deserve more gratitude than I can ever offer them.

Biographies of Contributors

Ariana E. Alexander is a doctoral candidate in History at New York University. Her dissertation—*Soles on the Sidewalk: the Bronx Slave Markets from the 1920s to the 1950s*—uses the lens of domestic day-labor markets to investigate migration, labor commodification, community activism, and local governance. She has won various awards including a Ford Dissertation Fellowship for her academic research. She holds a bachelors of arts in English and Ethnic Studies from Dartmouth College.

Houston A. Baker Jr. is Distinguished University Professor and Professor of English at Vanderbilt University. He has published or edited more than twenty books and is the author of more than eighty articles, essays, and reviews. He has served as editor of *American Literature*. His most recent books include *The Trouble With Post-Blackness*, edited with K. Merinda Simmons (Columbia University Press 2015), *Turning South Again: Re-Thinking Modernism, Re-Reading Booker T*, and *I Don't Hate the South: Reflections on Faulkner, Family, and the South*. His most recent book, for which he won the 2009 American Book Award, is a critique of Black public intellectuals titled *Betrayal: How Black Intellectuals Have Abandoned the Ideals of the Civil Rights Era* (Columbia University Press, 2008). Baker is a published poet whose most recent volume is titled *Passing Over* (Wayne State University Press, 2000). He has served in several administrative and institutional posts, including the 1992 Presidency of the Modern Language Association of America. His honors include Guggenheim, John Hay Whitney, and Rockefeller Fellowships, as well as several honorary degrees from American colleges and universities.

Leslie Bow is Mark and Elisabeth Eccles Professor of English and Asian American Studies at the University of Wisconsin, Madison where she specializes in ethnic American literatures and visual culture. She is the author of the award-winning, *'Partly Colored': Asian Americans and Racial Anomaly in the Segregated South* (New York University Press, 2010); *Betrayal and Other Acts of Subversion: Feminism, Sexual Politics, Asian American Women's Literature* (Princeton University Press, 2001); editor of the four-volume, *Asian American Feminisms* (Routledge, 2012) and a reissue of Fiona Cheong's novel, *The Scent of the Gods* (Illinois University Press, 2010). She is currently working on a book that explores race as a source of pleasure in the public sphere.

Angie Chabram is full professor of Chicana/o Studies and Cultural Studies at the University of California at Davis. She was raised by her mother in La Puente,

California, and attended UC Berkeley and UC San Diego. She has taught at Davis since 1986 and specializes in Chicana/o cultural representations as well as literature. She has edited several collections, including *The Chicana/o Cultural Studies Reader* and *The Chicana/o Cultural Studies Forum: Critical and Ethnographic Perspectives*. She recently published the first collection of Latina illness narratives entitled *Speaking from the Body*, with Adela de la Torre. She is working on a book about Chicana/o health narratives. In her classes, she seeks to create a bridge between students and community, scholarship and learning.

Andreana Clay is an Associate Professor in the Departments of Sociology and Sexuality Studies at San Francisco State University. Her book *The Hip-Hop Generation Fights Back: Youth Activism and Post-Civil Rights Politics* (NYU Press, 2012) explores how youth of color organize and identify as activists in the post-civil rights era. She has written articles on hip-hop culture, Black popular music, and queer sexuality that have appeared in several anthologies and academic journals.

Jane Chin Davidson is an art historian and researcher of the signification of race, gender, and sexuality in contemporary art, performance, and global exhibitions. Her essays have been published in leading journals, including *Journal of Visual Culture*, *Third Text: Critical Perspectives on Contemporary Art and Culture*, *n.paradoxa: International Feminist Art Journal*, and *Interventions: International Journal of Postcolonial Studies*. Her work has also been published in edited collections such as Meiling Cheng and Gabrielle Cody's *Reading Contemporary Performance* (2015) and Jonathan Harris's *Dead History, Live Art? Spectacle, Subjectivity and Subversion in Visual Culture since the 1960s* (2009). Dr. Davidson is a curator of art exhibitions, including *Inner Space, Global Matter* (2013) for three sites—NASA's Johnson Space Center, the University of Houston, and Miami International University—and the exhibition *Setting the Table: The 30th Anniversary of Judy Chicago's The Dinner Party at the University of Houston–Clear Lake* (2011). She was an Economic and Social Research Council postdoctoral fellow with the Cultural Theory Institute at the University of Manchester, where she also completed her PhD in Art History after receiving her BA at Reed College. She is currently Assistant Professor of Art History and Contemporary Art at California State University, San Bernardino.

Dr. April L. Few-Demo is Associate Professor of Family Studies in the Department of Human Development at Virginia Tech. Her research interests include adolescent and emerging adult sexuality, intimate violence, qualitative methodologies, rural women's reentry experiences, and diversity issues in academia. She has served on the editorial boards of the *Journal of Family Issues*, *Family Relations*, and the *Journal of Family Communication*. She is the recipient of awards for teaching, research, and diversity service. Her scholarship on the utility of Black feminist and critical race theories has resulted in plenary invitations to national conferences, book chapters on feminist family studies, and intimate violence in books such as the *Sourcebook of Family Theory and Research* (2005) and *Violence in The Lives of Black Women: Black, Battered and Blue* (2003) and a coedited book, *The Handbook of Feminist Family Studies* (2009) with Sally Lloyd and Katherine Allen. In addition, she has published in *Family Process, Journal of Family Issues, Violence and Victims, Family Relations, Sex Roles, Sexuality and Culture, National Women's Studies Association Journal, Journal of Family Communication, Journal of Family Theory and Review, Criminal Justice Policy and Research Journal*, and the *International Journal of International Journal of Offender Therapy and Comparative Criminology*.

Carmen V. Harris is a Professor of History at the University of South Carolina's Upstate Campus in Spartanburg, South Carolina. She holds a doctorate in History from Michigan State University. Her research focuses include African American women's, Southern, agricultural, and public policy history. Her first book chapter, "Grace Under Pressure: The Black Home Extension Service in South Carolina, 1919–1966," published in *Rethinking Home Economics in the Twentieth Century* (Cornell, 1997 and 2002), has been assigned reading in graduate classrooms. Her study of bureaucratic racism in the origins of the United States Cooperative Extension Service published in *Agricultural History* in 2008 won the Agricultural History Society's Vernon Carstenen Award for the best journal article published in the journal that year. She has also published on the overlap of 4-H and civil rights, and she recently published a chapter in *Beyond Forty Acres and a Mule: African American Landowning Families Since Reconstruction* (University Press of Florida, 2014).

Rashida L. Harrison completed her PhD in African American and African Studies from Michigan State University (MSU). She is a native New Yorker who received her BA from Cornell University. She taught for five years at MSU's James Madison College while completing her dissertation and then as a postdoctoral fellow. She currently works in an administrative capacity conducting civil rights investigations for the Office of Institutional Equity at MSU. She continues to actively teach for Central Michigan University's Global Campus in the Sociology Department and continues to build on her dissertation entitled "Towards a Transnational Black Feminist Discourse: Women Writing Against States of Imperialism, 1975–1989." She has interdisciplinary research interests in the areas focusing on Black women's political work throughout the African diaspora; interrogations of Black feminist discourse; intersections of race, class, gender, and sexuality; and theoretical inquiries of belonging.

Ayanna Jackson-Fowler is an Associate Professor of English at Tarrant County College Northwest Campus. She received her PhD from Texas Tech University in 2009. Her dissertation, "Repetition, Revision, and Appropriation: The Dialectical Relationship between Early Black Writing and the Romantic-Period British Literary Tradition," explores how Black writers such as Phillis Wheatley, Ignatius Sancho, Olaudah Equiano, and Ottobah Cugoano influenced nineteenth-century women writers. Her work has been included in *Transatlantic Literature of the Long Eighteenth Century* (Cambridge Scholars Press, 2011).

Patricia A. Matthew is Associate Professor of English at Montclair State University, where she teaches courses in nineteenth-century British literature and culture. She is writing a book about representations of the body and the discourse of disease and illness in Romantic-era fiction. She is coeditor with Miriam Wallace of a special issue for *Romantic Pedagogy Commons* ("Novel Prospects: Teaching Romantic-Era Fiction"). She writes, conducts workshops, and blogs about diversity in higher education. Her essays and reviews have been published in *Women's Writing*, *Nineteenth-Century Gender Studies*, *Signs*, the *Keats-Shelley Journal*, and *PMLA*. Her essays on race and feminism have been published in *The New Inquiry* and cross-posted in *Guernica*, *The Atlantic*, and *Harvard's Neiman Lab*. This work—*Written/Unwritten: Tenure and Race in the Humanities*—is her first book.

Dr. Fred P. Piercy is professor of family therapy in the Marriage and Family Therapy doctoral program, Department of Human Development, Virginia Tech, Blacksburg, Virginia. Dr. Piercy is also the current editor of the *Journal of Marital and Family Therapy*, the flagship journal of the American Association for Marriage and Family Therapy. Dr. Piercy's scholarship has involved family therapy education, family therapy of substance abuse, HIV social science research and prevention, qualitative research and evaluation, international family therapy, and infidelity treatment. Dr. Piercy has written more than 170 published journal articles and book chapters, five books, and forty-three funded grants. He has won national, university, and college teaching awards, as well as college awards for administration, outreach, and graduate student advising. He is the recipient of the 2015 Lifetime Achievement Award of the American Family Therapy Academy, AAMFT's 2007 Outstanding Contribution to Marriage and Family Therapy Award, and Virginia Tech's 2007 Alumni Award for Outstanding Graduate Student Advising. He also won NCFR's 2013 Kathleen Briggs Graduate Student Advising Award. Dr. Piercy has collaborated extensively with colleagues from the University of Indonesia and Atma Jaya University (in Jakarta, Indonesia).

Deepa S. Reddy is Associate Professor and Director of India Outreach Programs at the University of Houston. She has taught anthropology, cross-cultural studies, and women's studies at the University of Houston–Clear Lake since 2000. Between 2002 and 2004, she directed the Women's Studies program at UHCL and was responsible for reestablishing Women's Studies Week programming, helping to secure the Marilyn Mieszkuc Professorship, and writing the proposal to the Texas Coordinating Board for Higher Education that resulted in the establishment of UHCL's bachelor's degree program in Women's Studies. Her own research centers on identitarian, feminist, and caste politics in India and religious nationalism. Her book *Religious Identity and Political Destiny* was published in 2006. Since then, Deepa Reddy has also worked on a National Institutes of Health funded study on Indian community participation in the International

Haplotype Map project. She has published also on biopolitics, human substance donation, and most recently on the middle-class anticorruption movements of summer 2011. Finally, Deepa Reddy consults for Human Factors International, a company specializing in user experience design.

Lisa Sánchez González, Professor of English at the University of Connecticut, studied Classics and Comparative Literature at UCLA, where she received her PhD in 1995. She has taught at universities in the United States, Puerto Rico, and Brazil (as a Fulbright scholar). Sánchez is the author of *Boricua Literature: A Literary History of the Puerto Rican Diaspora* (New York University Press, 2001), *The Stories I Read to the Children: The Life and Writing of Pura Belpré* (Centro Press, CUNY, 2013), a bilingual collection of short stories entitled *Puerto Rican Folktales* (2Leaf Press, 2014), and various scholarly articles on issues of social justice, subaltern cultures, and American literature. She is currently writing a fantasy novel and doing research for a collection of essays, *Tribal Futurism*, on comparative colonialism, indigeneity, and literary history.

Wilson Santos (wsantosblog.com) is an Associate Course Director in the English Department at Full Sail University. He earned both his bachelor's and master's degrees in English at Montclair State University in New Jersey, where he also minored in Film Studies. A native New Yorker, Santos studied filmmaking at New York University and studied for a semester at Kingston University in England. He is a published spoken-word artist with several tracks released on notable dance music record labels such as Defected, Fluential, Stealth, and Ultra. As a writer, he has optioned two feature length screenplays. Santos's spoken-word short documentary film *My Verse* won first prize at the Enzian Film Slam festival in Maitland, Florida, and has been showcased at several international film festivals, as well as being nominated as an Official Selection of the Florida Film Festival. He is currently writing his fourth feature-length screenplay as well as compiling his poems into his first chapbook.

Sarita Echavez See teaches in the Department of Media and Cultural Studies and the SEATRiP (Southeast Asia: Text, Ritual, and Performance) program at the University of California–Riverside. She also is the founder and executive director of the web-based nonprofit organization called the Center for Art and Thought (http://centerforartandthought.org/). She is the author of the monograph *The Decolonized Eye: Filipino American Art and Performance* (University of Minnesota Press, 2009) and is at work on her current book project, *Accumulating the Primitive*.

Andrew J. Stremmel is Professor and Department Head in Teaching, Learning, and Leadership in the College of Education and Human Sciences at South Dakota State University (SDSU). He is former director of the Child Development Laboratory School at Virginia Polytechnic Institute and State University, where he was a faculty member for fifteen years prior to arriving at SDSU in 2004. He received both his PhD and MS degrees from Purdue University in Early Childhood Education and Child Development and earned his BA in Psychology from Pennsylvania State University. Dr. Stremmel's research interests are in the area of early childhood teacher education, in particular teacher action research, and Reggio Emilia-inspired, inquiry-based approaches to early childhood teacher education and curriculum. He has published more than sixty refereed journal articles and book chapters and has coedited two books, *Affirming Diversity through Democratic Conversations* (1999, Merrill/Prentice Hall) and *Teaching and Learning: Collaborative Exploration of the Reggio Emilia Approach* (2001, Merrill/Prentice Hall). He also has coauthored the book *Teaching as Inquiry: Rethinking Curriculum in Early Childhood Education* (2005, Allyn & Bacon), which is the first comprehensive early childhood education text provoked and inspired by the Reggio Emilia approach.

Cheryl A. Wall received her BA from Howard and her PhD from Harvard University and is a specialist in Black women's writing, the Harlem Renaissance, and Zora Neale Hurston. She is Board of Governors Zora Neale Hurston Professor of English at Rutgers, the State University of New Jersey. Wall serves on the editorial board of *American Literature* and the advisory board of *African American Review* and *Signs*. Her numerous publications include the seminal *Worrying the Line* (2005) and edited volumes about Zora Neale Hurston. She served as section editor for "Literature since 1975" in the *Norton Anthology of African American Literature* (2003), and coedited *Savoring the Salt: The Legacy of Toni Cade Bambara* (Temple University Press, 2007). A former chair of the Department of English, Professor Wall remains active in university affairs. In 2003, she was coprincipal with Mary Hartman of the Institute for Women's Leadership on "Reaffirming Action: Designs for Diversity in Higher Education" and was cochair with Rutgers University President Richard L. McCormick of the President's Council on Institutional Diversity and Equity. She is also the recipient of the Warren I. Susman Award for Excellence in Teaching.

E. Frances White is Professor Emeritx at the Gallatin School of Individualized Studies and the Department of Social and Cultural Analysis in the Faculty of Arts and Science at New York University. She served as NYU's Vice Provost for Faculty Development from 2005 to 2008 and Dean of the Gallatin School from 1998 to 2005. She has been awarded fellowships from the Danforth Foundation, the Mellon Foundation, and the National Endowment for the Humanities, among others. She has also been a Fulbright Senior Research Scholar in Sierra Leone and Gambia. Before coming to NYU, she taught at Fourah Bay College of the University of Sierra Leone, Temple University, and Hampshire College. Her awards include the Catherine T. and John D. MacArthur Chair in History (1985–1988) and the 1987 Letitia Brown Memorial Publication Prize for the best book on Black women. Her teaching and research interests include the history of Africa and its diaspora, the history of gender and sexuality, and critical race theory. Her books include *Sierra Leone's Settler Women Traders, Women in Sub-Saharan Africa,* and *Dark Continent of Our Bodies*. She is at work on a book about Afro-British Cultural Studies. She was awarded the 2013–2014 NYU Distinguished Teaching Award.

Jennifer D. Williams is Assistant Professor of English and Women's and Gender Studies at Morgan State University. Her research focuses on the interrelationships between gender, sexuality, race, and class, particularly as they intersect with urban geographies and cultural memory. Her book project *Sistas and the City: Black Women's Urban Literature and Culture after WWII* addresses these overlapping issues. Her recent article "Black American Girls in Paris: Sex, Race, and Cosmopolitan Desire in Andrea Lee's *Sarah Phillips* and Shay Youngblood's *Black Girl in Paris*" was published in *Contemporary Women's Writing* in 2015.

Index